LIBERALISM, JUSTICE, AND MARKETS

Liberalism, Justice, and Markets

A Critique of Liberal Equality

COLIN M. MACLEOD

CLARENDON PRESS · OXFORD
1998

Oxford University Press, Great Clarendon Street, Oxford OX2 6DP
Oxford New York
Athens Auckland Bangkok Bogota Bombay Buenos Aires
Calcutta Cape Town Dar es Salaam Delhi Florence Hong Kong Istanbul
Karachi Kuala Lumpur Madras Madrid Melbourne Mexico City
Nairobi Paris Singapore Taipei Tokyo Toronto Warsaw
and associated companies in
Berlin Ibadan

Oxford is a registered trade mark of Oxford University Press

Published in the United States
by Oxford University Press Inc., New York

British Library Cataloguing in Publication Data
Data available

Library of Congress Cataloging in Publication Data
Data available

ISBN 0-19-829397-6

1 3 5 7 9 10 8 6 4 2

Typeset by Best-set Typesetter Ltd., Hong Kong
Printed in Great Britain
on acid-free paper by
Bookcraft (Bath) Ltd
Midsomer Norton, Somerset

To
my parents

ACKNOWLEDGEMENTS

DURING the period which this book was written I received support from various institutions for which I am very grateful. A postdoctoral fellowship jointly funded by the Social Sciences and Humanities Research of Canada and the Killam Foundation assisted some of my research. The Centre for Applied Ethics and the Philosophy Department at the University of British Columbia sponsored my postdoctoral fellowship and provided me with various helpful resources. I also spent a very stimulating year as a visiting fellow at the Centre for Law and Society at the University of Edinburgh. While in Edinburgh, the International Social Sciences Institute provided me with an office and an intellectually rich environment in which to complete some of the final revisions to the book. Some of the material in the book is based upon some previously published material. A version of Chapter 7 appeared as 'Liberal Neutrality or Liberal Tolerance' in *Law and Philosophy* (1997) and Chapter 2 is derived in part from 'The Market, Preferences, and Equality' in the *Canadian Journal of Law and Jurisprudence*, 7 (1994).

The writing of this book has often been a very solitary affair but I have benefited enormously from the generous help I have been lucky to receive from so many friends and colleagues. Although it has changed in many respects, this project started life as a philosophy dissertation at Cornell University. So thanks first to my advisers and colleagues at Cornell who commented upon, discussed, and supported my research. In particular I am grateful to my supervisor David Lyons and to my committee members Richard Miller and Henry Shue.

A number of other friends and colleagues have commented on and discussed various aspects of this project. I have benefited greatly from their criticisms and suggestions. In particular I would like to thank Steve Andrews, Jerry Dworkin, Les Jacobs, John Russell, Peter Vallentyne, and the reviewers of the manuscript for the press. Thanks also to Sue Donaldson for more general encouragement and advice.

As always, there are a few people who deserve very special

thanks. First, I want to acknowledge the special contributions of my parents, Alistair and Ruth. They have always enthusiastically supported my academic endeavours. I have learned much about philosophy from my father and our frequent discussions of the material in this book have clarified my thinking on many issues. My mother has been the source of much wisdom not found in academic texts. I am also extremely indebted to Will Kymlicka. It was Will who, many years ago, first sparked my interest in Dworkin's work on equality. Since then he has been an extraordinarily generous source of advice, constructive criticism, and insight.

Finally, I wish to thank Avigail Eisenberg for her love, support, and encouragement. We have discussed my work on countless occasions and she has often pushed me to persevere in the face of seemingly daunting obstacles.

CONTENTS

1

Introduction

THE perfectly competitive market of economic theory, where economic agents are fully informed and perfectly rational, is a fiction. It does not exist, nor is it even approximated, in the real economic world. Yet this fiction exerts enormous influence in modern political theory. The seductive power of the ideal market lies in its capacity to model elegant and disarmingly simple solutions to complex problems. We can come to understand, for instance, how the uncoordinated activity of economic agents can lead to socially desirable states of affairs. Similarly, the ideal market enters normative political philosophy partly because it can be represented as illuminating important values. Defenders of the market claim we can learn much about individual liberty, the promotion of mutual advantage, and efficiency in the distribution of goods by studying it.[1] However, a principal limitation of the market for many theorists is its supposed insensitivity to the demands of egalitarian justice. This is in part because modern market societies exhibit a great deal of social and economic inequality. However, egalitarians have also been inclined to think that there is an inherent flaw in the ideal of a free market society. In traditional left-wing critiques, the market has been characterized as the enemy of equality on various grounds: it generates exploitation; it creates alienation; it is hostile to genuine freedom; and it is corrosive to the bonds of community.

---

[1] These themes are systematically pursued by J. Buchanan (1975), Gauthier (1986), and Narveson (1988). For these theorists the attraction of the market derives in large part from the idea that a theory of distributive justice concerns fundamentally a notion of mutual advantage. Justice, and morality more generally, is construed as an artifice through which mutually advantageous relations between self-interested individuals can be established and maintained. Mutual advantage theories of justice are often contrasted with theories that view justice as fundamentally a matter of showing impartial concern for all individuals. The debate between justice as mutual advantage and justice as impartiality is thoroughly explored by Brian Barry (1989). The arguments of this book all take for granted that the justice as impartiality perspective is correct.

It is remarkable then that the leading contemporary exponent of egalitarianism, Ronald Dworkin, vigorously defends the use of the ideal market as a theoretical device for the articulation of egalitarian distributive justice and liberal political morality. This book is about Dworkin's distinctive and influential theory of liberal equality. Its aim is to explore systematically and critically how Dworkin's conception of liberal equality is predicated on the market. I accept the view, articulated by Dworkin, that a successful theory of political morality must be predicated on an abstract but substantive conception of the equal moral standing of all persons. However, I challenge many of the theoretical connections which Dworkin attempts to establish between the ideal market and equality. Indeed, the theme which runs through the book is that Dworkin is mistaken to suppose that the market is intrinsic to the best interpretation of egalitarian justice.

Although I am principally interested in the theoretical dimensions of the relationship between ideal markets and equality, I do not think the project is without practical import. It is reasonable to suppose that support by liberals for actual free market arrangements as well as antipathy towards alternative economic models can be traced, at least in part, to the use in liberal theory of ideal models of market interaction. Whether we should be enthusiastic, from the point of view of justice, about extensive reliance on free market economic arrangements depends partly on the appropriateness of theoretically linking the market and justice. This is particularly true, I believe, given the recent political success which the New Right has had in expanding the scope of unfettered market activity and diminishing state action designed to assist the casualties of market forces. The market now occupies a central place in modern liberal democracies and its machinations have a profound effect on the character of the communities in which we live. Moreover, the global dominance of the market is increasing. The collapse of the communist states in Eastern Europe has been accompanied by a concerted effort to establish market economies in these countries. Burgeoning government debts and deficits combined with persistently high levels of unemployment have thrown the modest welfare provisions of most liberal democracies into crisis. There is pressure to reduce government spending on social programmes and to reduce government involvement in the functioning of the market.

The recent triumphs of the market are partly a testimony to the power of libertarian rhetoric to provide capitalism with a compelling basis in moral argument. Political philosophers sympathetic to the market have portrayed it as the guardian of individual liberty and the engine of material prosperity. The market is said to foster responsible, self-reliant citizens by providing handsome rewards to those who display initiative in entrepreneurial activity. Taxation for the purposes of redistribution is viewed as an unjust violation of private property rights and is even characterized as a cause of poverty. The welfare state, by contrast, is depicted as fostering dependency and undermining responsibility and self-reliance. In short, the credibility of the idea that a just society must be egalitarian in some fundamental sense has suffered while the putative moral virtues of capitalism have been articulated with renewed success.

Against this backdrop, Dworkin's contention that there is a surprising but nonetheless deep harmony between egalitarianism and the ideal market assumes a good deal of importance. After all, if traditional egalitarian antipathy to the market is fundamentally misplaced then perhaps egalitarian resistance to the expansion of unfettered market activity in the real world is also misguided. If, however, Dworkin is mistaken about the affinities between the market and egalitarian justice then egalitarians should remain cautious about embracing the market in the name of justice. In this respect, Dworkin's standing as America's 'leading public philosopher' (Scanlon 1993: 45) provides one reason to subject his arguments to sustained critical scrutiny. The suggestion by a figure of Dworkin's intellectual stature and political reputation that markets are, in principle, the ally of equality may contribute to the growing hegemony of market ideology.

I do not wish to overstate this point. I argue against Dworkin's contention that there is a deep and compelling theoretical connection between the market and equality. But my arguments, if successful, do not mean that a sensible version of egalitarian liberalism should be hostile to all actual market arrangements. My arguments do not support any kind of anti-market ludditism. However, the central claim which I try to establish, in a variety of different contexts, is that the criteria for assessment of the adequacy of market arrangements should not be ones which are parasitic upon incorporation of market paradigms into liberal principles.

A different, less explicit, theme which characterizes much of the argument of the book is a general scepticism about the fruitfulness of relying on artificial devices for the development of an adequate theory of justice. Of course, artificial devices have a venerable place in the history of political philosophy. The social contract tradition with its emphasis on hypothetical contracts as devices which can illumine various aspects of political morality is particularly important. There are countless variations on the contractarian theme. But there are other devices, such as the imaginary impartial spectator of utilitarianism, which have proved popular with political philosophers. One of the attractions of devices in political theory is that they offer the prospect of making progress on difficult and controversial issues by representing the solution to a problem as discoverable through use of a simplifying procedure. In the contractarian tradition, for instance, principles of distributive justice are represented as those which would be the object of agreement under specified hypothetical circumstances. By defining in some suitable way the circumstances and motivations of the hypothetical contracting agents, contractarians hope to be able to generate a fairly determinate answer to the otherwise perplexing question of what a just distribution of resources consists in. Of course, there are notorious controversies about how the circumstances of the contract should be described and there is the lingering suspicion that the answer to the problem is entirely determined by the specification of the conditions of the contract. Nonetheless, the idea that a procedural device of the right sort can solve substantive problems in the theory of justice remains attractive. The danger of devices is that they introduce distortions of the very ideals which we seek to understand and they divert attention from the tackling of substantive moral issues directly. Even though Dworkin has famously criticized the reliance on hypothetical contracts (Dworkin 1977: 150–4) which characterizes much modern political philosophy, his own theory, as we shall see, makes extensive use of similar procedural devices. Indeed, the suggestion which pervades his work is that the outcomes which would be generated by markets operating under various idealized conditions provide the best solutions to crucial problems in political philosophy. I believe some of the difficulties with device-driven theories of justice are exhibited in Dworkin's theory. The complex manipulations of the market around which Dworkin's theory is built appear to yield tidy solutions to difficult problems. In fact, they can distort our understanding of justice and divert our attention from the real underlying issues. Some idealizations and simplifying assumptions are inevitable in political philosophy but I believe that Dworkin's commitment to various kinds of market devices leads us astray.

Though the principal objective of this book is to develop a critique of Dworkin's account of liberal political morality, it is difficult to overestimate the importance and sophistication of his contributions to political philosophy. It is because Dworkin's arguments about the nature of justice are so interesting and compelling that it is appropriate to devote an entire book to his work. Indeed, I believe that Dworkin's work is as important as that of Rawls. Yet whereas every facet of Rawls's theory of justice has been examined in enormous detail, Dworkin's complex and subtle theory of distributive justice, unlike his substantial contribution to jurisprudence, has not received the attention it merits.

Before delving into the details of Dworkin's theory, it is worth considering some key features of his distinctive contribution to contemporary political philosophy. Dworkin's account of liberal theory begins with the controversial but compelling claim that all theories of political morality can and should be construed as interpretations of an abstract but fundamental requirement that all persons be treated with equal concern and respect.[2] The now famous equal concern and respect formula captures the idea that 'the interests of the members of the community matter and matter equally' (Dworkin 1983: 24).[3] This abstract egalitarian thesis is said to provide a common point of departure

---

[2] Dworkin identifies the egalitarian thesis as 'fundamental and axiomatic' (Dworkin 1977: xv) and speaks of the 'liberal's axiomatic principle of equal concern and respect' (Dworkin 1985: 210).
[3] Another formulation of the abstract egalitarian thesis supplied by Dworkin is 'government must act to make the lives of those it governs better lives, and it must show equal concern for the life of each' (Dworkin 1987: 7).

for all plausible theories of political morality. For Dworkin, developing a theory of political morality consists largely in developing a plausible and compelling interpretation of the fundamental egalitarian demand. This involves furnishing an account of people's interests 'most comprehensively construed' and determining what follows from 'supposing these interests matter equally' (Dworkin 1983: 25). Dworkin has claimed that the plausible forms of utilitarianism, libertarianism, Rawlsian contractarianism, and equal welfare theories can and should be represented as interpretations of the abstract egalitarian ideal (Dworkin 1981: 245–6; 1983: 24; 1987: 10–11).[4] He also thinks there are decisive objections to these theories qua interpretations of the egalitarian thesis. These are controversial and important claims which I will not discuss in any detail here. Nor do I explore the deeper philosophical foundations for the abstract egalitarian thesis which Dworkin has tried to defend. For the purposes of this book, I simply accept that a theory of justice must flow from acceptance of the concept of impartial moral concern captured by the abstract egalitarian thesis.

The idea that some principle of equality has a fundamental role to play in political philosophy is, of course, an old and familiar claim. However, it is only in the last twenty years or so that systematic efforts have been made to articulate explicitly egalitarian conceptions of justice. Much of the impetus for the exploration of the idea of equality can, of course, be traced to the work of Rawls. His suggestion that the central idea of distributive justice is that there is a strong presumption that primary goods should be distributed equally has generated remarkable interest in the idea of distributional equality.[5] Many theorists agree that equality must be accepted as a fundamental principle of distribution but they disagree both over how equality should be understood and what exactly justice requires be distributed equally. As Amartya Sen says we want an answer to the question: Equality of what? (Sen 1980). We want a

---

[4] Will Kymlicka pursues and develops this way of understanding competing theories of political morality as it applies to understanding the putatively fundamental distinction between deontology and teleology (Kymlicka 1988b: 173–90).

[5] The precise character of Rawls's general conception of justice is that 'all social primary goods—liberty and opportunity, income and wealth, and the bases of self-respect—are to be distributed equally unless an unequal distribution of any or all of these goods is to the advantage of the least favoured' (Rawls 1971: 303).

richer account of the egalitarian ideal and how it may be realized.

A number of different competing theories have tried to supply an answer to this problem. Even a cursory review reveals the lively debate surrounding the meaning of equality. Sen argues that Rawls's focus on primary goods is too narrow. He suggests that we should focus on a notion of basic capabilities and this leads him to a conception of 'basic capability equality' (Sen 1980). Richard Arneson believes that what egalitarians should really care about is welfare, but he also believes a conception of distributive equality must be sensitive to certain considerations of individual responsibility. As a consequence, he develops a theory of 'equality opportunity for welfare' (Arneson 1989). G. A. Cohen has reservations about Arneson's proposal and develops his own variant of it called 'equal access to advantage' (Cohen 1989). Dworkin has argued against a variety of versions of the view that it is welfare that egalitarians should aim to equalize. All versions of equality of welfare are, in Dworkin's view, defective conceptions of equality.[6] Instead he argues that it is resources that should be distributed equally. All these theories are interesting and important but in many respects Dworkin's theory stands alone in the field. What is noteworthy about Dworkin's contribution to egalitarian theory is its sheer breadth and depth. Where other egalitarian theories provide accounts of distributional equality, Dworkin uses his conception of equality as a basis on which to construct a comprehensive theory of political morality. His remarkable achievement has been to offer an explanation of how the apparently disparate ideals embraced by liberalism can be systematically articulated and defended through the adoption of an egalitarian conception of distributive justice.

---

[6] The equality of welfare theories discussed by Dworkin hold that resources are justly distributed when each person enjoys an equal level of welfare (Dworkin 1981: 185–246). There are different versions of equal welfare theories because there are different accounts of what welfare consists in. Dworkin argues that welfare might be taken to consist either in some kind of preference satisfaction, in some kind of conscious state (e.g. pleasure) or might be given some objectivist construal. Yet no matter how welfare is defined (and there are substantial puzzles in defining welfare adequately), Dworkin argues that equality of welfare is a defective conception of equality because such theories wrongly require the subsidization of expensive tastes.

As I have already indicated, at the heart of this theory of equality lies the ideal market. It is crucial to emphasize that the market does not appear in Dworkin's theory simply as a useful heuristic device. Rather it is intrinsic to the very interpretation of equality. As Dworkin puts it, 'the best theory of equality presupposes some actual or hypothetical market in justifying a particular distribution of goods and opportunities' (Dworkin 1983: 38). Yet the initial interpretation of the abstract egalitarian thesis does not begin with the market but with an account of the nature of our most fundamental interests.

Dworkin contends that our highest order interest is in leading a good life, the life that is in fact good. He also believes that an agent can only be successful in leading a good life if the projects, goals, ideals, etc. pursued by an agent are ones which are freely chosen and adopted by the agent. Indeed, the projects in which individuals engage must be endorsed by them if they are to contribute to the living of a genuinely valuable life.

While our most fundamental interest is in leading a good life, Dworkin is careful to note that actually leading a good life may be different from leading the life we (currently) believe to be good. Our views about what sorts of lives are valuable may be mistaken. Since our views about the good life are fallible, it is important that we have available the resources that would allow us to examine our views critically and to revise them if necessary. The basic problem which arises in light of this account of our fundamental interests concerns how social resources should be distributed and how, more generally, social and political institutions should be structured so as to ensure that everyone's interest in leading a good life is given full and equal consideration.

In addition to these useful observations about our fundamental interests, Dworkin has also furthered our understanding of some of the important demands of egalitarian justice. Perhaps his most important insight is that an egalitarian theory of justice must recognize a principle of individual responsibility. People are responsible for, and must accept the consequences of their choices about how to conduct their lives.[7] However, people

---

[7] By incorporating a principle of individual responsibility within egalitarianism G. A. Cohen thinks that egalitarian theories can capture what is attractive about certain libertarian approaches to justice (Cohen 1989: 933).

should not be penalized or have their interests set back by things over which they cannot reasonably be held to have control. (It is, of course, a tricky matter determining the choices and preferences for which people must be held responsible. Obviously, the degree of voluntariness will be a central determinant, but there is a lot of room for dispute about what constitutes voluntary choice.) Accommodation of this point about responsibility means that a theory of distributive justice must, to use Dworkin's terminology, be ambition-sensitive but endowment-insensitive. That is, it must accept as legitimate certain inequalities that are traceable to choices about how we live for which persons may be held morally responsible. But it must correct for inequalities that can be characterized as morally arbitrary, such as those which do not reflect our choices. Dworkin points out that many differences in the opportunities that people have to lead a good life are attributable to the effects of brute luck and are problematic from an egalitarian perspective. For example, the burden faced by a person with a serious congenital disability is arbitrary and entirely unchosen. An egalitarian theory of justice must therefore provide an account of the compensation that individuals who suffer disabilities are entitled to. Similarly, it must try to mitigate the impact on resource distribution of arbitrary differences in people's talents. However, differences in the life prospects of individuals that are attributable to their responsible choices must, as a matter of fairness, be permitted. A satisfactory account of justice must accommodate and give content to both these kinds of fundamental convictions.

Dworkin's theory has greatly advanced egalitarian theory precisely because it makes room for individual responsibility. Indeed, a notable limitation of much egalitarian theory prior to Dworkin is that it ignored or downplayed the significance of individual choice to the determination of distributive shares. Consider, for instance, the common suggestion that an ideal egalitarian distribution should be understood as directed at achieving and maintaining a predetermined equal pattern along a given dimension. On this approach equality might be understood as consisting in the equalization of welfare or primary goods or income. Traditional egalitarian theories are distinguished primarily by what they identify as the dimension over which equality as a distributive principle should reign. Theories of this sort are unsatisfactory because they give inadequate recognition to the idea that individual actions can create differential entitlements. It is both fair and reasonable that our shares of resources over a lifetime reflect, at least to some significant degree, the choices we have made about how to lead our lives. Suppose we are each situated in equal circumstances and you take advantage of opportunities to better your situation which are also open to me but which I decline. The result of our respective choices may be that you are happier or richer than I. Consider how the impact of choice is poorly captured by a theory which holds that resources should be distributed so as to equalize welfare. Suppose that you choose to brew some beer while I choose to spend the days watching TV. Now suppose that as a result of our respective choices you enjoy a higher level of welfare than I. I would be as happy as you if you gave me some of your beer but does equality require that you give me some? Similarly, suppose I choose to develop a taste for expensive wine while you remain satisfied with beer. My choice causes my welfare to decline relative to yours but does equality require that you subsidize my expensive taste? Whereas equality of welfare might condemn such inequalities as unjust because the outcome represents a departure from a standard of equal welfare, there is good reason to accept such inequalities as just because they reflect individual choice. To some important degree, we are responsible for our choices and we must accept the impact our choices have on our level of welfare or income. But once choice plays a role in determining distributive shares, there can be no simple specification of the pattern of holdings which best realizes egalitarian justice.

The failure of egalitarian theory in the past to accommodate responsibility has, in my view, substantially undermined its appeal both philosophically and politically by leaving egalitarianism vulnerable to libertarian critiques which place great emphasis on the moral and political significance of choice. Though libertarians are apt to exaggerate the degree to which entitlement is a matter of individual choice, they are right to insist that an account of justice which ignores or marginalizes responsibility for our own lives is unsatisfactory. Dworkin's highly innovative theory goes a long way to addressing the traditional deficiency of egalitarian theory in this respect because on his approach the choices of responsible individuals are important determinants of the resources to which they are entitled. The theory of equality of resources is really the first systematic and comprehensive attempt to tackle the problem of incorporating responsibility within egalitarianism. Because market-determined distributions of resources reflect, to an important degree, the choices of individuals, Dworkin is optimistic that idealized markets can be employed to craft a responsibility-incorporating form of egalitarianism. While Dworkin's insistence that egalitarian theory must accommodate responsibility is surely correct, I doubt whether the market mechanism at the heart of equality of resources permits us to track the significance of choice appropriately. Indeed, one of the main aims of the book is to show how the relationship between responsible choice and entitlement is distorted by even idealized models of market interaction.

Dworkin believes that his vision of a liberal society can satisfy, in large measure, the requirements of egalitarian justice. The type of liberalism Dworkin champions is characterized by three basic commitments. First, a liberal society must ensure that 'each person have an equal share of resources measured by the costs of the choices he makes, reflecting his own plans and preferences, to plans and projects of others' (Dworkin 1987: 27). He thinks that the requisite kind of distributive equality can be achieved, to a great extent, through fairly extensive free market economic arrangements. There is some need for market outcomes to be adjusted—through a suitable system of redistributive taxation—so as to eliminate or at least render acceptable the effects of arbitrary differences in native endowment and luck. But Dworkin does not imagine that providing fair compensation for disabled and untalented persons will substantially upset a market economy. Second, appropriate political structures must display neutrality between different conceptions of the good life. '[G]overnment must be neutral on what might be called the question of the good life ... [P]olitical decisions must be, so far as it is possible, independent of any particular conception of the good life or of what gives value to life' (Dworkin 1985: 191). Third, the political system must provide and protect a broad range of liberty rights which give individuals widespread discretion over matters of great personal concern.[8]

These commitments—to choice-sensitive distributive equality, neutrality, and liberty—form the core of Dworkin's liberalism. Although he has argued in more piecemeal ways for these constitutive doctrines of his liberalism, the most sustained and systematic philosophical argument for them is found in the elaborate equality of resources theory of justice. Indeed, it is this theory that provides Dworkin's most direct and complete interpretation of the abstract egalitarian ideal. As I have suggested, the theory of equality of resources makes explicit and extensive use of a theoretical model of market interaction. 'The idea of an economic market, as a device for setting prices for a vast variety of goods and services, must be at the center of any theoretical development of equality of resources' (Dworkin 1981: 284). In the course of our investigations, I will explain exactly how and why Dworkin believes that the market is crucial to the articulation of liberal egalitarianism. But since the material we will cover is often complex, it may be useful to provide a brief overview of the various dimensions of Dworkin's theory explored in the following chapters.

The first element of Dworkin's theory is an account of what constitutes an equal initial distribution of resources. This problem occupies my second chapter. Dworkin argues that the outcome of an imaginary auction which displays the features of a perfectly competitive market and in which all participants have equal purchasing power provides a perfect model of a fair initial distribution of resources. The market is favoured because the price system provides a measure of the value of resources, one that can be used to give content to the idea that the legitimacy of individual claims to resources is dependent on the impact of these claims on other members of the community. I argue that

---

[8] There is a fourth component to Dworkin's egalitarian liberalism—democracy. In this work, I do not directly discuss the nature of Dworkin's interesting views on democratic theory (Dworkin 1988). He clearly believes that the best interpretation of equality entails a strong commitment to democratic institutions. However, in a striking departure from the rest of his egalitarian theory, he does not argue that the market has any crucial role in the articulation or defence of an egalitarian conception of democracy. Since the focus of my project is the intimate theoretical connections Dworkin claims to detect between the market and equality, I shall not examine his contributions to democratic theory.

this account of initial equality fails because it depends on mistaken assumptions about the way in which fair distributive shares can be predicated on individual preferences. A theory of justice needs an account of the circumstances under which individuals form their preferences and how the distribution of resources affects these circumstances. Dworkin's solution to the problem of initial equality is unsatisfactory because it wrongly supposes that the issue of appropriate preference formation can be addressed independently of distributional issues.

The third chapter takes up a different dimension of distributional equality. Egalitarians now generally recognize that differences in our choices about how hard we work, what we work at, and the sorts of risks we are willing to assume may all legitimately ground differences in the resources to which we are entitled. This means that a theory of distributive justice must have a dynamic component. It must explain the way in which individual choices about the consumption and production of current resources may affect entitlement to future resources. Dworkin argues that the operation of a perfectly competitive market provides a unique model of how an egalitarian distribution of resources can be maintained through time as individuals with equal initial distributive shares make choices resulting in complex patterns of trade and production. Because differences in the rewards which accrue to ongoing market activity simply reflect differences in the choices individuals make about the sorts of lives they wish to lead, a market-determined distribution of resources is 'ambition-sensitive'. Equality is preserved through time because the market ensures that each person's aggregate opportunity costs, as measured by their choices about what to consume and produce, are equal. I dispute the significance of this result. By considering the impact of various kinds of high-stake and high-risk gambling permitted in the ideal market, I show how unregulated market activity may result in significant distributive unfairness and erode the control individuals should be able to exercise over their lives.

In the fourth chapter, I consider Dworkin's analysis of and solution to the problems posed for the theory of justice by disabilities. It is widely accepted that justice requires special recognition and accommodation of the interests of disabled persons. However, it is difficult to explain the exact nature and extent of societal obligations to persons with disabilities. Dworkin suggests that a complex hypothetical insurance market can be used to determine the extra resources to which disabled individuals are entitled by way of compensation for the special disadvantages they face. I identify many objections to this approach. I suggest that it is unlikely that we can make the complex counterfactual judgements on which the insurance scheme relies. There is also a real danger that the sort of compensation yielded by this scheme would reflect irrational attitudes to risk. Among other things, this means that the scheme can also generate obviously unfair outcomes in which disabled individuals are denied adequate compensation. Finally, I show that because Dworkin's theory views compensation as mainly a matter of adjusting individual ownership of resources, it is insensitive to broader concerns about the complexion of the social environment in which persons with disabilities must live.

In market societies differences in income tend to track differences in talent. But egalitarianism insists that differences in income that are traceable to arbitrary differences in talent are not justified. Therefore, liberals who defend a market economy need a theory of how market interaction should be adjusted to mitigate the impact on resource distribution of arbitrary differences in individual talent. This is the problem explored in the fifth chapter. Dworkin argues that another, more complex, hypothetical insurance market can be used to design a system of redistributive taxation that meets this need. I argue that no coherent theory of fair market adjustment emerges from this strategy. This hypothetical market scheme proceeds from a misdiagnosis of the problem of unequal natural endowment which obscures the distinction between talents and disabilities. It suffers a number of internal inconsistencies and thus either has no determinate implications or yields results that violate egalitarian criteria of justice.

In the sixth chapter, I consider a central problem for liberalism. It concerns the reconciliation of the apparently divergent ideals of equality and liberty. For Dworkin the key to defending liberty while affirming the theoretical primacy of equality lies in showing that a commitment to liberty is actually a constitutive component of his theory of equality of resources. To show this he develops a very complex argument called the 'constitutive bridge strategy'. It seeks to link defence of individual liberty to the market structure invoked in equality of resources. I argue that this strategy fails both because it depends on too many ad hoc premisses and because, even in its most plausible version, it does not lead to a recognizably liberal conception of liberty. I also defend a rival interest-based strategy for the defence of liberty against a number of Dworkinian objections. I attempt to establish that it provides a better place for liberty within the ideal of abstract equality than the market-based defence offered by Dworkin.

The element of Dworkin's liberalism that I examine in the seventh chapter is his view about the appropriate relationship of the state to the different conceptions of the good that may be adopted by its citizens. A characteristic feature of liberalism is that the state must exhibit a kind of impartiality towards different conceptions of the good. The state must respect the fact that its citizens have chosen to adopt diverse conceptions of the good. Dworkin argues that his theory embraces and provides a compelling justification of this sort of liberal doctrine. I argue, however, that his account of the relationship between liberalism and the good is ambiguous. Specifically, I argue that he conflates an ideal of liberal neutrality with an ideal of liberal tolerance. I suggest that the ideal of tolerance provides a better interpretation of egalitarian considerations than the market-driven ideal of neutrality.

A common theme of these chapters is the connection between markets and liberal justice. As I have indicated, the market performs a variety of important functions in Dworkin's distinctive brand of liberalism. First, it provides an account of distributive equality in which individual choices about the production and consumption of goods are important determinants of each person's entitlement to resources. Second, it provides a framework for identifying and rectifying undeserved inequalities which are associated with disability and differences in talent. Third, it illuminates the relationship between the ideals of liberty and equality. Fourth, it provides a model of state neutrality. I will argue that these attempts to reveal a deep affinity between justice and markets are vulnerable to a number of related objections. The focus on the market distorts crucial issues concerning the circumstances of authenticity—i.e. the social conditions under which we form and deliberate about preferences and beliefs about the good. The market is an unreliable device for articulating the demands of egalitarian justice because the resulting theory is insensitive to various unfair consequences of certain market activities. The attempts to establish a link between the market and justice are also often burdened by unduly demanding and unrealistic epistemic requirements. Equality of resources does not adequately accommodate children and other easily marginalized groups.

I believe that the difficulties which Dworkin's theory repeatedly encounters teach us some broader lessons about the market and justice. First, the determination of the proper role of the market in a just society can only be effected after we have a non-market account of the circumstances of authenticity. The criteria for assessing the moral adequacy of market arrangements are independent of idealized models of market interaction. Second, there are domains, such as the cultural arena, where we should resist the push towards full marketization. Finally, we should be more aware of the many ways in which real world markets fall well short of meeting the demands of justice. The happy reconciliation between the market and justice which Dworkin's arguments purport to provide, at least at a theoretical level, is not successful.

A few final prefatory remarks are in order. First, although Dworkin's theory is centred around the model of a perfectly competitive market drawn from economic theory, his presentation of this idea is fairly informal. That is, he does not dwell on the precise formal details or mathematical theorems which define the market in economic theory. Nor does he address standard problems in economic theory such as externalities, market failure, and the provision of public goods. In Dworkin's view, establishing the appeal of the market as a device for the articulation of egalitarian justice does not depend on close examination of the technical aspects of the market. Instead, he thinks that we can describe the essential features of the market for his purposes in a fairly non-technical manner. This is appropriate, I think, since Dworkin's arguments, though influenced by economic theory, do not fall within the ambit of professional economics. My examination of Dworkin's arguments accepts this presupposition. Thus, so far as possible, I follow Dworkin's characterization of the market and I avoid the use of economic jargon which might be appropriate in a different context.

Second, while the focus of this book is on the specific arguments of Dworkin which I examine in great detail, I try to situate the main elements of his theory within the broader context of contemporary political philosophy. I do not pretend to offer a comprehensive comparison of Dworkin's theory with competing theories but, where appropriate, I indicate both what distinguishes Dworkin's approach from others and how Dworkin has advanced our understanding of important issues. Similarly, where I believe Dworkin's solutions to problems fail, I do not attempt to advance fully developed alternatives. In various chapters, I tentatively indicate directions which might be explored in pursuit of better solutions. However, this book does not advance a novel or comprehensive theory of egalitarian justice. Nor does it attempt to describe, in any detail, the role the market should play in a genuinely just society. These are crucial issues but they cannot be addressed here in any thoroughgoing way.

Finally, some of the criticisms developed in this book appeal to moral intuitions about fairness and judgements about the nature of human interests. Frequently, I explain and motivate the underlying judgements by constructing hypothetical examples which are designed to sharpen and motivate various intuitions. The hazard of this strategy, of course, is that one's audience may not share the intuitive judgements upon which an argument depends. However, in normative political philosophy there is no way of avoiding this approach to argument. Here I share the view of Thomas Nagel, who notes that in political philosophy

the use of moral intuition is inevitable, and should not be regretted. To trust our intuitions, particularly those that tell us something is wrong even though we don't know exactly what would be right, we need only believe that our moral understanding extends farther than our capacity to spell out the principles which underlie it. Intuition can be corrupted by custom, self-interest, or commitment to a theory, but it need not be, and often a person's intuitions will provide him with evidence that his own moral theory is missing something, or that the arrangements he has been brought up to find natural are really unjust. (Nagel 1991: 7)

Beyond this commitment to testing arguments in the court of reflective and considered judgement, I employ no special method of moral enquiry. This is consistent with Dworkin's own approach to normative argument and I am unaware of any genuine alternative. I hope readers will share my intuitions and find my criticisms persuasive.

2

Initial Equality

THE examination of the relationship between liberalism, justice, and markets begins in this chapter with consideration of the first dimension of the various complex connections Dworkin draws between the economic market and equality. The suggestion under examination is that what justice requires by way of an initial distribution of resources can be established by considering the operation of an ideal market. I identify an objection to this claim. It holds that, even in the restricted circumstances in which Dworkin believes the claim obtains, the market may fail to yield an equitable distribution. This is because the individual preferences on which a market-driven distribution depends are not sufficiently reliable indicators of individual interest to serve as the determinants of fair distributive shares. I then examine two arguments through which it might be thought that the appropriateness of relying on preferences expressed in the market could be re-established. I suggest that these arguments succeed in preserving the credibility of the market only to the degree that they obscure an important problem concerning the conditions under which individual preferences can assume ethical significance. Once this problem is given proper recognition the market cannot be employed as a device for the articulation of egalitarian justice in the way envisaged by Dworkin.

THE PROBLEM OF INITIAL EQUALITY

Dworkin believes we can may make considerable progress in constructing a comprehensive theory of distributive justice by first considering the simpler problem of determining a fair distribution of resources amongst a fixed population of individuals, each of whom has the capacity to devise and pursue some conception of the good life. I will call this the problem of initial equality. The idea is that by articulating this element of distributive equality we will garner a richer understanding of the character of egalitarian justice. To avoid obvious complications that would otherwise arise immediately, Dworkin simplifies the problem of initial equality by making the tacit stipulation that individuals are not differentially affected by 'brute luck' (Dworkin 1981: 293). In effect, this amounts to assuming that no one suffers a disability and that there are no morally relevant differences in the benefits that accrue to individuals through exercise of their varying talents. Dworkin also sets aside questions about what resources should be publicly owned and controlled (Dworkin 1981: 285). The focus of equality of resources, in the first instance, is on what constitutes equality in the private ownership of resources. My discussion does not challenge this assumption.

In these admittedly highly artificial circumstances, Dworkin claims that the outcome of a special imaginary auction of social resources describes an initial distribution of privately owned resources which will secure for all individuals an equally valuable share of resources with which to conduct their lives. It might immediately be objected that the counterfactual simplifying assumptions which give shape to the problem of initial equality involve so great a departure from real problems of distributive justice as to rob the problem of any relevance. Issues of distributive justice should be tackled, so the objection goes, in the actual historical, social, and economic contexts in which they arise and have practical urgency. Indeed, liberal theory is often assailed for its reliance on highly contrived theoretical devices ranging from Hobbes's fictitious state of nature to Rawls's original position. These devices are said to yield principles which are appropriate not for genuine human communities but only for the peculiar beings and circumstances conjured by the philosopher's imagination. I think there is some merit in this charge. Indeed, a common thread that runs through many of the criticisms developed in this book is that too great a reliance on the artificial device of the perfect market for the purposes of interpreting equality leads to a distorted and inadequate theory of justice. Nonetheless, I accept that the development of a theory of justice inevitably involves some abstraction and idealization. Obviously, the application of ideal theory to the real world raises difficult interpretive problems that multiply the complexity of the subject-matter. But in the final analysis since justice is an *ideal* we aspire to and seek to realize, even if only imperfectly, it is appropriate that we explore the ideal in circumstances in which some of the confounding complexities of the real world are temporarily set aside. Thus I shall provisionally accept as reasonable the main idealizations which are necessary to take Dworkin's arguments seriously.

In the artificial context which defines the problem of initial equality, Dworkin suggests that providing each person with an equally valuable share of resources best satisfies the demands of abstract egalitarian concern. This may seem like an easy requirement to meet but there are substantial puzzles involved in determining the true value of distributive shares. It is to solve these puzzles that Dworkin appeals to the market. In what follows I shall not challenge the supposition that an appropriate objective of justice is to devote equal resources to each person's life. Rather, I will argue that Dworkin's auction cannot be relied upon to generate an initial distribution of resources that realizes this objective appropriately.

THE ENVY TEST AND THE AUCTION

The exposition of the theory of equality of resources begins with that favourite of philosopher's fictions: a desert island shipwreck. Dworkin imagines that the propertyless immigrants to the desert island are faced with the problem of fairly dividing the various resources they discover on the island. They provisionally agree upon a criterion for an equal distribution of resources which stipulates that 'no division of resources is an equal division if, once the division is complete, any immigrant would prefer someone else's bundle of resources to his own bundle' (Dworkin 1981: 285). Dworkin dubs this the envy test and the envy test largely defines the conception of distributive equality at the heart of the theory of equality of resources.[1] However, it

---

[1] There is a large literature in economics that employs some version of the envy test as a criterion of 'equity'. It is clear that Dworkin has been influenced by at least some of this literature. Hal Varian provides a very useful overview of much of the relevant economic literature and its relationship to Dworkin's theory (Varian 1985).

is crucial to note that the envy test alone does not provide a sufficient criterion of a just distribution in these circumstances. Dworkin argues that there may be distributions of resources achieved through certain means which pass the envy test yet fail to treat people as equals. For example, a distribution of resources that is devised by a single person who is charged with the task of dividing the resources may satisfy the envy test yet be unfair because it favours some tastes over others (Dworkin 1981: 285–6).[2] There is, in other words, a possible problem concerning arbitrariness in the composition of bundles to which the simple envy test is not sensitive. In distributing resources a divider must determine what combination of resources will make up each bundle. There can, however, be more than one combination that will satisfy the envy test and individuals can have conflicting preferences about the most desirable combination. Here is a simple illustration of the problem of arbitrary bundle composition. Suppose the divider is faced with the task of distributing 99 oranges and 99 apples to three people—A, B, and C. One distribution that will pass the envy test is to give each person 33 oranges and 33 apples. Since each person's bundle of resources is identical, no one can prefer the bundle held by someone else. However, this division might arbitrarily favour some tastes over others. Suppose, for instance, that A likes apples and oranges equally well, while B likes only apples, and C likes only oranges. A's taste for a mixed diet is favoured over the tastes of B and C who would prefer a different ratio of oranges and apples in their own bundle. Clearly, this initial distribution satisfies the envy test but because it arbitrarily favours A's tastes over the tastes of B and C it is unfair.

So a division of resources secured by a divider may be open to the charge that it arbitrarily privileges some people's preferences (about the composition of resource bundles) over the preferences of others. The introduction of a special auction of the island's resources in which individuals have equal bidding power is Dworkin's favoured solution to overcoming the problem posed by the simple envy test. The island's resources are divided into lots and auctioned off. Bidding on the resources

---

[2] Strictly speaking, Dworkin cannot rule out the possibility that a divider would arrive at the same distribution as that generated by an auction. He must hold that whereas a divider may make a mistake the auction is infallible.

provides each person with an equal voice in the construction of bundles and arbitrariness in the composition of bundles is thereby avoided. The distribution of resources is deemed to be complete and equal when all lots have been sold and when no one envies the bundle of resources held by anyone else. In effect, the auction operates as a perfectly competitive economic market. As Dworkin makes clear in a brief footnote, it is supposed to exhibit all the characteristics such markets display in standard microeconomic theory.[3]

I mean to describe a Walrasian auction in which all productive resources are sold. I do not assume that the immigrants enter into complete forward contingent claims contracts, but only that markets will remain open and will clear in a Walrasian fashion once the auction of productive resources is completed. I make all the assumptions about production and preferences made in G. Debreu, *Theory of Value*. (Dworkin 1981: 287, n. 2)

The distribution of resources secured by the operation of this market seems to display a number of egalitarian virtues. First, it does not arbitrarily favour some tastes, because everyone plays an equal role in determining the distribution of resources. Hence the arbitrary bundle composition problem is solved. Second, it effectively avoids the problem of expensive tastes which plagues equality of welfare accounts of distributional equality. Equality of resources is, therefore, a superior conception of distributive equality to 'equality of welfare', which is viewed by Dworkin as the chief rival to equality of resources as a conception of

---

[3] John Bennett argues that Dworkin's discussion of the auction is not, in fact, consistent with some of the technical assumptions made in economic theory. For instance, equilibrium proofs in economics standardly assume that resources are continuously divisible but Bennett notes that Dworkin explicitly makes mention of 'nondivisible resources, like milking cows' (Bennett 1985: 196–7; Dworkin 1981: 285). Bennett's criticism that Dworkin cannot assume that all markets will clear at prices which match supply to demand without also assuming continuous divisibility of resources is technically correct. But I do not think it is sufficient to undermine the intuitive appeal of the auction device. The assumption of divisibility of resources could be built into the auction without jeopardizing the idea that an auction conducted from a position of equal initial bidding power treats persons as equals. And for our purposes it is the putative egalitarian credentials of ideal market distributions which matter most. For it is the intuitive attraction of the seemingly fair procedure of an auction operated from a position of equal bidding power that makes the market seem like a promising device to solve the problem of initial equality. The problem of continuously divisible resources does not therefore undermine the appeal of Dworkin's argument.

distributive equality. To understand this important claim, we must briefly examine the ideal of equality of welfare.

The label 'equality of welfare' actually refers to a family of theories because there are various interpretations of how human welfare should be understood.[4] Equality of welfare theories have two components. Each version of equality of welfare provides a particular interpretation of welfare and, in light of this interpretation, a criterion for the distribution of resources which 'holds that a distributional scheme treats people as equals when it distributes or transfers resources among them until no further transfer would leave them more equal in welfare' (Dworkin 1981: 186). The initial appeal of equality of welfare as a conception of equality is evident. Since everyone's most basic interest is in leading a good life, it seems plausible to suppose that impartiality demands that everyone, so far as is possible, enjoy an equally successful life. After all, it is human well-being and not resources per se which is morally fundamental. Resources have only instrumental value—they are useful in generating welfare. It might seem obvious therefore that the appropriate locus of egalitarian concern is the distribution of welfare. Resources should be harnessed in the equal promotion of well-being. A sound conception of equality must therefore be built around a sound conception of welfare which provides a metric in virtue of which we can determine the true value of resources to different individuals (Dworkin 1981: 188). Equality of welfare is initially attractive because it shows direct concern for everyone's well-being. Moreover, it provides us with a measure of the value of resources which in turn permits us to determine how a distribution of resources best realizes the ideal of impartial moral concern.

[4] In his examination of equality of welfare, Dworkin considers a wide variety of conceptions of welfare. Three main types of theories are canvassed: success theories of welfare, conscious state theories of welfare, and objective conceptions. Success theories of welfare define welfare in terms of the satisfaction of various kinds of preferences. Here Dworkin distinguishes between political preferences, personal preferences, and impersonal preferences. Success accounts of welfare will vary depending on which kinds of preferences are thought to be important to an agent's well-being. Conscious state theories vary with respect to how the mental states associated with enjoyment and dissatisfaction are understood. So Bentham's hedonism is but one possible version of a conscious state theory of welfare. Objective theories of welfare define welfare in terms of a non-subjective account of the elements of a person's life which render it valuable. On this type of theory, a person's life can be improved by the achievement of goods that she does not believe to be valuable (Dworkin 1981: 191–4).

Notwithstanding these attractions, equality of welfare falls prey to a devastating objection in the form of the problem of expensive tastes. The difficulty is that equality of welfare yields deeply counter-intuitive results because it requires that resources be lavished on individuals who have deliberately cultivated tastes whose satisfaction involves a substantial drain on social resources. A person with expensive tastes requires a greater share of resources to achieve a given level of welfare than someone with more modest tastes. So in order to achieve an equal level of welfare the person with expensive tastes must be given a greater share of resources than the person with modest tastes. Yet in cases where expensive tastes are deliberately cultivated, the distribution of resources required by equality of welfare is patently unfair. Dworkin illustrates this difficulty with the following thought experiment (Dworkin 1981: 228–35). We begin by imagining a community in which equal welfare has been achieved through a distribution of wealth which, coincidentally, gives everyone equal wealth. We now consider the case of Louis who deliberately cultivates expensive tastes—e.g. for exotic wine and gourmet food. Given these new tastes, Louis will experience a lower level of welfare than his fellow citizens unless he receives a transfer of extra wealth from the other members of the community. Equality of welfare requires that the other members of the community subsidize Louis's more expensive lifestyle but the required subsidy is unfair. Our egalitarian intuitions tell us that Louis is not entitled to a larger share of resources simply to satisfy his taste for 'plover's eggs and prephylloxera claret'. The particular aetiology of Louis's tastes— i.e. they are deliberately cultivated—disqualifies his claim to extra resources. As Dworkin says, equality 'condemns rather than recommends compensating for expensive tastes' (1981: 235).

FAIR SHARES AND OPPORTUNITY COSTS

The failure of equality of welfare because of the problem of expensive tastes is instructive. It suggests that a theory of distributive equality must provide a theory of fair shares—that is, an account of the share of resources each person can lay claim to in pursuit of their chosen life plans—which is suitably sensitive to choice-based dimensions of well-being. Equality of welfare distorts the distributional significance of choice because it compensates those who make expensive choices rather than holding them responsible for the costs of their own choices.

The brief detour into the problem of expensive tastes further illuminates the attraction of reliance on the market as a device for the articulation of an egalitarian theory of fair shares. The market provides a non-welfarist mechanism through which the value of scarce resources may be gauged and fair distributive shares determined. The price system of the market establishes how important or valuable resources are to individuals as this is reflected in their willingness to pay for them. The resources a person can acquire are a function not only of the importance she attaches to them but also of the importance attached by others to them. For example, scarce resources for which there is high demand will command a high price in the market. Equality of resources employs what Dworkin calls 'the special metric of opportunity costs: it fixes the value of any transferable resource one person has as the value others forgo by his having it' (Dworkin 1987: 26). This metric seems to provide a way of giving content to the important idea that the legitimacy of individual claims to resources is dependent on the impact of these claims on other members of the community. It seems reasonable, for instance, that a person who acquires scarce resources which other people want must accept, as fair, a smaller share of other resources. The metric of opportunity costs seems to provide a good way of tracking this aspect of a theory of fair shares. Since everyone has equal purchasing power in Dworkin's auction, everyone can acquire an equally valuable bundle of resources and thus no one will prefer the bundle someone else has acquired to the bundle she has acquired. Phrased in the language of opportunity costs, the auction ensures that aggregate opportunity costs are equal. As Dworkin sees it, then, the market has a special role to play in the articulation of egalitarian justice because, provided individuals have equal purchasing power, the market can accurately measure the value of goods and ensure that resources of equal value are devoted to the lives of all persons. Since, in the circumstances depicted, providing individuals with equally valuable bundles of resources seems a reasonable interpretation of the abstract requirement that a distribution of resources must treat individuals as equals, the market would appear to be a helpful device for understanding the demands of equality. Dworkin represents this sort of market-driven solution to the problem of equal initial distribution as *uniquely* satisfactory. He suggests that no other egalitarian distributive proposal can supply an appropriate metric for the accurate and fair identification of the value of resources.

SUBJECTIVE PREFERENCES AND OBJECTIVE INTERESTS

This is a difficult position to sustain. In assigning value to a resource, the market responds only to subjective individual preferences. This might be unobjectionable if we could assume that individual preferences correspond neatly to actual individual interests. But this would be an unwarranted assumption. As Dworkin recognizes, individuals can be, and often are, mistaken in their judgements about what is in their own interest. (At a metaethical level, liberal equality is not predicated on subjectivism or scepticism about the good.) Resources for which they express a strong preference may fail to contribute to the possibility of their leading a decent life. Consequently, the metric supplied by Dworkin's auction is quite likely to fail to achieve the goals set for it—namely, determining how important, in fact, resources are to individuals and providing everyone with an equal share that represents a fair accommodation of divergent individual claims to a common stock of resources. Since the market valuation of resources is predicated on subjective preferences, it can yield only a subjective measure of the value of resources. Thus the special metric of opportunity costs which equality of resources depends on will be an unreliable guide to the value of resources if individual preferences about what resources have value are mistaken. Yet surely, what is relevant here is the actual value of the resources in question. What is essential is the real as opposed to perceived contribution resources can make to the leading of a good life. A plausible rendering of the egalitarian objective must hold that genuinely equal and fair shares of scarce resources are shares that really contribute equally to the possibility of each person leading a decent life. It is crucial to note here that I refer throughout to the role resources play in securing the *possibility* of leading a good life. I assume, with Dworkin, that individuals have some responsibility for forming their own preferences and more generally for ensuring that their lives go well. I am not, of course, suggesting that fair initial shares must, in the event, result in equal objective welfare. A fair initial distribution can be compatible with unequal levels of welfare.[5] Nonetheless, the ethical significance of preferences for resources is partly dependent on there being a sufficient correspondence between those preferences and the actual value of the resources to persons.

Once the unreliability of merely subjective preferences as indicators of individual interests is acknowledged, it is easy to see how Dworkin's auction can be incompatible with securing the goal that resources of equal value must be devoted to the life of each person. In an auction where there is equal bidding power, a person who purchases a resource that she prefers to other resources because she falsely believes it can contribute to her leading a good life will, at the conclusion of the auction, have a less valuable bundle of resources than the person whose preferences do not reflect mistaken beliefs about the value of available resources. In normal circumstances, my bag of dross is less valuable than your bag of gold, even if I prefer my dross to your gold. My belief in the value of dross is not self-validating. Satisfaction of the envy test does not ensure that each party's share of resources is equally valuable.

There are at least two different ways in which mistaken beliefs may render preferences unreliable guides to individual interest.

---

[5] Dworkin is clearly mistaken when he says that '[a]nyone who insists that equality is violated by any particular profile of initial tastes, therefore must reject equality of resources, and fall back on equality of welfare' (Dworkin 1981: 289). The dichotomy between equality of welfare and equality of resources is far too simplistic. A conception of equality may insist that initial tastes or preferences satisfy certain minimal welfare motivated conditions without adopting equality of welfare. A concern for minimal welfare might lead us, for instance, to want to screen an initial profile of preferences for self-destructive preferences. After screening for such preferences we might then rely on some market-determined distribution of resources. The resulting distribution could easily diverge from equality of welfare but would, nonetheless, proceed from the recognition that a distribution of resources based on the profile of initial tastes would form an unsatisfactory conception of equality.

First, there are what might be called *intrinsic* mistakes. A person may have mistaken beliefs about the sort of life which is worth leading or what sorts of projects have inherent value. Preferences for resources may be formed in light of this belief. I might form a preference for various exotic and expensive pieces of sports equipment if I believe that I should devote my life to sports. If, in truth, such a life would prove disastrous—unfulfilling, shallow, frustrating, etc.—then although my preference for sports equipment would be in line with my plan for the good life, its satisfaction would not contribute to the possibility of my leading a good life because of the intrinsic defectiveness of my conception of my own good. Second, there are what might be called *instrumental* mistakes. A person may have plausible beliefs about the sort of life which is worth pursuing but have mistaken beliefs about the resources needed to pursue such a life satisfactorily. Perhaps my plan to be a musician is sensible. However, I will not be able to pursue this plan successfully if I falsely believe that it is best pursued by the acquisition of a large collection of expensive instruments when what I really need is good musical instruction.

Clearly, mistaken beliefs of either sort undermine the authority of preferences as indicators of the value of resources. It is also reasonable to suppose that at least some of the participants in Dworkin's auction will have such beliefs. The immigrants are fallible humans and are prone, therefore, to both intrinsic and instrumental mistakes. Moreover, Dworkin cannot evade the difficulty generated by mistaken convictions simply by stipulating that the immigrants' preferences are fully rational and error free.[6] Tempting though such a simple rejoinder might seem, it is

[6] The assumption that the auction operates as a perfectly competitive economic market does imply that the preferences of the immigrants satisfy certain formal conditions. We are to suppose, for instance, that preferences for resources form a complete transitive ordering over all available resources. That is, for all possible bundles of resources a person prefers one bundle to another or is strictly indifferent between bundles. Transitivity requires that if a person prefers A to B and B to C, she must also prefer A to C. It is, of course, unrealistic to suppose that the preference orderings of actual humans satisfy these formal conditions and thus Dworkin's theory even in this regard may depend on unreasonable assumptions about the formal properties of preferences (Bennett 1985). My argument does not depend on challenging the propriety of assuming that preferences satisfy these formal conditions. Mistaken beliefs of the sort which I believe create difficulties for Dworkin's argument are consistent with the formal constraints on preferences presupposed by the perfect market.

not available because, as we shall see, it begs a fundamental question about the role resources play in the formation of preferences. In short, the problem of initial resource distribution is too intimately intertwined with the problem of rational preference formation to permit the problems to be treated as independent. We cannot simply assume that the preferences of the immigrants are well formed in the requisite sense—i.e. that they are not predicated on either mistaken intrinsic beliefs or mistaken instrumental beliefs—because whether preferences are well formed depends partly on how resources are initially distributed. Given the imperfect match between subjective preferences and objective interests, the envy test cannot be relied upon to generate a sound interpretation of the underlying egalitarian ideal. The market, in the form of the initial auction, does supply an adequate solution to the problem of initial equality.

One obvious theoretical solution to this problem is to abandon market-determined opportunity costs as measure of the value of resources. Perhaps instead we should search for purely objective criteria for determining the contribution resources are actually likely to make to the leading of a good life. After all, if we are trying to ascertain how important a given resource *in fact* is to an individual, appealing to the actual benefit an individual might derive from it seems appropriate. An objectivist account of the value of resources could then be employed to tackle the problem of initial equality. An initial distribution of resources could be judged equal when the resources devoted to each person contribute equally to the possibility of each person leading a good life.

Devising a suitable objectivist account of the value of resources for individuals would be theoretically complex and demanding. At the level of ideal theory, however, this approach is not unattractive. Moreover, Dworkin's own strategy involves extravagant informational assumptions—that is, all the incredible informational assumptions embedded in the model of the perfectly competitive market. For instance, the model of the perfectly competitive market assumes that all individuals have full information about the prices and quality of all available goods and services. It also assumes that individuals incur no costs in obtaining this information (Buchanan 1985: 14–15). It is therefore difficult to see how his approach can be favoured simply on the ground that it is theoretically less demanding than some suitable objective alternative. My point is not, however, to articulate and defend a complete objectivist account of fair distributive shares. Rather, I wish to emphasize the hazards of a strategy which makes egalitarian justice a simple function of the interaction of individual subjective preferences.[7] The problem of initial equality cannot be adequately solved without some appeal to an account of the value of resources which is preference-independent. We need a richer account of the relationship between resources and human interests than is provided by merely subjective preferences.

There are, however, two important lines of argument suggested by Dworkin which might be thought to undermine the present objection to the market as a device for determining fair initial distributive shares. Both suggest that greater ethical significance can be assigned to merely subjective preferences for the determination of fair distributive shares than my objection admits.

RESPECT FOR PERSONS

According to the first of these lines of argument, valuations of resources, of the sort relevant to distributive justice, must be predicated on individual preferences because otherwise the fundamental principle that individuals must be treated as equals and respected as persons would be violated. On one statement of what this principle requires we 'must impose no sacrifice or constraint on any citizen in virtue of an argument that the citizen could not accept without abandoning his sense of equal worth' (Dworkin 1985: 205). A theory of fair distribution that was guided, even partly, by an objective account of individual interests might seem to violate this principle because it would respect the judgements of people with plausible views of what is valuable while overriding the judgements of those with mistaken

[7] It is interesting that Dworkin seems to identify the objectivist approach as one potentially suitable way of fleshing out the abstract idea of equality of resources (Dworkin 1981: 226). Surprisingly, however, he does not elaborate or pursue his own suggestion. Thomas Scanlon also argues that objectivist criteria of well-being have an important role to play in a theory of distributive justice (Scanlon 1975: 655–69).

views. Those whose views are overridden or disregarded (because, let us say, they are mistaken) may be denied the opportunity to pursue the convictions that are partly constitutive of their personality. Dworkin seems to hold that a person cannot maintain her sense of equal worth and hence cannot be treated as an equal if her own view of what makes life valuable (as this is reflected in her preferences) is not taken as authoritative for the purpose of determining what sorts of resources it would be valuable to acquire. Each individual's personality—that is, her particular tastes, convictions, and view of the good life—must play a role in determining distributive shares. Consequently, even though people may be mistaken about what is of value to them, it is their own perceptions of value which, on this view, must underlie their sense of equal moral worth and it is these perceptions, accordingly, which must be given full recognition if they are to be treated with genuine respect.

THE ENDORSEMENT CONSTRAINT

Second, Dworkin articulates an interesting thesis about the relationship of the self to its ends which might seem to undercut any criticism of his reliance on people's de facto preferences. As it stands, the objection I have presented seems to have force not simply because the auction may lead to a distribution that fails to achieve the appropriate egalitarian objective, but also because it seems theoretically possible to incorporate an objectivist account of interests into the theory of distributive justice in a way that would obviate the need to predicate equal distributive shares on the potentially unreliable information furnished by preferences. If it is possible to undermine the relevance of any preference-independent strategy for the identification of the value of resources to individuals, then the objection is greatly weakened.

According to the endorsement constraint argument, it can be acknowledged that individual preferences may fail to reflect an individual's actual or objective interest in leading a good life. However, it can still be maintained that when there is a divergence between the conception of the good life held by an individual and that individual's actual interest, it is impossible to secure the individual's genuine interest by simply supplying, directly, the resources which it would *in fact* be in the individual's interest to acquire. Resources can only serve an agent's interest in leading a good life if their use is informed and guided by an appropriate conception of the good life which is actually *endorsed* by the agent. Yet, it does not seem possible to provide agents with substitute conceptions of the good life in anything like the way in which one might provide them with different bundles of resources. A conception of the good life must be chosen and endorsed by a person. It cannot be supplied from outside. We can only lead our lives in light of our own convictions about what sort of life is worth leading, even if these convictions are, in fact, mistaken. There are, then, two general necessary conditions which must be satisfied if a person is to lead a genuinely good life. First, the conception of the good through which the value of given resources and activities to an agent is gauged must be sound. A life predicated on a wholly misconceived conception of the good will fail to be genuinely good, even if an agent endorses the misconceived plan of life as valuable. Second, the agent must endorse the conception of the good at which her life is aimed. The genuine value which may be reflected in a sound conception of the good cannot be transmitted to the person who is the actual subject of a life unless the agent consciously accepts the conception as valuable. Given these conditions, a life can fail in different ways to be good. My life will be bad if I devote it to counting blades of grass. It will be bad even if I firmly believe that counting blades of grass has great value. I may be content but that does not ensure that my life is good. As J. S. Mill pointed out there is a difference between mere contentment and genuine happiness. In this case, my life will be bad because my belief about what is worthwhile for me is false. Similarly, it might be true that my life would be better if I took up painting and that there is thus a sense in which painting *is* an objectively valuable activity for me. However, if I think painting is a waste of time then I will not be able to derive the genuine value of the activity by purchasing oil and canvas and painting landscapes. In this case, the endorsement constraint is not met.

Dworkin explains the endorsement constraint by distinguishing between our 'transparent' and 'opaque' interests in leading a good life. Our 'transparent interest' is our interest in leading the life that is in fact good, while our 'opaque interest' is our interest in leading a life that matches our own view of what sort of life would be good. He argues that although we can, as philosophers, distinguish these interests, agents cannot in the course of leading their lives choose between them. He says that 'even though their highest-order interest is, in the sense we are using, a transparent interest, they can only pursue that interest by falling in with their own beliefs about what kind of life is good' (Dworkin 1983: 28; see also 1989: 85–6). Our opaque interests which are reflected in our subjective preferences enjoy a kind of ethical priority because our transparent interests cannot be realized unless our opaque interests match our transparent interests.

There are different ways in which the endorsement constraint as a general thesis might be defended. One strategy is simply to form a generalization about the endorsement constraint based on the strong intuitive support it receives in a range of representative cases. There are, after all, many examples, both trivial and serious, in which the endorsement constraint seems to command powerful intuitive support. On the trivial side, Raz notes that we cannot 'make someone who does not wish to see a Bogart film enjoy watching it without also making him want to watch it' (Raz 1986: 291–2). On the more serious side, liberals frequently claim that forced participation in even genuinely valuable religious practices cannot succeed in improving a person's life unless she has the relevant religious convictions. As Kymlicka says of the value of prayer, 'we can coerce someone into going to church and making the right physical movements, but we will not make her life better that way' (Kymlicka 1990: 204). This will be true even if prayer is genuinely valuable for the agent—i.e. even if prayer is one of her transparent interests. The obstacle to the achievement of value in these and other similar cases seems to be the absence of an appropriate conviction about the value of the activity in question. The endorsement constraint is credible because it provides a compelling general explanation of our intuitive reaction to these cases.

In more recent work, however, Dworkin tries to supplement the basic intuitive argument with a related but different strategy which aims at providing a deeper philosophical basis for the endorsement constraint. Dworkin now links acceptance of the endorsement constraint to a more comprehensive and complex theory of the nature of ethical value. He contends that the best account of how our lives can have ethical value is captured by a quasi-Aristotelian theory in which 'a good life has the inherent value of a skillful performance' (Dworkin 1991: 57). The good life consists not simply in the achievement of objectively valuable ends but also in a kind of 'skillful response to a complex challenge' which is generated by the circumstances in which we find ourselves. We must, however, direct the performance of our own lives from the inside, according to our own convictions about how to live well. On the *model of challenge*, as Dworkin labels it, 'the connection between conviction and value is constitutive: my life cannot be better for me in virtue of some feature or component I think has no value' (Dworkin 1991: 77). Hence the model of challenge embraces the endorsement constraint. The model of challenge accepts that there is an objective dimension to our interest in leading a good life. Our convictions about what gives value to our lives are fallible and can be mistaken. So our beliefs about the good are not self-validating. Nonetheless, genuine ethical value can only be transmitted to our lives through our convictions. Dworkin believes that the principal alternative account of ethical value is provided by the *model of impact* (Dworkin 1991: 43–57). On this rival account, ethical value is *additive*, in the sense that the goodness of a person's life is a simple function of the sum of its objectively valuable components. Here the overall success of a person's life is to be evaluated in terms of the contribution the life makes to, or the impact it has on, the realization of objective value in the world. On the impact model, endorsement does not serve as a necessary condition for the achievement of good life.[8] Ultimately, Dworkin thinks we should accept the model of challenge in preference to the impact model because the former offers the best overall interpretation of the diverse and complex phenomenology of ethical value. This is, of course, a very controversial claim and I cannot here hope to evaluate the success of the model of challenge in furnishing a satisfactory theory of ethical value. The topic could easily occupy an entire book. However,

---

[8] Endorsement is not irrelevant to the goodness of a life on the impact view. Endorsement can contribute to the goodness of a life but it is not a necessary condition of a good life (Dworkin 1991: 50).

I doubt very much whether the plausibility of the endorsement constraint really stands or falls with the success of the model of challenge. After all, one of the main reasons Dworkin gives for adopting the model of challenge is that it makes sense of our convictions about the constitutive dimension of ethical value. In other words, our convictions about the role of endorsement as a requirement for the achievement of goodness are prior to and distinguishable from the model of challenge. It is, in the first instance, because we think the endorsement constraint has some force that the model of challenge is initially plausible, not vice versa. This, of course, is consistent with the fact that other liberals like Kymlicka and Raz accept the importance of endorsement without expressing any commitment to the challenge model of ethical value.

At any rate, for the purposes of this chapter the issue is how far acceptance of the endorsement constraint provides a suitable basis for predicating a solution to the problem of initial equality on merely subjective preferences. In this context, Dworkin can appeal to the endorsement constraint in the following way. If we assume that preferences for resources expressed in the auction are reflective of convictions about the good life then, given the endorsement constraint, even mistaken subjective preferences assume ethical significance for distributive purposes. In effect, the claim is that in addressing the problem of initial equality, there really is no alternative to relying on subjective individual preferences. The endorsement constraint shows that the attempt to rely upon any alternative account of the true value of resources would be self-defeating insofar as there is a divergence between 'objective' valuations and individual preferences. And insofar as there is a happy convergence between subjective preferences and objective valuations, the latter are superfluous to the solution of the problem of initial equality.

Both the respect for persons argument and the endorsement constraint argument seem powerful. The first argument points to the plausible requirement that, as a matter of respect for persons, distributive shares must be sensitive to individual preferences and to the choices which reflect fundamental individual convictions. The endorsement constraint argument complements and deepens the respect for persons argument. It suggests that distributive shares must be a function of de facto individual preferences because the contribution a resource can make to an individual's life depends on the agent's recognition and acceptance of its value. Since the market responds to and respects individual preferences, it might seem that Dworkin is justified in linking equality and the market after all. However, these considerations seem to support a market-driven theory of fair initial distribution of resources only because a crucial problem concerning the conditions under which preferences are formed has been obscured.

The force of the foregoing arguments in defence of Dworkin's market-based strategy is largely dependent on the tacit assumption that any issue surrounding the ethical significance of preferences can be addressed independently of the problem of equitable initial distribution. Individual preferences (and preference orderings) are treated as fixed ingredients in the problem of determining an equitable initial distribution of resources. The respect for persons and endorsement constraint arguments focus only on the implications for the determination of distributive shares of the assumption that individuals have already formed preferences. In effect, preferences are taken as givens around which the problem of initial distribution must be solved. In the context of the problem of initial equality, however, it is a mistake to privilege preferences in this way.

PREFERENCE FORMATION AND AUTHENTICITY

If, as Dworkin maintains, abstract justice requires demonstrating equal concern for each person's interest in leading a good life, then justice must concern itself with the circumstances under which individuals form their preferences and their views about the good life. The ethical significance which can ultimately be assigned to preferences is partly dependent on their being formed under favourable circumstances. In addressing the problem of how resources should be distributed we cannot assume that favourable circumstances exist or that they cannot be affected by the distribution of resources. A comprehensive theory of distributive justice must confront the problem of what might be called the *circumstances of authenticity*. This is the problem of determining the circumstances under which it is reasonable to suppose that individuals will be able to form what might be termed 'authentic preferences'. Authentic preferences are preferences which accurately reflect an individual's objective interest in leading a good life. Authenticity in this sense is a matter of degree. Though we want our preferences to be authentic, it is unlikely that we can ensure that all our preferences correspond exactly to our objective good. However, some circumstances will be more conducive to the realization of this ideal and the distribution and deployment of social resources can profoundly affect the degree to which the circumstances of authenticity are achieved. It is precisely this dimension of the problem of initial distribution that is obscured by Dworkin's discussion.[9]

At least two conditions must be met if the circumstances of authenticity are to be adequately secured. First, social structures must be conducive to the formation of authentic preferences. Second, distributional arrangements must be such as to ensure that all who have the requisite cognitive capacities are afforded the same opportunity for the formation of authentic preferences. Meeting these conditions requires addressing some problems concerning the initial distribution of resources that cannot be resolved by reference to the standing preferences of individuals. Protecting everyone's interest in being able to form sensible preferences places demands on the distribution and deployment of resources that are prior to fair accommodation of the preferences that persons have. This is easily illustrated.

Consider the value of education. It seems reasonable to assume that justice requires the provision of educational resources to the members of society. But how is this requirement of justice to be explained? The following considerations seem relevant. It is plausible to suppose that a person denied a decent education will be less able to form sensible views about the good life than a person who has enjoyed the benefits of education. The sort of provision and distribution of educational resources secured by a society can clearly affect the degree to which individuals are able to form preferences which are in line with their interest in leading a good life. Thus, it is because we wish to guarantee the

[9] Dworkin is not oblivious to the issue concerning the authenticity of preferences but his discussion is, in my view, too thin. I examine his treatment of the issue a little later in the chapter.

conditions under which everyone can develop sensible views about the good life that we think the provision of education is important. (This is not, of course, the only reason.) This shows that a special resource distribution problem arises when the resources in question—like those involved in the provision of education—have an important impact on the capacity of individuals to form sensible preferences. In order to address this problem, we must identify the sorts of resources which play an important role in facilitating preference formation. However, what makes the problem special is that it cannot be resolved simply by appeal to de facto individual preferences. We think it is crucial to provide individuals with educational resources partly because of the role such resources play in the formation of preferences. We do not think that the importance that attaches to the provision of educational resources is predicated on an expressed preference for them. Individual entitlement to such resources is independent of the expression of individual preference for them.

It is worth noting that education is not the only area in which the market cannot be relied upon to ensure that the circumstances of authenticity are adequate. For instance, the media, especially television, radio, and newspapers, have a significant impact on the formation of preferences. In this area, market forces can work against diversity in a way which can be detrimental to the circumstances of authenticity. One reason for government regulation of the media is to ensure that a variety of viewpoints and programmes, and not just those for which there is current market demand, are readily available to the public. As with the case of education, our interest in being exposed to a variety of perspectives on different issues is not always reflected in our current preferences. Similarly, the artistic and cultural environment in which we develop our views about what is valuable does not always receive adequate support through the market. Valuable cultural institutions are often worth preserving even if there is little immediate demand for them revealed in consumer preferences. Thus state subsidies of the arts and culture may be justifiable because of the contribution they can make to the circumstances of authenticity.[10]

[10] I discuss the case for state support of art and culture in greater detail in Ch. 7.

Dworkin's use of the market as a means of resolving the problem of the initial distribution of resources fails, ultimately, because it is insensitive to this dimension of distributive justice. The market secures a distribution which responds to extant individual preferences. It ignores the distributive issues associated with the problem of adequately securing the conditions under which meaningful individual preferences can be formed. This point about the connection between justice and preference formation furnishes a suitable rejoinder to Dworkin's two arguments for relying exclusively on subjective preferences in the determination of fair initial shares. To begin with, my argument partly circumvents Dworkin's arguments by challenging the idea, implicit in his discussion, that the whole problem of initial distribution should take for granted that individuals have determinate preferences. It may be true that, *once* individuals have preferences, then considerations of the sort Dworkin identifies mean that some distributive problems must be resolved by reference to de facto individual preferences—even if some of these preferences are irrational. But to concede this does nothing to justify the bypassing of problems concerning the acquisition of preferences in the first place. There is, in other words, still a crucial issue which bears upon the initial distribution of resources and which cannot be broached by the market apparatus.

However, my argument also bears more directly on the force of Dworkin's claims about the status of subjective preferences. The claim that respect for persons simply entails respect for the de facto preferences of persons is too sweeping. In fact, whether preferences should be taken at face value depends upon the conditions under which they are formed. For instance, showing appropriate respect for the participants in Dworkin's auction surely does not mean letting them bid for resources while they are intoxicated—even if they indicate willingness to participate while in such a condition. Preferences formed under the influence of drugs or alcohol do not have the same ethical significance as preferences formed under more favourable conditions. My argument suggests that other factors, including the influence of resource distribution on preference formation, are also relevant to assessing the ethical significance of expressed preferences.

The suggestion that subjective preferences must be relied upon in the determination of distributive shares because the contribution a resource can make to a person's life depends on the person's endorsement of the value of the resource is also too broad. The endorsement constraint argument is important and I shall return to it in other contexts. But it only establishes the ethical significance of a subset of subjective preferences, namely those which are related to the implementation of a particular conception of the good held by an agent. In some instances, deriving value from a resource depends on subjective recognition and acceptance of the value of the resource. In these cases, the endorsement constraint explains why merely substituting more valuable resources of some sort for the less valuable resources which are, in fact, preferred by someone cannot contribute to improving a person's life. However, the endorsement argument does not apply with full force to allocations of resources which improve a person's capacity to assess the value of different options and to form sensible preferences. The contribution of resources like basic education to leading a good life does not depend on active endorsement of their value. This is because such resources are largely instrumental to preference formation.[11] They provide us with the wherewithal to make judgements about the sort of life which is worth leading. People can benefit from the provision of education even if they fail to recognize the value of education, which is not true of resources of various other kinds. This means that some distributive issues, especially those associated with securing the circumstances of authenticity, can be addressed without running foul of the endorsement argument.

I should emphasize that I do not wish to be interpreted as arguing that individual preferences (or more generally the market) can have no legitimate role to play in determining fair distributive shares in even an ideal theory of justice. As Scanlon correctly observes, 'the proponent of an objective criterion of well-being need not deny the relevance of subjective preference altogether. A high objective value may be attached to providing those conditions which are necessary to allow individuals to develop their own preferences and interests and

[11] This point is developed in greater detail in Ch. 7, where I discuss the role that the endorsement constraint plays in Dworkin's rejection of perfectionism.

make these felt in the determination of social policy' (Scanlon 1975: 658).

I have not yet explicitly addressed what Dworkin has to say about the authenticity of preferences. In his original presentation of equality of resources, his remarks are cursory. He says:

It might be said . . . that the fairness of an auction supposes that the preferences people bring to the auction, or form in its course, are authentic—the true preferences of the agent rather than the preferences imposed upon him by the economic system itself. Perhaps an auction of any sort, in which one person bids against another, imposes an illegitimate assumption that what is valuable in life is individual ownership of something rather than more cooperative enterprises of the community or some group within it as a whole. Insofar as this (in part mysterious) objection is pertinent here, however, it is an objection against the idea of private ownership over an extensive domain of resources, which is better considered under the title political equality, not an objection to the claim that a market of some sort must figure in any satisfactory account of what equality of what private ownership is. (Dworkin 1981: 290–1)

In this passage, Dworkin rather confusingly conflates at least two distinct issues. One concerns the question whether preferences in the auction are exogenous or endogenous. The other concerns the attractiveness of extensive private ownership of resources. In either case, the kind of authenticity which is identified and dismissed is quite different from the conception of authenticity which I have identified. I am not concerned directly with whether an agent's preferences are really hers but rather with whether the actual preferences of an agent correspond sufficiently closely to her actual interests. Moreover, the problem about the circumstances of authenticity which I have raised speaks directly to the problem of the distribution of privately held resources. So it cannot be dismissed as a problem of political equality which can be broached independently. In this passage, Dworkin gives us no reason to believe that the character of the preferences held by participants in the auction is not relevant to assessing the fairness of the outcome determined by the auction.

In subsequent work the importance of authenticity is given greater recognition. Indeed, Dworkin articulates a *principle of authenticity* which stipulates that prior to entering the auction parties must have ample opportunity to form their convictions rationally (Dworkin 1987: 34–6). This principle did not play a role in Dworkin's original exposition of the connection between the market and initial equality. The principle of authenticity is introduced in the context of his attempt to accommodate a strong commitment to liberty within his egalitarian theory. But it might also seem that this principle rescues Dworkin's account of initial equality from the foregoing criticisms. If we could, courtesy of a prior principle of authenticity, ensure that the pre-auction preferences of the immigrants are authentic, in the sense of being rationally formed, then the outcome of the auction could more plausibly be viewed as representing a just initial distribution of resources. So by invoking a principle of authenticity as a necessary precondition of the auction, Dworkin seems to provide a way around the difficulty with the auction identified above. Convictions that are formed under the conditions required by the principle of authenticity could not be ill-conceived in the sense required to get the argument of this chapter off the ground. After all, Dworkin says that the principle of authenticity requires the protection of 'the parties' freedom to engage in activities crucial to forming and reviewing the convictions, commitments, associations, projects and tastes that they bring to the auction' (Dworkin 1987: 35).

Unfortunately, appeal to the principle of authenticity merely evades and does not respond to the basic difficulty. The reason is simple. We cannot ensure that the principle of authenticity is satisfied without broaching problems concerning the initial distribution of resources. As my argument shows, individuals must be provided with resources if they are to come to develop authentic preferences. There is then a distributive issue about how resources needed to create conditions of authenticity are to be distributed. How should resources be distributed in order to ensure that people can form sensible plans, goals, and convictions where this in turn will allow them to make sensible purchases in the auction? But this problem is, in effect, just one aspect of the problem of initial equality restated. We face all the problems of determining what a just distribution would consist in and how we should determine the value of different resources. Presumably, Dworkin would think that the resources needed to generate the conditions which satisfy the principle of authenticity should be distributed in a manner which is consistent with each person's interest in leading a good life receiving full and equal consideration. Perhaps the egalitarian ideal requires that resources of equal value should be devoted to each person in facilitating sensible preference formation. We are back to where we started from. Now, however, it seems impossible to invoke the idea of an auction as a compelling way of solving the problem of distributive equality because the metric of opportunity costs cannot be relied upon to determine the value of resources relevant to securing the circumstances of authenticity. Indeed, in order to solve this aspect of the problem of initial equality, we need to appeal to some preference-independent account of interests by reference to which the value of the relevant resources can be gauged. In spelling out the connection between the market and equality of resources, Dworkin reminds us that 'it is sovereign in this argument . . . that people enter the market on equal terms' (Dworkin 1981: 289). Yet people cannot enter the market on genuinely equal terms unless the problem of authenticity has been addressed and the market offers no solution to this problem.

The general conclusion to be drawn from the argument of this chapter is that a preference-sensitive market distribution of resources cannot address all the relevant dimensions of the problem of fair initial distribution. The need to consider the impact of resource distribution on the formation of preferences, to which I have drawn attention, is, of course, only one aspect of justice. We must also consider how to distribute resources for the pursuit (as opposed to the formation) of preferences. It is possible that the market, because it is sensitive to opportunity costs, has some role to play in providing a solution to this problem. Yet the demonstration that the market equalizes opportunity costs is probably not sufficient to save equality of resources. An initial distribution of resources in which opportunity costs, as measured by the market, are equal will not ensure that everyone has a fair share of resources if the preferences to which the metric of opportunity costs respond are not authentic. Dworkin's market-based theory encounters problems because it does not adequately distinguish the different elements of distributive justice implicated in the problem of fair initial distribution. As a consequence it offers a distorted picture of the way in which preferences have ethical significance. And thus in this respect, the market does not succeed as a device for illuminating the demands of egalitarian justice. We must now consider how well it handles other aspects of justice.

3

Equality through Time

A COMPREHENSIVE theory of distributive justice must have a dynamic component. It should explain how an equitable distribution of resources can be maintained through time. This problem has different dimensions. At one level, we want to know what criteria of justice we should employ to assess the fairness of the outcomes generated by the complex interplay of exchange, production, and luck. After all, it need not be the case that the criteria in virtue of which we judge an initial distribution of resources to be just are identical to the criteria we employ to judge subsequent distributions.[1] Even the apparently simple demand that a distribution of resources through time be equal is subject to a variety of interpretations. At another level, we want to know what sorts of institutions are required to ensure that an equitable distribution is maintained. There is a long tradition in liberal theory of supposing that the market will be central among the requisite institutions. Even theorists further to the left are increasingly exploring ways in which the market can be harnessed and manipulated in the pursuit of various egalitarian objectives.[2] The fact that the market, in some form, will inevitably occupy a central place in contemporary societies raises various issues about the capacity of the market to sustain justice on an ongoing basis. If the requirements of justice can be identified independently of the market, then we will be interested in determining the degree to which the market is able to achieve justice.

[1] For instance, Nozick's historical entitlement theory of justice has three distinct components: (1) an account of justice in initial acquisition; (2) an account of justice in transfer; and (3) an account of the rectification of injustices arising out of violations of either (1) or (2) (Nozick 1974).

[2] With respect to the problem of equality through time there are a variety of theorists who argue that the market can, in principle, maintain a fair distribution through time. See for instance Carens (1985: 55), Varian (1985: 115), and Rakowski (1991: 70–1). Krouse and MacPherson even argue that Rawls can be interpreted as committed to this idea (Krouse and MacPherson 1988: 92–3; cf. Rawls 1971: 305).

Where the market fails to preserve justice, we will be interested in determining what sorts of interventions or adjustments to market-derived outcomes are necessary. The striking feature of Dworkin's theory, in the context of these issues, is the idea that the ideal market converges perfectly with the requirements of justice. In its capacity to preserve justice through time the market is inherently, not merely contingently, egalitarian. The ultimate objective of this chapter is to explain and challenge Dworkin's contention that the market, albeit in an extremely idealized form, provides the solution to this problem of distributive justice. First, however, I want to discuss some of the underlying issues that motivate and give shape to the general problem of equality through time.

RESPONSIBILITY AND ENTITLEMENT

One of the common criticisms levelled at left-liberalism, at both a theoretical and political level, is that it fails to give sufficient recognition to the importance of individual responsibility. As a consequence liberal theories allegedly do not capture the compelling idea that the determination of distributive shares through time should be affected by choices for which individuals can be held responsible. At the political level, liberalism's supposed disregard of the significance of individual responsibility is thought to be reflected in various welfare-state programmes which implicitly deny that the poor who benefit from such programmes should accept responsibility for ameliorating their material condition. Right-wing critics frequently allege that welfare rolls are filled with able-bodied individuals who are capable of providing adequately for themselves but who choose to take advantage of overly generous social programmes. Many of the recipients of social assistance are characterized as undeserving and as placing unfair burdens on those members of the community who accept responsibility for their lives. Since I am principally concerned with liberal theory, I shall not attempt to refute the sociological mythology upon which this popular piece of conservative rhetoric is based. However, some sympathetic commentators have suggested that liberal egalitarian theory, by giving short shrift to notions of individual responsibility, leaves itself open to the kind of criticism that fuels conservative attacks on the welfare state.

The charge that contemporary liberal theory does not adequately accommodate individual responsibility is in large part traceable to the rejection by Rawls of the idea that a notion of desert has a role to play in determining distributive shares.[3] Rawls's argument against making a distributive scheme sensitive to considerations of desert depends on emphasizing the moral arbitrariness of the distribution of the sorts of individual characteristics that are often thought to ground desert claims. Since no one can 'claim credit' for their native endowment or the features of their character determined by social circumstance, no one can advance a valid claim that they deserve or are entitled to resources in virtue of features they arbitrarily have and others arbitrarily lack (Rawls 1971: 104). The question which the familiar Rawlsian argument raises is whether the recognition of the moral arbitrariness of social and natural contingency effectively eliminates any substantial conception of individual responsibility from liberal theory. Recently, Samuel Scheffler has offered a pessimistic assessment of liberalism's resources in this regard (Scheffler 1992). He argues that the sort of naturalism to which liberals appeal in defending claims about the determination of individual traits by social and natural contingency leads to general scepticism about ascriptions of individual responsibility. If, as naturalism might seem to imply, we really have no legitimate philosophical basis for holding individuals responsible for any of their actions, decisions, or preferences—because all such choices are determined by forces outside the control of the individual—then we cannot claim that individuals are differentially entitled to resources in virtue of responsible choices they make.

Although acceptance of the general soundness of a broadly naturalistic explanation of human action inevitably shrinks the range of actions for which individuals can legitimately be held responsible, it does not necessarily eliminate the category of individual responsibility altogether. Even in the face of naturalism, there may be many responsibility-generating choices. Nagel, for instance, insists that 'apart from pathological condi-

---

[3] The utilitarian strain of liberal thought is also generally hostile to considerations of desert.

tions, the level of someone's effort is the result of free choice' (Nagel 1991: 118). Yet, whether liberal theory actually gives suitable recognition to a conception of individual responsibility that plays a role in determining entitlement to resources is a matter of some controversy. Consider the ambiguity about this issue in Rawls's theory. On the one hand, Rawls insists that individuals be 'regarded as taking responsibility for their ends and this affects how their various claims are assessed' (Rawls 1985: 243). But on the other hand, the distribution of income secured by the difference principle is not sensitive to an entitlement-grounding principle of individual responsibility. The difference principle instructs us to distribute income equally, unless an unequal income improves the situation of the worse-off representative group. The possibility that members of the worse-off representative group owe their situation to ends they have chosen and could have reasonably not chosen does not play a role in determining what share of income they should receive. The tension evident in Rawls's theory reflects a general difficulty in much liberal theory. Few liberals wish to abandon the idea that individuals may be held responsible for many of the choices they make. Yet there has been little work on how a suitable principle of individual responsibility can be systematically incorporated into a theory of distributive justice.

AMBITION-SENSITIVITY

Insofar as liberals recognize the legitimacy of making distributive shares sensitive to the choices made by responsible agents, they need a theory of how this requirement can be tracked. Such a theory should explain the way in which individual choices about the consumption and production of current resources affect entitlement to future resources. Dworkin's theory makes a particularly important contribution to liberal theory precisely because it speaks directly to this issue. Recognition of the importance of individual responsibility is given through the requirement that the distribution of resources be *ambition-sensitive*. That is, the distribution should reflect choices freely made by individuals about how to lead their lives. There are, of course, many sorts of decisions that bear upon the sort of life we choose to live, but in the context of the distribution of resources secured in some kind of market setting we can roughly distinguish three kinds of choices which may legitimately ground differences in the holdings of individuals. First, there are choices concerning the mix of work and leisure in one's life. A person may be able to earn more income by working harder or by putting in longer hours. Second, there are what might be called 'production choices'. These are decisions about what sorts of goods and services to produce or provide. The more we make available what is in demand by others, the more resources we may acquire through market transactions. Often these decisions are reflected in our choice of occupation. We may decide whether to be a doctor or an artist and our decision will affect the resources available to us. If our chosen occupation produces something highly valued by other members of the community then we can acquire more resources than if we had chosen a less highly valued occupation. Third, there are choices concerning the sorts of risks one is prepared to take in leading one's life. While one person may choose to run high risks with a small chance of a huge payoff, another may prefer to minimize risk in order to secure a more modest but more likely payoff. To some degree, one's life will be affected by the risks one is prepared to undertake and by how luck plays itself out through such decisions. The fact that luck plays a role in determining a distribution of resources does not necessarily mean that the distribution is morally arbitrary. In this context, Dworkin makes a useful distinction between different kinds of luck. 'Option luck is a matter of how deliberate and calculated gambles turn out— whether someone gains or loses through accepting an isolated risk he or she should have anticipated and might have declined. Brute luck is a matter of how risks fall out that are not in that sense deliberate gambles' (Dworkin 1981: 281). Some inequalities which reflect the operation of option luck are fair whereas those attributable to brute luck are generally problematic.

Dworkin does not carefully distinguish the kinds of choices which are relevant to resource entitlement. Nor does he analyse any relevant differences there may be in the degree to which these choices provide legitimate grounds for differences in resource holdings. What is crucial for him is that they represent ways in which people may differ in their ambitions. A genuinely egalitarian distribution should be sensitive to differences in the ambitions of individuals and this means that differences in the size of resource bundles (e.g. income) held by individuals can be consistent with, and indeed may be required by, the best interpretation of equality. So whereas differences in resource holdings that arise from unequal natural endowment—as when the services of the talented command a higher price—are not fair, those which reflect differences in freely made decisions about how to live one's life are fair and represent no departure from a commitment to distributive equality.

Generating an account of how ambition-sensitivity can be accurately tracked is made considerably more complicated by the arbitrary differences in native endowment that actually obtain in the real world. Consequently, Dworkin first approaches the problem of tracking ambition-sensitivity under the idealizing assumption that each person's capacity to earn resources is unaffected by disabilities or by differences in talent. In this admittedly abstract context, Dworkin claims that the perfectly competitive market can preserve equality and track ambition as parties with initially equal shares engage in trade and production. Equality of resources 'supposes that if people begin with the same wealth and other resources, then equality is preserved through market transactions among them, even though some grow richer than others and some happier through these transactions' (Dworkin 1986: 297). The argument which supports this claim depends on linking a conception of individual responsibility with a view of the procedural fairness secured by the market. It claims that differences in the rewards which accrue to market activity fairly reflect differences in the choices individuals make about the sorts of lives they wish to lead and for which they must assume responsibility. It is fair to hold individuals responsible for the consequences that their decisions have for their lives because the market, from a position of initial equality, offers every individual the same (initial) opportunities. In this way the market displays a kind of procedural fairness. Differences in resource holdings generated by market activity are thus simply the upshot of the different choices individuals make as they respond to opportunities which are open to all in light of their preferences about what sort of life they wish to lead. So there are two related claims that form the core of this part of

Dworkin's theory. First, individual entitlements should be a function of choices about how to lead one's life. Second, the market can, from a position of initial equality, fairly and accurately gauge the degree to which decisions about one's life should affect one's entitlements.

Unless we succumb to across-the-board scepticism, inspired by naturalism, about choice and responsibility, there is clear intuitive support for the first of these claims. It simply seems to follow from accepting the principle that individuals capable of self-direction must assume an important measure of responsibility for the ends they pursue and for the consequent shape of their lives. This principle is not unqualified. Most importantly, the degree to which individuals may be held accountable for their lot in life is influenced by the degree to which their lives are conducted in circumstances where justice obtains and by the degree to which they exercise effective control over their lives. Yet in the hypothetical circumstances envisioned by Dworkin, circumstances in which initial equality has been established, it is reasonable to suppose that different choices by individuals can justify differences in individual entitlement to resources. It is reasonable, in other words, for resource holdings to be influenced by willingness to work hard, to produce what others value or to undertake risks.

It is less clear, however, that the entitlements that might be established over time by even a perfectly competitive market match our intuitions about the degree to which the principle of individual responsibility requires or permits the distribution of resources to be affected by these factors. I will attempt to demonstrate that considerations of fairness arising out of acceptance of a principle of individual responsibility can be violated by the unfettered operation of the market, even when a position of initial equality is presumed and when distribution is not influenced by arbitrary differences in natural endowment. In challenging Dworkin's analysis, my strategy will be to construct a series of counter-examples designed to reveal a divergence between the market-driven account of ambition-sensitivity and our pre-theoretical convictions about the appropriate impact of choice on important human interests. Let's begin by examining the rationale for the market theory of ambition-sensitivity and equality through time more closely.

A MARKET THEORY OF AMBITION-SENSITIVITY

Dworkin believes that the market is the appropriate device for tracking the idea that a distribution should be ambition-sensitive primarily because the results it secures are sanctioned by the envy test when it is applied synoptically (Dworkin 1981: 304–5). This test ensures that aggregate opportunity costs, over a lifetime, are equal.[4] A distribution of resources that satisfies this test provides each person with an equally valuable bundle of resources as measured by each person's preferences. Such a distribution can plausibly be billed as satisfying the abstract demand that each person is to be treated as an equal in the distribution of resources and opportunities. This does not necessarily mean that each person's bundle of resources at any given time is identical. Instead, the idea is that the envy test should ideally apply to the bundle of resources that a person holds over an entire life and that in applying the test we must focus not only on the actual resource holdings of individuals but on the decisions that gave rise to them. For example, even though a person who preferred a life of leisure to one of hard work might prefer the material holdings of someone who worked hard throughout her life, she does not prefer the bundle of the hard worker if that includes a life of hard work. The envy test, synoptically applied, is satisfied because each person prefers the life she leads over-all—including the mix of resources and labour that sort of life requires—to the lives lived by others. In a similar way, while the non-gambler may desire the winnings of the gambler, she prefers a life with fewer risks and no gambling winnings to that of the gambler which, though it may include great gains, also presents the risk of great losses.

Given a background of initial equality, the perfectly competitive market can ensure that the envy test is satisfied on an ongoing basis because the market provides each participant with the same initial opportunities. All differences in income and other resources are traceable to a pattern of individual decisions concerning consumption and production. What individuals derive from market interaction will depend on the decisions they

---

[4] Remember that the special metric of opportunity costs 'fixes the value of a transferable resource one person has as the value others forgo by his having it' (Dworkin 1987: 26).

make but since each individual is, at least initially, faced with the same range of alternatives, differences in income and other resources reflecting different individual choices will pass the scrutiny of the envy test and thus be fair. Distribution tracks choice and the requirement of ambition-sensitivity is thereby met. Obviously no real market comes close to providing individuals with initially equal options, so this argument does not provide any assurance that real markets are consistent with maintaining equality through time. Nevertheless, it is worth considering whether this theory of ambition-sensitivity really is faithful to our egalitarian convictions. After all, the degree to which the theory is sound will affect our judgements about how equality through time might be approximated by actual institutions.

It is certainly true that the ideal market is responsive to choices exhibited in people's preferences. The difficulty is that it is not always responsive in the right way. The general problem I identify here is most pronounced in economies in which technological innovation and other factors have an impact on the production, supply, and value of resources. However, we can detect difficulties with the market theory of ambition-sensitivity even in economies concerned only with the exchange of a fixed supply of goods. The objections I raise revolve around difficulties with supposing that the market can appropriately accommodate conflicting individual preferences about risk-taking and the exertion of effort in economic settings. In the exchange economy example with which I shall begin, only different preferences concerning risk will be scrutinized. Specifically, I shall suggest that some types of gambling permitted in unregulated exchange economies can have unfair consequences.

There are, and can be, no non-paternalistic restrictions on the running of lotteries in Dworkin's scheme.[5] Moreover, Dworkin is committed to viewing the distribution of resources secured by a fair lottery, against a background of initial equality, as a distribution consistent with the demands of equality. A fair lottery is one which is open to all at the same odds. As we have already noted, the envy test, applied comprehensively, is satisfied by a fair lottery and its outcome. That 'fair' gambles gener-

---

[5] Dworkin seems to allow that gambling may be restricted on paternalistic grounds but he does not develop the suggestion (Dworkin 1981: 295).

ate fair outcomes is a popular view. Rakowski, for instance, states that 'gambling poses no threat to a just distribution of goods, so long as equality of resources prevails and all have an equal chance to wager' (Rakowski 1991). I suspect, however, that our convictions about the fairness of some lottery-generated outcomes does not extend to all such outcomes. Indeed, I think it is only when individuals are adequately insulated from the potentially adverse consequences of certain types of gambling that we are prepared to endorse the outcome of lotteries as fair. The objection I develop here assumes both that we can assess the relative significance of at least some kinds of human interests and that we can assess, at least roughly, the rationality of different kinds of risk-taking. By considering whether the operation of a lottery within a simple exchange economy can generate results that are problematic from the perspective of an egalitarian conception of fairness, we can begin to evaluate this dimension of Dworkin's theory.

So let us return to the artificial world of Dworkin's imaginary desert island after the original auction of resources. Since the envy test is satisfied, no one will want to exchange the resources they control for other resources. Therefore, trade amongst the immigrants can only take place after the immigrants use their initial allotment of goods to produce goods for which there is demand. I want to set aside, for the time being, complications that are introduced when there is uncertainty about what sorts of goods can be produced by current and future methods of production and technology. So we will stipulate: (1) that everyone knows exactly what goods can be produced by the current means of production; (2) that the available means of production will not change; and (3) that returns to production are constant in that there are no economies of scale. Later we will see what happens when these conditions are relaxed. In these circumstances, the immigrants, having introduced money as a convenient medium of exchange, will be able to trade the new goods they create from their initial share of resources through various market transactions. To keep the example fairly simple let us suppose that among the many goods that have been produced from the initial allocation of resources are two retirement communities, one that provides tennis facilities and another that provides golf facilities. A dozen of the islanders are interested in

these options. Each of them has $10,000 in retirement savings
and each retirement community has 600 hours per year of
recreational activity to allocate amongst its guests on a user-pay
basis.

Each person is faced with a choice about the community to
which she would prefer to retire. We can imagine, following
Dworkin, that each person's decision will be shaped by beliefs
about how available goods might contribute to the leading of
a good life. The decision to choose a tennis resort over a golf
resort will be influenced by a number of factors (e.g. how much
one likes golf or tennis) but one of the important factors will be
each person's sense of the degree to which she will be able to
satisfy her tastes given the tastes of others. As individuals who
are capable of assuming responsibility for their ends, the immigrants can adjust their preferences in light of information about
the expected availability of some good. For instance, a person
might decide to take up tennis instead of golf because, given
other people's interest in golf and how that can be expected to
affect opportunities to play golf, she might not be able to play as
much golf as she might like. Let's suppose in our example that
six islanders are interested in tennis and six in golf. All the
islanders acknowledge that they are responsible for the tastes
they choose to adopt and they recognize, consequently, that they
must be prepared to adjust their expectations in light of the
tastes of others. If individuals are to be held responsible for and
bear a fair share of the costs of their consumption choices they
need to know what the relevant menu of choices contains and
they need to be able to form reasonable expectations about what
they will be able to acquire given the tastes of others.[6]

In these circumstances, the market does appear to provide
a suitable mechanism for conveying the relevant information
and for providing an allocation of resources that fairly reflects
the degree to which each person's share of goods is a complex
function of freely made choices. The price system of a market
sends signals to consumers about what they can expect given the
tastes of others. As Dworkin says, the market is 'an institution-

---

[6] There is the logical possibility that no determinate pattern of tastes will be
generated in this way since mutual adjustments in tastes in response to the perceived
tastes of others might go on *ad infinitum*. I think, however, that we can view this as
merely a logical possibility.

alized form of the process of discovery and adaptation at the center of equality of resources' (Dworkin 1981: 314). Moreover, the prices that are established when the market is in equilibrium can be plausibly represented as fairly tracking the cost that each person's choices impose on others. Why does the market distribution strike us as eminently fair? I suspect the principal reason is that we have no compelling reason to suppose that there is any morally relevant difference between the taste for tennis and the taste for golf. With such commodities we have no plausible basis either for privileging individual islanders (e.g. by guaranteeing some a fixed share of their favoured resource) or for privileging the satisfaction of certain tastes over others (e.g. by supposing that the satisfaction of tennis preferences has greater intrinsic importance or urgency than golf preferences). The market can work in an egalitarian fashion here because, against a background of initial equality, it assigns equal weight to the equally morally significant preferences of each person. Where tastes between tennis and golf are evenly distributed, the market will permit each person to acquire the same number of hours per year of their preferred retirement activity. Of course, if more of the islanders are interested in tennis than golf then the market will provide each tennis player correspondingly fewer hours of play. Golfers, by contrast, will be able to buy more time on the links. In this way, the market provides a choice-sensitive way of gauging the expense of different tastes.

EXCHANGE GAMBLES

It is possible, however, to construct variations on the foregoing example in which market activity, even when it is confined to voluntary exchange of resources amongst equally situated individuals, does not yield a distribution that seems acceptable from an egalitarian point of view. Consider how the introduction of a certain form of gambling might lead us to lose confidence in the adequacy of a purely market-driven distribution. Suppose that our dozen islanders are ten years from retirement and suppose that their preferences have the following complexion. As before, half of the islanders are interested in golf and half are interested in tennis. However, four of the would-be tennis players and four of the would-be golf players are also prepared to enter a lottery in which they each risk all of their retirement savings for the chance of increasing their retirement income eightfold. We can call this an *exchange gamble*. The chances of winning the lottery are poor—only 1 in 8—and the stakes are very high, but we may suppose that each gambler is willing to lose everything in order to acquire the small chance of substantially increasing the number of hours of recreation she will be able to enjoy in retirement. The gamblers decide to hold the lottery ten years from now on the eve of their retirement. Before they actually retire, the islanders have an interest in practising golf or tennis in anticipation of retirement. Those who expect or hope to retire to the tennis community will naturally develop tennis skills appropriate to their planned retirement activity. Similarly, golfers will hone their drives, chips, and putts. Indeed, one reason the gamblers decide to hold the lottery ten years hence is that the losers of the lottery might lose any satisfaction from the leisure activities currently open to them if they knew now that they could not pursue those activities in retirement. So suppose the lottery is set up and is ultimately won by one of the tennis enthusiasts, leading to the distribution of resources described by Table 1.

The tennis player, T3, is the big winner of the lottery. With her winnings she can purchase much more court time than the other tennis enthusiasts. Of course, more time for her means considerably less time for T1 and T2. Similarly, after the lottery, there are fewer golfers with resources to devote to golf. Consequently, G5 and G6 have access to much more time on the course. Dworkin's theory implies that the consequences of running such a lottery are consistent with securing each person a fair share of resources. The envy test is satisfied because the non-gamblers prefer playing it safe to running the reckless risks of the gamblers and vice versa. Nonetheless, it is not obvious that a distribution so heavily determined by the excessively risk-tolerant preferences of the immigrants is really fair to those who did not wish to gamble. After all, the lives of the non-gamblers are significantly affected by decisions to gamble which are utterly irrational. Before the lottery, both the risk-averse tennis players (T1 and T2) and the risk-averse golfers (G5 and G6) run a 50 per cent risk of being unable to enjoy a satisfactory retire-

TABLE 1. *The lottery*

	Pre-Lottery Distribution		Post-Lottery Distribution	
	$	Hours tennis/golf	$	Hours tennis/golf
T1	10,000	100	10,000	60 tennis
T2	10,000	100	10,000	60 tennis
T3	10,000	100	80,000	480 tennis
T4	10,000	100	0	0
T5	10,000	100	0	0
T6	10,000	100	0	0
G1	10,000	100	0	0
G2	10,000	100	0	0
G3	10,000	100	0	0
G4	10,000	100	0	0
G5	10,000	100	10,000	300 golf
G6	10,000	100	10,000	300 golf

ment because their fellow consumers are willing to accept a very bad bet. (Suppose that everyone agrees that a minimum of 75 hours of recreational activity of either golf or tennis is necessary to have a satisfactory retirement.)

In this sort of exchange setting there is reason to believe that the unrestricted gambling permitted by the market may generate consequences that are objectionable from the point of view of justice. The most obvious concern is that gambling may introduce an unacceptable degree of uncertainty about the sorts of lives persons who are not gamblers can reasonably expect to be able to pursue. We might believe that the gambler must accept the uncertainty that goes with her decision to gamble along with the eventual outcome of her gamble. If she wins, she enjoys good option luck and if she loses she has bad option luck. However, we cannot suppose that it is fair to require non-gamblers to acquiesce in whatever degree of uncertainty (about, for example, the kinds and quantities of goods that will be available for consumption) that can be generated under free market conditions because of the willingness of some to gamble. Individuals have an important interest in securing conditions under which they are able to form and implement plans in light of reasonable expectations about the sorts of lives that are available to them. We can call this the interest in reasonable predictability. This interest can be unfairly jeopardized if there are no market-independent limits on the degree of uncertainty arising out of the willingness of some to gamble. This is not to say that *any* degree of uncertainty is inconsistent with fair recognition of the interest in forming reasonable expectations. The point, rather is that the market itself provides no assurance that this interest will be given *adequate* recognition. Indeed, the market allows this substantial interest to be undermined by irrational and unreasonable attitudes to risk-taking.

The above example illustrates this point. The reasonably risk-averse islanders' interest in being able to plan for the future is significantly undermined by the willingness of others to accept a manifestly irrational high-stake bet. It is unfair to penalize individuals who assume reasonable attitudes to risk simply to accommodate the unreasonable attitudes of others. Indeed, such treatment would seem plainly inconsistent with a plausible interpretation of the abstract egalitarian thesis. We fail to treat individuals as equals, in the relevant sense, if we give equal weight both to the expression of irrational attitudes to risk and to protecting conditions conducive to forming and implementing plans. The interest we have in enjoying an environment in which we can successfully form and implement plans is an aspect of our most fundamental interest in leading a good life. By contrast, preserving the opportunity to act on irrational attitudes to risk hardly qualifies as a comparable interest. Justice requires us to distinguish between the reasonableness of different attitudes to risk and to determine, in light of these distinctions, the degree to which the consequences of risk-taking should be permitted to affect the interest that members of the community have in maintaining a relatively stable environment.

In the foregoing example, I have emphasized the threat to the interest in reasonable predictability posed by *highly irrational* risk-taking. Yet there may be cases in which the interest in reasonable predictability is threatened by risk-taking which is perfectly reasonable. For example, there may be investment opportunities which are reasonable to pursue but which have extremely uncertain and potentially adverse consequences. Whereas the importance which attaches to the interest in reasonable predictability is obviously greater than preferences for irrational risk-taking, determining the relative significance of the interest in reasonable predictability and preferences for reasonable risk-taking is more difficult. This raises the question as to how the claim to protection of the interest in reasonable predictability should be interpreted. One possibility is that fairness only requires protection of the interest when it is jeopardized by the side-effects of irrational risk-taking. A stronger interpretation is that individuals can insist upon protection of the interest in reasonable predictability from threats stemming from *both* rational and irrational risk-taking.[7] Although I am unsure how this issue should be resolved, I am inclined to the weaker interpretation. It seems arbitrary to limit reasonable risk-taking in order to safeguard reasonable predictability because the significance of the competing interests here seems quite comparable. At any rate, the objections to Dworkin's argument will go through on the weak interpretation and it is this interpretation upon which my analysis relies.

The failure of the market to give appropriate weight to different preferences also suggests that the market will not track ambition-sensitivity properly. In this case, the relationship of the choices made by individuals and the burdens they face is inappropriate. The non-gamblers who exercise due care and prudence in planning their lives face the frustration of a significant interest whereas the gamblers who choose to act foolishly are able to satisfy their preferences even though this imposes costs on responsible members of the community. The market can be too accommodating of irrational choices and thus not sufficiently responsive to rational choices. However, the crucial distinctions between different kinds of choice needed to track the distributional implications of choice cannot be drawn by the mechanism which is supposed to ensure fairness in the market— namely, the envy test.

The failure of the envy test to provide a basis for the distinction between reasonable and unreasonable forms of risk-taking is easy to diagnose. Dworkin's metric of opportunity costs

---

[7] It is possible that the potential tension between the interest in reasonable predictability and preferences for reasonable risk-taking is more illusory than real. After all, a lot of reasonable risks have consequences that can be reasonably anticipated. If this is generally the case then there will be no need to choose between the weak and strong interpretations of the claim to protection of the interest in reasonable predictability.

assigns equal weight to all personal preferences,[8] reasonable and unreasonable, rational and irrational, in gauging the value of resources and opportunities. The degree to which preferences of any sort can be satisfied is simply a matter of what the market will bear and this, in turn, is a function of the interaction of existing preferences. Thus the irrational preference for engaging in high-stakes gambling at poor odds can be satisfied only to the degree that others share this preference. But the fact that the preference is irrational plays no role in determining whether it can be satisfied. The envy test, because it is merely a function of these preferences, is necessarily insensitive to independent assessment of the relative moral significance which attaches to their satisfaction. The seeming virtue of the market for the tracking of ambition-sensitivity is that because it does not systematically privilege any preferences it seems to provide an impartial mechanism for determining how each person's choices should affect entitlement to resources. In this way it might seem that no person's preferences are unduly favoured over others. Certainly, it is plausible to suppose that a genuinely egalitarian theory should not *arbitrarily* privilege any preferences. However, from the fact that preferences should not be *arbitrarily* privileged it does not follow that we should make no effort to determine the moral significance of different personal preferences. And insofar as we have reason to think that certain preferences are weightier than others then we do not abandon our commitment to impartiality by treating such preferences differently.

OBJECTIONS

(a) Are irrational preferences special?

I must anticipate two objections to the foregoing analysis. First, it might be suggested that although some tastes (e.g. for some

---

[8] Although he does not make the point explicitly, I assume that Dworkin believes that only 'personal preferences' should have any weight in this context. So-called 'external preferences' should not be permitted to influence the determination of opportunity costs. The distinction between personal and external preferences was initially drawn by Dworkin in the context of a criticism utilitarianism. A personal preference is a preference for goods or opportunities for oneself whereas an external preference is a 'preference for the assignment of goods and opportunities to others' (Dworkin 1977: 234).

types of gambling) may be irrational the consequences of those tastes need be no different from the consequences of reasonable tastes. Since we would not be justified in voicing objection to outcomes generated by reasonable tastes we cannot be justified in objecting to the identical outcomes if they happen to be generated by irrational tastes. The point here is that, in the exchange economy example, the distribution of resources which is generated by the lottery *could* have arisen simply out of a different pattern of individual tastes for the available resources. One difficulty with this argument is that the unfairness detected in the lottery is not with the distribution of resources per se but rather with how the uncertainty generated by the lottery affects individual plans. As I have indicated, Dworkin argues that, in the ideal conditions under which his scheme operates, individuals will adjust their tastes for goods in light of the tastes of others and that a kind of equilibrium will emerge from this process of mutual adjustment. For this process to work, individuals must be reasonably confident about the goods that will be available given the tastes of others. Yet it is this confidence which is threatened by some forms of destabilizing market activity. Moreover, even if some degree of uncertainty about how the tastes of others will affect the availability of goods is inevitable, it is appropriate that we distinguish between more and less reasonable sources of uncertainty. Whereas some disruption of certainty which is traceable to changes in tastes caused by rational reflection on the value of goods is tolerable and unavoidable, extensive uncertainty arising from irrational, high-stakes gambling is much more difficult to defend. While some level of certainty is an important good, it is not always an overriding good. Nonetheless, if levels of uncertainty are too great and if they are generated by irrational behaviour then people have a claim of fairness that uncertainty be controlled.

I should emphasize that my arguments are not designed to show that all gambling need be inconsistent with securing an environment which is conducive to forming and implementing individual plans or that any degree of uncertainty is antithetical to fair accommodation of this interest. Some degree of gambling-induced uncertainty may be acceptable. And in many cases the effects of irrational gambling behaviour on more significant interests may be negligible. Moreover, there are likely to be difficult problems in determining how much weight the interest in preservation of a level of certainty should have as against the interest some individuals have in pursuing high-stakes gambles. My claim is that the market gives insufficient recognition to the importance of reasonable predictability. The market cannot, by itself, distinguish between reasonable and unreasonable sources and levels of uncertainty or determine properly the degree to which certainty should be preserved. The relevant standards for making these judgements are complex and probably imprecise but whatever they are, they are independent of the market.

(b) The real world

A second possible objection to the foregoing argument is that the example from which it proceeds is rather contrived in that it depends on the concentration of a rather unusual pattern of tastes within a numerically small segment of the population. Perhaps in the real world the problematic irrational tastes for gambling would be more diffuse and thus would not generate, at least in any significant form, the sort of problem I have drawn attention to here. This is a fair enough point, and it suggests we should not exaggerate the significance of the damage to Dworkin's position established by my argument. I have not shown that, in more realistic settings, market institutions would not provide the most feasible approximation to arrangements for the tracking of ambition-sensitivity. Nonetheless, Dworkin makes a substantial theoretical claim which I believe we now have grounds for doubting, namely that the perfectly competitive market perfectly tracks ambition-sensitivity. We can distinguish the question of the technical accuracy of Dworkin's claim from the practical overall significance of any technical failings we detect. If counter-examples of the sort constructed here seem plausible, then we have at least one reason to think that a market account of ambition-sensitivity needs to be supplemented by considerations about the moral significance of the ways in which different kinds of personal preferences are expressed through the market.

It is worth noting that there may be rough real world analogues to the sort of problem identified above in the ideal market. Consider, for instance, how interest rates on borrowed money may be affected by high-stakes gambling. If the banks lend huge sums of money to investors who engage in highly speculative and risky business ventures, then ordinary borrowers (e.g. homeowners with mortgages) may have to assume the costs—in the form of higher interest rates or even bank failures—of the lost gambles of the banks. Similarly, interest rates can be affected by the highly speculative activity of international currency traders. People with reasonable aspirations may find it difficult to plan and pursue their goals—e.g. homeownership—because risk-taking by the banks creates uncertainty about whether or not they will be able to finance their plans safely. Part of the justification for regulating financial institutions lies in the need to insulate consumers from the unpredictable and potentially devastating consequences of unrestrained risk-taking in the market. Notice that in these sorts of cases the fact that the envy test could be satisfied from a background of rough equality does not provide a sufficient reason to judge the situation fair. It may be true that the ordinary consumer, armed with knowledge of the gambling proclivities of her bank, would prefer the option of not assuming a mortgage at all to the option of borrowing money in a potentially unstable investment climate. It may also be true that she would prefer her situation, all things considered, to that of her neighbour who is prepared to accept the perils of borrowing. But even if the community's resources are at this point in time equally distributed, it surely does not follow from these facts that the situation is fair. To the contrary, the situation may be unfair if individuals must either forgo the pursuit of reasonable objectives or acquiesce in the risks created by the unreasonable tastes of others. In these instances, our views about fairness will not be determined by the envy test. They will be influenced by supplementary judgements about the relative weightiness of the different interests at stake. For we can recognize the possibility that the market-determined weight of the relevant interests may be mistaken.

The highly artificial pure exchange economy affords Dworkin the best chance of substantiating the market's claim to preserve equality through time. The objections I have urged so far present a serious challenge to this claim by raising an important point neglected by Dworkin. This is the idea that there are some market-independent standards that are relevant to the tracking of ambition-sensitivity in appropriate ways. The significance of the failure of the market to supply the relevant criteria is, I believe, even more apparent when we consider an economy in which resources are produced and not merely exchanged.

PRODUCTION GAMBLES

In the foregoing section I challenged the view that there could be no fairness-based objection to gambling in an exchange setting. The sorts of gambles at issue there are what I called *exchange gambles*. These are gambles in which the distribution of some fixed supply of resources is determined through some chance scheme in which individuals voluntarily choose to participate. Lotteries are prime examples of exchange gambles since they merely redistribute some fixed sum of money amongst participants. Letting the costs of exchange gambles fall where they may seems fair partly because such gambles appear to affect only the individuals who decide to participate in them. If my decision to enter a lottery cannot affect the share of resources held by someone who does not gamble, it seems reasonable enough to hold me responsible for the consequences for my life of my decision to gamble. While I have tried to show above that the purely self-regarding appearance of exchange gambles can be illusory, it must be conceded that it is only in quite unusual circumstances that freely entered-into exchange gambles are problematic from the point of view of justice. However, it must also be recognized that in a production economy exchange gambles play an insignificant role in comparison with what I will call *production gambles*. Whereas exchange gambles are purely redistributive in their effects, production gambles have the potential either to increase or decrease the total amount of available resources. A prime example of a production gamble is investment in the development of technology. (Exploration for the purposes of discovering new reserves of natural resources is also a kind of production gamble. A successful gold prospector affects the supply of gold and can thereby affect the value of existing gold reserves.) A successful new technology may expand productivity dramatically or generate innovations that render formerly valuable goods obsolete. However, there is usually some risk, especially at the stage of development, that the proposed technology will not succeed and hence will not contribute to improved productivity. In some cases, where technology goes awry, new technology may even retard productivity. Because production gambles may affect productivity, not merely distribution, they have a different character from exchange gambles and may give rise to a different sort of unfairness.

Dworkin's analysis does not explicitly accommodate this distinction. And it may be that one of the reasons Dworkin's argument initially appears so compelling is that it focuses almost exclusively on exchange gambles. Although his brief discussion of option luck uses some examples which might be interpreted as production gambles,[9] most of the analysis seems to proceed on the assumption that exchange gambles are representative of the choices to run risks that are typical of market interaction. That this is so seems evident in his claim that 'the life chosen by someone who gambles contains, as an element, the factor of risk; someone who chooses not to gamble has decided that he prefers a safer life' (Dworkin 1981: 294). As a general statement this is only true of exchange gambles. All other things being equal, the non-participant in the lottery does have a safer life than the gambler. But this need not be true of certain production gambles. Consider the case of investment in technological innovation. Suppose there is a market for recorded music large enough to sustain two record manufacturers. Smith purchases the resources needed to set up a record manufacturing business. The tastes of others provide the basis for a reliable market for records and partly because of this expectation Smith enters the record business. Now suppose that Jones decides to invest her resources in what, in this imaginary world, is the yet unproven technology of compact discs. There is a 50 per cent chance that she will be unable to develop marketable compact discs and will therefore lose all of her investment. But there is also a 50 per cent chance that the technology will be so successful that it will make records obsolete. If this happens, then Smith will lose her investment because she will be unable to compete with Jones's product. Of course, Jones's investment decision makes Smith's

[9] Dworkin uses one example about growing risky crops that might be construed in this way (Dworkin 1981: 293).

decision risky. In fact, it has been made just as risky as Jones's decision—both have a 50/50 chance of losing everything.[10] We might try to say that both Smith and Jones have chosen to gamble—Smith is gambling that Jones's investment will not pay off. But in the context of Dworkin's argument this would be a somewhat misleading description because Smith would prefer not to gamble at all. Yet she must acquiesce in the risks created by Jones's decision to gamble. She would prefer a safer life but that is not available to her in the market because of the production gambles of others. Now we might think that Smith could avoid facing the risks generated by Jones's production gamble by investing elsewhere. However, it is always possible that the risks involved in pursuing other ventures are equally high. The existence of safer investment opportunities depends on the extent to which producers in other areas take production gambles. The degree to which one can insulate oneself from the production gambles of others will depend on the gambling proclivities of the rest of the population and we cannot be assured that we will be able to preserve the value of the resources we currently hold. Moreover, even if it seems unlikely that the population would be dominated by risk-takers we must also remember that the impact of production gambles is frequently not isolated to discrete sectors of the economy. As the defence industry often reminds the public, developments in technology in one area frequently spill over to other areas in quite unexpected ways. The point here is not that production gambles in a market setting necessarily generate unfairness, still less that technological innovation is a bad thing. I mean only to illustrate the point, glossed over in Dworkin's theory, that in an environment in which unregulated production gambles are permitted, it may be impossible for risk-averse individuals to insulate themselves from risks arising from the choices of others. So whereas exchange gambles do not directly affect the value of the resources of those who choose not to participate in them, the same does not hold true of production gambles.

Once this feature of production economies is recognized it is even more difficult to see how even an ideal unregulated market

---

[10] Notice that Jones can make Smith's investment *more* risky than Jones's investment. Suppose, for instance, that there is a 60% likelihood that the innovation will succeed. Smith will now face a 60% chance of losing.

can be regarded as correctly tracking the impact of choice on distributive shares. The principal problem lies with the fact, noted above, that Dworkin's market-driven egalitarianism offers no way of discriminating between reasonable and unreasonable choices or between their distributive consequences. In a free market, reasonable, risk-averse individuals may unduly suffer because some individuals are prepared to take very risky production gambles. Related difficulties also arise insofar as the market is unable to distinguish adequately between the consequences of different kinds of attitudes towards hard work or between the consequences of different views about the hardships associated with different types of employment. Some people may display an eccentric willingness to work unusually hard or to work in unpleasant or dangerous settings. There are arguably cases in which it would be unfair to expect individuals to accept as fair the sort of remuneration that the market would yield when individuals with moderate and reasonable attitudes have to compete with individuals with unreasonable attitudes. However, I shall focus primarily on the sort of unfairness associated with unregulated production gambles of the sort compatible with the free market, commenting only very briefly on the related difficulties that arise with regard to attitudes to work.

The sorts of production gambles which are most problematic from the point of view of distributive fairness are those which are very risky and which have a dramatic impact on the supply and value of resources in the economy. The most acute difficulties arise in cases where the legitimate interests of individuals who, with good justification, are unprepared to engage in high-stakes gambling are adversely affected by the gambling activity permitted by the market. In an interactive market economy the success or failure of production gambles can affect the opportunities and resources available to individuals. Simply put, what other people do affects the value of the resources we control. It is not obvious that it is reasonable for the value of a person's resources to be significantly influenced by market forces without regard to the character of these forces. It is unfair and inconsistent with the egalitarian ideal for one person's opportunity to lead a decent life to be held hostage to, or undermined by, another person's willingness to assume great risks. Most of us would accept that you would be unfairly treated by a scheme of distribution if your interest in leading a good life were significantly set back by my willingness to live dangerously. As I have already suggested, individuals are not treated as equals, in the relevant sense, when reasonable and unreasonable attitudes towards risk are allowed to play an equal role in determining the distribution of resources. Unreasonable attitudes to risk which jeopardize important interests should not be treated on a par with reasonable and more benign attitudes to risk. Since the market imposes no antecedent constraints on the sorts of risks individuals may undertake and provides no mechanism to mitigate adverse consequences of risk-taking, it provides no barriers to this sort of unfairness. The metric of opportunity costs is insensitive to this difficulty. It cannot discriminate between the distributional consequences of risk-taking in production settings that are legitimate and those which, if left unadjusted, are illegitimate. The threat that production gambles can pose to distributive fairness can be illustrated by a couple of simple examples.

First, consider the case of a very risky production gamble that succeeds—i.e. a gamble in which the gambler obtains her desired outcome. For example, until very recently real vanilla extract could only be manufactured by using real vanilla beans. However, recent advances in biological engineering have made it possible to produce real vanilla extract (i.e. vanilla extract that is chemically indistinguishable from vanilla extract made from vanilla beans) without using vanilla beans. Moreover, the biological manufacturing process is dramatically more efficient in creating vanilla than traditional methods. The new process is so superior that traditional producers of vanilla cannot possibly compete with producers who employ the new manufacturing techniques. It is realistic to suppose, however, that at some earlier point the successful development of the new technology seemed most improbable. So let us suppose, for the sake of argument, that investment in vanilla biotechnology was extremely risky. Say, for instance, that at the time investors were faced with decisions about how to allocate their resources, the odds of an investment in biotechnology yielding a feasible manufacturing process were judged by reliable experts to be 100 to 1 against. Now consider the situation of two people interested in entering the vanilla business. Prudence decides to devote her resources to the established and reliable method of manufacturing vanilla, while Feodor gambles his resources on the development of biological technology. Luck, for once, is on Feodor's side. Against the odds, his investment proves successful. Unfortunately, Feodor's good luck is very bad luck for Prudence. She is forced out of business and into poverty because she cannot compete with the huge quantities of cheap vanilla that Feodor can now produce. By the criteria supplied by Dworkin's theory this outcome is perfectly fair. Opportunity costs, as measured by the market, are equal because Prudence preferred the investment option she chose to the rather reckless gamble of Feodor. Yet surely the outcome is unfair. Prudence suffers even though she made a very sensible and reasonable decision about how to conduct her life.[11] But according to Dworkin's theory she must accept her lot as fair because she was unprepared to accept a gamble that was very likely to result in her ruin. This is not plausible. It is unfair to penalize people for acting reasonably simply because others are prepared to gamble, quite irrationally, with their own source of livelihood.

Now consider a second sort of case, in which a risky production gamble fails dramatically. Suppose instead of speculating on vanilla, Feodor decides to devote half his resources to the purchase of an orange grove. The other members of the community like oranges and as long as the grove is capable of producing oranges they can engage in mutually advantageous trades of goods. Now Feodor realizes that if he could protect his orange trees from frost damage he could increase his annual yield and acquire more in trade with his neighbours. So Feodor invests his remaining funds in the development of a special virus which he hopes will protect his crop from frost and thereby increase his yield. Since Feodor is willing to run high risks in the pursuit of great profits, he decides to test a potentially dangerous virus on his orange grove. The odds of its succeeding are not good and the costs of its failure high. This time Feodor is unlucky. The

---

[11] It might be argued that Prudence's investment is really not prudent. Perhaps she should have a diversified investment portfolio that would insulate her from the dire consequences of Feodor's successful gamble. Although diversification may in general be a sensible principle of investment, it can offer no guarantee against the possibility of disastrous outcomes of the sort faced by Prudence. After all, other investments are vulnerable to the consequences of gambling activity. In the unregulated market there is no guarantee that safe havens for investment exist.

virus destroys his entire orange grove and he is unable to engage in trade with his neighbours. In this case, it is less clear that the outcome is directly unfair to Feodor's neighbours because although they are made worse off by his irresponsible gambling they are only marginally worse off. Nonetheless, there is clearly something problematic about the social consequences of Feodor's gambling and a sort of unfairness may be lurking in the background.

The problem is not simply that Feodor's neighbours suffer because of his irrational willingness to gamble but that the market provides an inadequate and unfair mechanism for the avoidance of loss to the community. One way to deal with this sort of problem is to impose regulations concerning the sorts of risks individuals may assume in developing the resources they control. For instance, governments may regulate the way lumber companies tend forests so as to ensure that the renewable resource is not destroyed.[12] However, regulations of this sort are incompatible with the market model at the centre of Dworkin's theory because they favour some preferences about the use of resources over others. Regulation makes gambling with biotechnology more expensive and this means that individuals who are prepared to gamble must expend more of their resources than non-gamblers to pursue their plans. Put in different terms, regulation disturbs market determination of opportunity costs. On Dworkin's theory, the only mechanism available to the community for holding Feodor's gambling proclivities in check is the price system. Members of the community who are uneasy about the prospects of Feodor experimenting on the orange grove with biotechnology may outbid Feodor for the orange grove or they may directly pay him not to engage in the experiments. But this sort of strategy seems to amount to little more than requiring that the community capitulate to extortion. Individuals with reasonable preferences about the use of valuable resources must bribe an individual with an irrational attitude towards risk so as to ensure that he acts reasonably. A distribu-

---

[12] Such regulations may be partly motivated by a concern for future generations. We may have an obligation to ensure that 'as much and as good' is available for subsequent generations. However, it is still plausible to suppose that members of the current generation have a legitimate grievance from the point of view of their own interest in leading a good life if a valuable resource (like a lumber-producing forest) is destroyed through irresponsible management.

tion of resources secured by what is tantamount to extortion is obviously unfair. Yet it is just such a distribution which is licensed as legitimate by Dworkin's market model of equality.

In order to illustrate the specific difficulties that Dworkin's argument encounters I have once more relied upon fairly simple and admittedly artificial examples. Again it might be asked: Is the force of the critique weakened by the use of such simplifying examples? I do not believe so. To begin with, the strategy deployed here is faithful to the method employed by Dworkin in the exposition of his own theory. The central examples used to elaborate the theory of equality of resources all involve many unrealistic, simplifying assumptions. Thus it is reasonable to test the theory against similarly simplified examples. Remember that under the ideal conditions stipulated by Dworkin the market should be able to track the acceptable impact of choice on distribution perfectly. Technically, a single plausible counter-example is sufficient to throw the adequacy of the theory in doubt. This is not to say, however, that the problem with Dworkin's argument brought out by the examples is merely technical and thus lacking in significance. After all, unlike the case of exchange gambles, in more realistic settings the fairness-disrupting consequences of production gambles in the market are likely to be more pronounced.

From the industrial revolution on, the dislocating impact of rapid technological development on different sectors of the economy has been a recurring theme in human history. Consider an obvious contemporary example. We are all familiar with how rapid developments in computer technology have had a profound impact on the relationship of labour to the means of production. Changes have proceeded at a remarkable pace and in many unanticipated directions. It is difficult to say that workers dislocated by technological developments which seemed no more that a remote possibility only a few years ago should alone bear the costs of changes in production techniques that render them redundant. Suppose it were true that such workers *could have* insulated themselves from the impact of rapid technological development by, say, investing in the very production gambles that threatened to create labour redundancy. The mere existence of such an insulating investment opportunity in the market is not sufficient to show that those who did not avail themselves of it must accept the resulting, market-determined outcome as a fair reflection of their choices. For although it is fair to hold individuals responsible for costs they face that they could have *reasonably* foreseen and could have taken reasonable measures to insulate themselves from, it is not fair to hold individuals responsible for costs that they could not have reasonably anticipated. So the mere fact that the market may present opportunities through which the potential costs of technological development can be mitigated does not show that individuals who failed to avail themselves of such opportunities must accept that the share of resources supplied to them by the market fairly reflects their choices. The choices made possible by the market have to be *reasonable* ones. And many gambles on the development of technology available in the market—even many of those that eventually pay dividends—are bad or extremely uncertain gambles. We cannot suppose that the principle of individual responsibility requires individuals to bear the costs of bad bets or even of the very unreasonable choices they fail to make. The idea that attributions of responsibility depend not only on what an agent could have done but on what she could reasonably have done is recognized in plenty of non-market cases. I am responsible for the loss of my money if a man on the street simply asks me for my wallet and I comply with the request. However, I am not responsible for the loss if the man makes his request at gun point, even if it is true that I could have disarmed him and refused the request. The ideal market provides every person with the same initial menu of opportunities. So it will be true that the choice made by one person could have been made by any other. However, the market does not ensure that any choice made by one person could reasonably have been made by another. It is this latter condition, not the mere equivalence of possible choices, which must be satisfied before we can tightly link fair shares with market choices.

In assessing the probable significance of production gambles in complex economic settings, it is also worth pointing out that successful production gambles can be accompanied by a multiplier effect which can distort to an even greater degree the appropriate relationship between choice and fair shares. Big winners of production gambles are better placed to take advantage of investment opportunities unavailable to smaller, less lucky players. They may, for example, be able to realize economies of scale. The market advantages secured by successful production gambles may permit individuals to attain a position of dominance in the market that further erodes any intuitive link between their market choices and their market successes. The difference between a Rockefeller and a pauper can be one lucky choice that antecedently seemed quite insignificant.

The analysis of production gambles supplements the case against the claim that the ideal market can be relied upon to track choice and preserve equality through time. The market is an imperfect device for gauging the appropriate relationship between choice and resource entitlement because there is not always a sufficient correspondence between the reasonableness of choices and the benefits and burdens that flow from such choices. The principle of responsibility that gives rise to the requirement of ambition-sensitivity is attractive partly because insisting that individuals be accountable for the consequences of deliberate decisions about how to lead their lives reflects a view of agency in which individuals are capable of securing their interests through their own efforts. It thereby establishes limits on the degree to which we are obliged to promote and secure the well-being of others. At the same time, we accept that no one can exercise effective control over all aspects of her life—the options available to a person are affected both by blind luck as well as the complex interaction of choices made by others. However, the value of responsible self-direction remains a function of the degree to which we are able to lead a genuinely good life through our choices. So while we accept that the choices of others may constrain the degree to which we can achieve a good life, we may legitimately seek to insulate ourselves from some of the bad consequences of choices which threaten substantial interests, without adequate justification. Specifically, the interest we have in preserving a stable environment in which reasonable choices can give rise to reasonably confident expectations about the future should not be jeopardized by preferences that reflect an irrational predilection for risk-taking.

There can be a clear divergence between a market-determined distribution of resources over time and the distribution which is consistent with the principle of individual responsibility that motivates the requirement of ambition-sensitivity. It is reasonable to conclude that there are market-independent standards of the degree to which individual shares of resources should be affected by a willingness to undertake various risks. I have not developed a theory which would permit egalitarians to make the requisite judgements in a systematic fashion. Nor have I rejected the claim that willingness to take risks can provide a legitimate basis for unequal resource entitlements. However, I have pointed out the perils of assuming that an adequate theory of the distributional significance of choice is built into the idea of an ideal market.

EFFORT, OCCUPATIONAL CHOICE, AND ENTITLEMENT

The foregoing arguments are intended bear out my contention that unregulated exchange and production gambles of the sort compatible with Dworkin's theory may generate distributive unfairness. Of course, choices about what sorts of risks one is prepared to undertake are not the only choices with which individuals in a market setting may be faced. I noted earlier that decisions about how hard to work and what sort of work to do are also important to determining the resources that may be acquired in the market. If my theoretical reservations about the capacity of the ideal market to track appropriately the way resource distribution should be affected by risk-taking choices are sound then there are parallel difficulties about supposing that the market-determined remuneration for hard work and occupational choice will necessarily be fair. I will not explore these further limitations of the market in any detail. Instead I shall conclude this chapter by merely pointing to a couple of examples which are illustrative of the sort of related difficulties I think Dworkin's theory faces.

Consider first how the market may treat individuals unfairly with regard to the way hard work should affect remuneration. While it is undeniable that, other things being equal, a person who works harder than a colleague (e.g. puts in longer hours) is entitled, to some degree, to more pay, it is not obvious that the market always provides the appropriate standard of remuneration. In particular, it seems unfair to ask individuals to accept a lower wage because the workforce includes some whose attitudes towards work are arguably so extreme as to be unreasonable or foolish. We might wonder, for instance, whether the preferences of individuals who would be glad to accept starvation wages and an 80-hour work week should be given equal weight in a market context when it comes to determining what constitutes a fair wage. Second, consider the similar situation of individuals who must perform unpleasant work. It would be unfair to require individuals to face costs, in the form of an unpleasant workplace, simply because some members of the workforce have extremely eccentric attitudes to the rewards of unpleasant work. It is not obvious, for instance, that all workers in pubs should have to accept the costs of working in a smoke-filled environment simply because a sufficiently large percentage of workers are prepared to tolerate the smoke. In both these sorts of cases the market seems an imperfect device for gauging appropriate remuneration. As with the case of risk-taking, Dworkin's theory fails to make morally relevant distinctions about the nature of the attitudes and choices which shape market forces and outcomes. Sketchy as these examples are, they nonetheless suggest that some market-independent theory is needed to provide a framework from which to draw the distinctions which are blurred in Dworkin's analysis.

These examples depend on accepting a potentially controversial premiss, namely that we can sometimes distinguish reasonable and unreasonable personal preferences about effort and the character of the workplace. However, I do not think this represents a departure from Dworkin's general egalitarian framework. It is true that Dworkin insists that, at a certain point, we must accept the tastes of others and we must be prepared to adjust our preferences accordingly. We can always wish that others had preferences more congenial to the pursuit of our own plans and it is our bad luck that they do not have tastes that accommodate ours. Yet we cannot insist that the preferences of others be manipulated simply out of deference to our preferences. There is, of course, enormous diversity across the class of reasonable preferences and within this wide range we must be prepared to adapt our preferences to the preferences of others. However, nothing in the deeper theory of equality that animates Dworkin's theory requires us to ignore morally relevant differences in the character of individual preferences. We operate under the constraint that we must treat like preferences alike but that does not imply that we must treat *all* preferences and choices alike. We can mount an objection to the weight given by the market to relevantly different preferences. The objection is not to the content of the preferences per se but to the weight given by the market to relevantly different preferences.

Dworkin's insistence that a theory of the equitable distribution of resources through time must be ambition-sensitive is correct and important. I believe it shows, *pace* Scheffler, that there is a conception of individual responsibility alive within liberalism. I have shown, however, that the theory of ambition-sensitivity provided by the ideal market is inadequate. Even when the complicating fact of differential native endowment is set aside, the problem of the appropriate relationship between choice and entitlement cannot be solved without sensitivity to the different sorts of choices involved. The ideal market is appealing because it appears to provide a precise algorithm for tracking ambition-sensitivity and indeed there are settings in which ideal market outcomes do track choice fairly. In other contexts, however, it does not. Fixing the parameters within which the market can be left to run and determining how choice should determine entitlement outside these parameters calls for the tackling of problems about which the market and Dworkin's theory are silent.

4

Disabilities

THERE is a widespread conviction that it is somehow unfair that some persons, through nothing but sheer brute bad luck, must live their lives with the burden of serious physical or mental disabilities[1] while others, through only good fortune, face no such hardship. Most of us believe that justice requires special recognition and accommodation of the interests of

---

[1] I prefer to speak of 'disabilities' or 'persons with disabilities' rather than 'handicaps' or 'handicapped persons' since the latter terms may suggest that 'disabled persons have their caps in hand' (Rosenberg 1987: 3). There is an interesting and complex debate concerning the political significance of the terms which are employed in this context. For example, some theorists argue that the phrase 'person with a disability' is preferable to the phrase 'disabled person' because the latter phrase may wrongly suggest that a person is entirely defined by their disability. By contrast, the former phrase suggests that disability is only one aspect of the person. For helpful discussions of these matters see Bickenbach (1993: 20–3) and Tremain (1996: 350 n. 48, 356–8). Interestingly, Tremain endorses the locution 'disabled person' partly because she believes it more accurately captures the way in which the social classification of certain differences as disabilities generates disadvantages for persons who display such differences. There is a different important terminological and conceptual issue which my analysis does not directly address. In my discussion I refer to disabilities and the disadvantages which accrue to persons with disabilities. I believe that some of these disadvantages are, in a sense explained more fully in the next chapter, inherent while other disadvantages are generated by the social response to the traits of disabled persons. I think this simple usage of these terms is adequate for my discussion. However, the more complex term 'disablement' is often employed in discussion of these matters. *The International Classification of Impairments, Disabilities and Handicaps* (ICIDH) prepared by the World Health Organization distinguishes three dimensions of disablement: impairment, disability, and handicap. Bickenbach offers the following summary of the ICIDH account of disablement: 'an impairment is any abnormality of physiological or anatomical structure or function. A disability is any limitation (resulting from an impairment) in the ability to perform any activity considered normal for a human being or required to perform for some recognized social role or occupation. And, finally, a handicap is any resulting disadvantage for an individual that limits the fulfillment of a normal role or occupation' (Bickenbach 1993: 10). There is considerable controversy both over the adequacy of this classification and of the appropriate analysis of disablement more generally. Though some of the remarks I make in the course of my discussion are not neutral with respect to these controversies, I think my analysis of Dworkin does not depend on entering into the intricate debates surrounding disablement. For more on this topic see Bickenbach (1993) and Tremain (1996).

persons with disabilities. However, it is difficult to explain theoretically, at least with any precision, the nature and extent of our
obligations to disabled persons. Indeed, in most accounts of
justice this problem is either relegated to the periphery or ignored altogether. Rawls clearly recognizes that differences in
natural endowment need to be addressed by a theory of justice
(Rawls 1971: 100–2). However, he offers no explicit account
of the compensation to which disabled persons are entitled.[2]
Ackerman (1980: 129–33) and Sen (1992) both give explicit
recognition to the problem of compensatory justice for disabilities. However, neither Ackerman's claim that 'genetic domination' is a basis for compensation,[3] nor Sen's insistence that a
sound theory of equality must give direct consideration to 'capabilities' and 'functioning', supply much guidance about the crucial questions about how much and what sort of compensation
should be provided to disabled persons. Libertarians such as
Gauthier, Fried, and Narveson simply reject the idea that disabilities create a problem for a theory of justice. Gauthier claims
that 'the congenitally handicapped and defective, fall beyond of
the pale of a morality tied to mutuality' (Gauthier 1986: 268).
Fried says, 'I deny that handicaps or differences in talents are
morally arbitrary in any sense which would provide a basis for
redistribution' (Fried 1983: 49; see also Narveson 1983: 15–19).

    In contrast to the general inattention to the issue of justice and
disability that characterizes mainstream political philosophy,
Dworkin's theory addresses this matter directly and systemati-

----

[2] Kymlicka points out that Rawls's difference principle does not adequately deal
with disabilities because the distribution of primary goods it secures does not
mitigate the extra burdens disabled persons face in living a satisfactory life
(Kymlicka 1990: 72). In Rawls's most recent work, *Political Liberalism* (1993) the
problem of justice and disability receives no consideration.

[3] Rakowski correctly argues that Ackerman's theory in which compensation is
owed to individuals who suffer 'genetic domination' is clearly defective. The difficulty is that Ackerman's definition of genetic domination is far too demanding
because it requires that compensation be paid only if '*everyone* conscientiously
believes that his genetic endowment places him in a superior position to pursue what
the person making the evaluation regards as the good life' (Rakowski 1991: 96). The
disturbing consequence of this theory is that many profoundly disabled individuals
simply would not be entitled to any compensation. Rakowski's own theory of
equality of fortune does address the problem of compensatory justice for persons
with disabilities. His own theory, though distinct in some respects, is closely related
to Dworkin's theory (Rakowski 1991: 97–106).

cally.[4] In this chapter, I consider Dworkin's significant but ultimately problematic account of compensatory justice for disabled persons. The critical component of my discussion focuses
primarily on the proposal that a hypothetical insurance market
should be used to illuminate the degree to which justice requires
the provision of compensation to persons with significant physical or mental disabilities. The hypothetical insurance market
scheme is principally conceived of as an analytical device for
tracking the abstract demands of justice vis-à-vis disabled persons from the perspective of Dworkin's theory of equality of
resources. However, Dworkin also suggests that his approach
may provide officials of actual communities with guidance in
structuring appropriate schemes of compensation for disabled
persons. He also thinks that his theory can be used to solve other
important practical problems. Indeed, he has recently argued
that the insurance market theory of compensation can be extended to illuminate the requirements of a just health care
policy. The theory provides a way of addressing the two most
basic problems that contemporary democratic communities
must face in designing a just health system: How much should
the community spend on health care? And how should health
care resources be distributed? Since many Western nations are
currently grappling with these questions with a renewed sense of
urgency, Dworkin's account of justice in health care has a direct
bearing on important practical problems. So although I am
principally interested in assessing the adequacy of the insurance
market theory of disability compensation, my arguments do
challenge the usefulness of this approach as even a rough
guide to the design of actual institutional arrangements such as
health care systems and compensatory programmes for disabled
persons.

[4] This is not to imply that the issues surrounding disability have not received
careful attention. Although most prominent political philosophers largely ignore the
topic, there is a large literature from a variety of disciplinary sources which addresses
the nature and social significance of disabilities. A more comprehensive examination
of justice and disabilities than I can hope to offer here would require careful
consideration of this literature. My narrow focus on Dworkin's theory does not
address many crucial problems and it is not meant to diminish the importance of
other work in the field. Bickenbach (1993) provides a good overview of many of the
central issues.

I begin by briefly reviewing some central components of Dworkin's diagnosis of the problem posed for egalitarians by disabilities along with a description of the hypothetical insurance market scheme and the considerations supporting its use. The hypothetical insurance scheme faces a number of serious difficulties. Together they provide ample reason to reject the scheme as a strategy for the articulation of the requirements of justice for disabled persons. Although I offer some tentative suggestions about more fruitful approaches to the basic problem of compensation, I do not attempt to develop any alternative theory of fair compensation.

One further note. There is generally held to be an important parallel between the problem posed for egalitarians by disabilities and a similar problem rooted in the fact that people are endowed with different talents. In both cases it seems unfair that some individuals are in a better position to lead a good life than others simply in virtue of the arbitrary natural distribution of capacities. Despite this apparent similarity, I shall follow Dworkin's lead and proceed on the assumption that it is reasonable to maintain a distinction between and treat independently the sorts of distributive issues raised by disabilities and unequal talents. I will reserve full discussion of the rationale behind treating problems posed by unequal talents and disabilities as distinct until the next chapter. For now, suffice it to say that treating these problems independently is justified because the obstacles that disabilities may present to the leading of a good life are more direct, pervasive, and intractable than those posed by the fact that people differ in their talents. Disabilities merit special attention from the point of view of egalitarian justice.

PERSONAL AND IMPERSONAL RESOURCES

Dworkin's analysis of the challenge for a theory of justice posed by disabilities proceeds from the basic premiss that justice requires that an equal share of resources be devoted to the life of each person. Dworkin develops this idea along two dimensions. First, he identifies the sorts of things that should be considered resources and that should, ideally, be distributed equally. Second, he articulates criteria for determining what constitutes a genuinely equal distribution of these resources. Two basic kinds of resources are distinguished: personal and impersonal. 'Personal resources are qualities of mind and body that affect people's success in achieving their plans and projects: physical and mental health, strength and talent. Impersonal resources are parts of the environment that can be owned and transferred: land, raw materials, houses, televisions sets and computers, and various legal rights and interests in these' (Dworkin 1991: 37). Dworkin notes that this understanding of the resources with which distributive justice is concerned leads to a striking view of the distinction between a person and her circumstances. According to this picture, a person's physical and mental powers (i.e. her personal resources) along with the impersonal resources which she controls, belong to her circumstances. By contrast, the person is defined principally by her personality. The personality consists essentially of the particular tastes, ambitions, and views about the good life that a person holds. So whereas aspects of personality lie within the realm of attributes that a person may choose to adopt, a person's circumstances are unchosen. From the point of view of ideal theory, it is the person, so construed, who is entitled to an equal share of personal and impersonal resources. This distinction between the person and her circumstances is significant partly because it facilitates a simple comprehensive statement of the general objective of Dworkin's liberal egalitarianism. The ideal of 'perfect liberal equality' is to make circumstances equal overall.

It is within this framework that Dworkin locates the problem posed by disabilities. In effect, he explains the unfairness associated with disabilities in terms of the distribution of personal resources. Individuals with disabilities have fewer personal resources than those without disabilities. For the most part, these differences in personal resources cannot be attributed to responsible choices made by individuals and thus must be viewed as morally arbitrary. For example, other things being equal, people who are blind lack a personal resource that sighted people enjoy. Since differences in personal resources are unchosen—a matter of brute luck—they can be represented as ways in which overall circumstances are unequal. The specification of what constitutes equal overall circumstances must therefore be sensitive to the impact of disabilities on people's circumstances.

At first glance, the distinction between a person and a person's circumstances appears helpful in understanding the problem posed by disabilities. At least some of the obstacles which disabled persons face in leading a good life seem traceable to aspects of a person's natural endowment as reflected in their personal resources. However, before we consider how Dworkin develops the distinction in the context of equality of resources, it is worth considering an important challenge to Dworkin's analysis which has been developed by Shelley Tremain. In a very insightful critique of Dworkin's theory of disability compensation, Tremain contends that the understanding of disability which is presupposed by the person/circumstances distinction is deeply flawed (Tremain 1996).[5] Specifically, Tremain raises an important challenge to the idea that the disadvantage associated with disabilities should be conceived as one arising out of the personal characteristics of disabled persons. Indeed, she contends that Dworkin's approach to disability compensation should be abandoned because the very way the problem is framed is demeaning to disabled persons.

As we have seen, Dworkin locates the problem of disability in the 'qualities of mind and body' of persons. The physiological and psychological attributes which some persons have (either as a matter of natural endowment or as the consequence of calamity) create obstacles to the living of satisfactory life which are not faced by others who are more fortunate. Tremain contends that the representation of disabled persons reflected in the person/circumstances distinction is degrading to them because it implies that disabled persons, in virtue of their natural attributes, are defective or suffer from some kind of personal inadequacy. By locating the problem of disability in the physical and psychological attributes of disabled persons, disabled forms of life are depicted not simply as different but as deficient. According to Tremain, the attempt to locate the disadvantages associated with disability in the personal characteristics of per-

---

[5] In fact, Tremain raises a number of objections to Dworkin's approach some of which parallel my criticisms of his theory. For instance, we both emphasize epistemic difficulties which Dworkin's hypothetical insurance market theory encounters and we both argue that Dworkin's scheme of compensation is insensitive to social and political dimensions of the disadvantages faced by disabled persons. Nonetheless, as my discussion of her argument indicates, Tremain's critique diverges in important respects from mine.

sons means that compensation must be viewed as a response to the damaged condition of the disabled person. There are two related dimensions to Tremain's objection. First, Dworkin's analysis mistakenly supposes that the forms of life exhibited by a disabled persons are necessarily deficient (e.g. because they have a personal resource deficit) rather than merely different. Second, it wrongly implies that the disadvantages faced by disabled persons are not creations of the discriminatory practices which dominate the social environment in which they conduct their lives. As Tremain puts it: 'When the "problem" of disablement is represented in the way that Dworkin represents it, viz. as one which arises from some natural "defect" ("circumstance") of disabled persons, then the onus for the social injustices that are inflicted upon disabled persons is inadvertently redirected onto those citizens themselves' (Tremain 1996: 356). Tremain urges that we adopt a different conception of disablement according to which the disadvantage associated with disability arises from schemes of social classification rather than from features of a person's endowment which are 'naturally' burdensome. Indeed, she claims that disability itself is created by a process of social classification of difference. 'The classification *disability* effectively installs the category as a particular type of difference where certain persons become recognizably and understandably *disabled* ones. That is to say, the symbolic, aesthetic, and practical significance given to certain forms of embodiment, modes of communication, appearances, bodily comportment, cognition, and gesture systematically *disable* certain persons ("viz. disabled persons")' (Tremain 1996: 357). On this view, the disadvantages associated with disability are socially generated from the arbitrary classificatory schemes of difference. By contrast, Dworkin's analysis suggests that disadvantages arise directly out of natural attributes.

I think Tremain's analysis is useful in revealing a limitation of Dworkin's theory. As I argue later in the chapter, Dworkin's focus on personal resources leads him to neglect the social and political dimensions of the unfair disadvantages which are faced by disabled persons. However, I am more sceptical that the person/circumstance distinction itself generates a demeaning representation of disabled persons. It is true that many of the disadvantages faced by disabled persons are inaccurately described as attributable to brute bad luck in the distribution of natural attributes. Some unfair and discriminatory forms of social classification can create significant disadvantages. The discriminatory social response which is encountered by persons with disabilities is not really an instance of the disadvantage created by the natural attributes of persons. Nonetheless, I think Tremain overstates the case against Dworkin. It is a mistake to suppose that *all* the disadvantages which accrue to persons with disabilities arise out of the natural attributes of such persons. However, in my view, it is also distorting to deny that there is a physiological and psychological basis of some disadvantages. Some forms of life have burdensome components which are not socially generated. Many significant disadvantages are appropriately attributed to features of a person's physical or psychological constitution. I think this is true, for instance, of the disadvantage faced by individuals who suffer chronic pain. The crippling pain of serious arthritis is a genuine disadvantage which arises not from arbitrary schemes of social classification of difference but from features of a person's physiological make-up. Dworkin's approach, even if it is incomplete, provides one way of capturing this dimension of disadvantage. Moreover, accepting the idea that some such disadvantages are, in one sense, internal to the person need not imply that the person is defective. Indeed, Dworkin's person/circumstance distinction arguably allows us to preserve the integrity of persons with disabilities because although circumstances profoundly affect persons, they do not fully define them. In my view, persons can accept that some qualities of their body or mind give rise to serious burdens without supposing that they are diminished or defective persons on that account. If this is right then the supposition about the source of disadvantage reflected in the person/circumstances distinction is not entirely discredited. Tremain's critique does not provide adequate justification for wholesale abandonment of Dworkin's approach.

With this (partial) defence of Dworkin's analysis in place, let us now consider how he develops the rest of his account of compensation for disabilities. The basic criterion specified by Dworkin for determining when circumstances are equal overall, or equivalently when equal resources are devoted to the life of each, is the envy test. It stipulates that resources are equally distributed when no person prefers the total set of resources—both impersonal and personal—she controls to the total set of resources controlled by anyone else. In the previous chapters, we have seen how Dworkin argues that a distribution of impersonal resources which satisfies the requisite version of the envy test can be generated and maintained, at least in principle, through the use of a perfectly competitive market. The plausibility of these results depends crucially on the simplifying counterfactual assumption that personal resources are equally distributed.[6] The market can only be represented as securing a fair distribution of resources on the assumption that individuals enjoy an equal natural endowment—i.e. that each person has equal personal resources. Once this simplifying assumption is dropped the theory of equality of resources becomes much more complex. The immediate difficulty is that the market cannot be directly invoked as a mechanism through which the problem of unequal personal resources can be remedied.

The market is unavailable here because the physical and mental powers of people cannot be transferred from one person to another or distributed among people like impersonal resources. This is not merely because such transfers would, for the most part, be practically infeasible but because such transfers would be inconsistent with preserving the legitimate bodily integrity of persons. Dworkin realizes that recognizing some principle of bodily integrity complicates the person/circumstances distinction on which the ideal of liberal equality depends. But he suggests that we must view it as a 'flexible notion, more a matter of degree, according to which someone's eyes are part of him *as well as* part of his circumstances, and are in that way different from his clothes' (Dworkin 1983: 39). This characterization of the distinction helps explain why perfect liberal equality should not be interpreted as justifying compulsory redistribution of body parts even where technically possible. Equality of resources can, therefore, be defended from the charge made by some critics that it sanctions forced organ transplants (Narveson 1983: 15–19). Some of an individual's personal resources are partly constitutive of the person *qua* moral agent. Physical

---

[6] Of course, I argued in the previous chapters that Dworkin's arguments concerning the egalitarian virtues of the market are unsuccessful even if this simplifying assumption is granted.

attributes cannot always be sharply distinguished from the self. We accept a principle of bodily integrity that places prohibitions on highly invasive measures such as forced transplants partly because we recognize that the distinction between a person and a particular body is imprecise in this way. Removing a person's eyes represents a change to the person and not merely to her circumstances, and liberal equality does not require that *persons* be made equal. Consequently, where equalizing personal resources runs up against the constraint imposed by the principle of bodily integrity, equality must be pursued through other means. There are, therefore, good reasons to distinguish personal and impersonal resources. Only the latter are subject to redistribution in the name of equality. Nevertheless, given that human capacities are unequally distributed, a prohibition on redistributing them directly means that the requirements of perfect liberal equality cannot be satisfied. Some people will prefer the mental and physical powers enjoyed by others to their own bundle of powers. The blind will prefer the sight of others to their blindness and so on. Yet, if the envy test is not satisfied then the distribution of resources is, from the perspective of perfect liberal equality, unfair.[7]

The failure of the envy test signals a problem for the egalitarian liberal. Note, however, that even the abstract application of the envy test in this context can be an unreliable measure of fairness. There are readily imaginable cases in which the full envy test could be satisfied, even with regard to personal resources, but where we must doubt that resources are equitably distributed. Consider the case of the mentally disabled blind person whose sight could be restored by special but relatively inexpensive eyeglasses. Let us suppose, however, that because of her mental disability, she is unable to appreciate how being able to see would improve her life. We can imagine that this person prefers her total set of resources—personal and impersonal—to anyone else's total set and that everyone else is also satisfied

---

[7] We have to be careful about how we interpret the envy test here for there may be cases in which a blind person does not prefer the sight that others have. There can be tremendous psychological costs for congenitally blind persons who gain their sight. A person who is blind from birth may, therefore, rationally prefer continued blindness to sight. But cases like this should not be interpreted as signalling the absence of disadvantage or disability. After all, it will probably be true that a blind person would have preferred to have been born sighted than blind.

with their share of resources. By strict application of Dworkin's criterion, the existing distribution of resources is just and justice would not require that resources be devoted to providing the blind person with the special eyeglasses she needs. This shows that the envy test, even if it could be applied to personal resources, is an inadequate guide to justice in the distribution of resources. To reiterate a point made in the second chapter, the mere fact that a person is satisfied with her lot is not a guarantee that she has been fairly treated.

Clearly, the ideal of perfect liberal equality cannot be fully realized. Arbitrary inequalities in personal resources are ubiquitous and they cannot be eliminated through any scheme of redistribution. Yet Dworkin insists that some progress towards a reasonable approximation of the ideal can be made. We cannot eliminate all troublesome inequalities or even provide full compensation for disabilities. But we can provide individuals with disabilities extra resources that will at least mitigate, to a reasonable degree, some of the adverse effects of their disabilities and provide fair compensation for this variety of undeserved disadvantage. So the problem we face in pursuing liberal equality is determining 'how far the ownership of independent material resources should be affected by differences in physical and mental powers' (Dworkin 1981: 301).

THE HYPOTHETICAL INSURANCE MARKET

Dworkin argues that a solution to this problem can be developed by speculating about the answer to the following question: 'If (contrary to fact) everyone had at the appropriate age the same risk of developing physical or mental handicaps in the future (which assumes no one has developed them yet) but that the total number of handicaps remained what it is, how much insurance coverage against these handicaps would the average member of the community purchase?' (Dworkin 1981: 297). So the suggestion is that we can determine the share of impersonal resources to which disabled persons are entitled in the way of compensation for their disability by speculating about the sort of coverage individuals would purchase in a hypothetical insurance market operated under the following counterfactual conditions. First, at the time the insurance market is operated, individuals participating in the market are assumed to have no disabilities. Second, every individual knows the general odds of developing a given disability and everyone is assumed to face the same risk of developing a given disability. Third, everyone has equal purchasing power in the hypothetical insurance market. That is, the material resources each person can devote to the purchase of insurance are equal.[8] Dworkin claims that a fair level of compensation for actually suffering a given disability is equivalent to the level of insurance coverage against suffering that disability which would be purchased in such an insurance market by the average person. Speculation about the sort of coverage that would be purchased in such an insurance market against suffering a disability provides the basis for designing real systems of compensation for individuals who are actually disabled. Premiums to finance a system of redistribution modelled on such a scheme would be collected through some compulsory process (e.g. taxation) and the resulting funds would be devoted to providing compensation to persons with disabilities. Dworkin also argues that this mechanism can be extended to the case of health care more generally.[9] The requirements of a just health care system can be modelled by asking what sort of health insurance would be purchased by average people who make insurance decisions in similar counterfactual conditions.[10]

[8] Dworkin actually equivocates on whether the hypothetical insurance market scheme requires that consumers have equal purchasing power. In his more recent accounts of the theory Dworkin suggests that his scheme will still work if it proceeds from other background distributive conditions. He says, for instance, that the background distribution of resources need only satisfy whatever theory of economic justice is favoured by a particular reader. Thus he asks readers 'to imagine an economic distribution that is fair according to your own view' (Dworkin 1994: 22; see also Dworkin 1993: 888). I think that Dworkin only advances this proposal in the expectation that his readers will share a fairly egalitarian conception of fair economic distribution. After all, it is clear that Dworkin would not view an account of compensation as fair if it was derived from a libertarian conception of distributive justice in which the purchasing power of individuals was grossly unequal.

[9] Indeed, Dworkin used the hypothetical insurance market argument to provide a guarded endorsement of the health care reform package proposed by the Clinton administration in 1993 (Dworkin 1994).

[10] There are three minor qualifications to this claim. First, Dworkin anticipates that the health care provisions arrived at through the hypothetical insurance market scheme might have to be modified by some paternalistic considerations. Second, accommodation of the health care interests of future generations may also lead to modifications to the theory. Third, the scheme might have to be adjusted to accom-

Speculation about the insurance purchases which would be made under these conditions permits us to determine how many resources a just community should devote to health care, how these resource should be distributed, and what sort of basic health care services must be provided to citizens as a matter of justice.

There are various reasons why the hypothetical insurance theory of compensation is initially compelling. First, the counterfactual condition it exploits secures a kind of impartiality. By stipulating that each party faces the same risk of developing a disability, the insurance market ensures that concern for the consequences of disabilities is equally shared and prevents individuals from favouring their specific interests over the interests of others. Second, the compensation that this procedure yields is the product of the aggregation of individual choices. Each person has equal influence and equal responsibility in determining a fair level of compensation. The resulting standards of compensation may thus be characterized as reflecting a fair consensus about the appropriate accommodation of competing needs. Third, the theory provides a basis for deriving a fairly determinate answer to the elusive question of how much compensation each variety of disability merits. The theory goes beyond mere recognition of the general legitimacy of compensation. It aims at furnishing a principled basis for determining the extent of the obligation to assist disabled persons. Finally, the theory has the attraction of treating the problem of compensatory justice as one that is amenable to a purely procedural solution. Since there is no obvious antecedent specification of fair compensation for disabilities, relying on a fair procedural device to generate an account of compensation might be the best strategy for devising an account of fair compensation. In cases of pure procedural justice, the fairness of an outcome is wholly determined by the fairness of the procedure that generates it. The hypothetical insurance market speaks directly to the issue of compensation and seems procedurally fair. The counterfactual condition ensures that everyone is equally situated and the outcomes that it generates are not morally arbitrary. In this way, the account of

---

modate the relevance of voluntary behaviour in creating health care costs. For instance, perhaps smokers should face heavier health care premiums if their chosen lifestyle puts them at greater risk of imposing costs on the health care system.

compensation it yields can plausibly be billed as a theory of *fair* compensation.

Despite these virtues, Dworkin is careful not to represent this as a perfect solution to the problem of disabilities. He says only that it is superior to other approaches[11] and that 'it would have the merit of aiming in the direction of the theoretical solution most congenial to equality of resources' (Dworkin 1981: 299). Does the hypothetical insurance market scheme provide the best way of illuminating our obligations to persons with disabilities? Can it illuminate the requirements of a just health care system? It is vulnerable to a number of objections.

EPISTEMIC OBSTACLES

To begin with, there are various epistemic difficulties that face strategies which depend on making complex counterfactual judgements to generate answers to moral problems. The hypothetical insurance market poses very complex counterfactual questions. Yet it is difficult to believe that we could have, even in ideal circumstances, any very good basis on which to supply sufficiently determinate or accurate answers to these questions. It is doubtful, for instance, that we could accurately calculate the amount of insurance an average person would purchase against blindness, if she did not have any information about disabilities she might actually suffer, except general statistics about the incidence and general nature of various disabilities in the population. Remember that the scheme will not provide any distinctive solution to the problem of disability compensation unless it yields fairly determinate results about the resources to which disabled persons are entitled. After all, the deep puzzle posed by disabilities is not whether compensation is required but rather how much and what sort of compensation is owed to disabled persons. Yet the hypothetical insurance market scheme

[11] Dworkin does not provide a comprehensive examination of alternative theories of compensation. But as I noted above there are not many competing theories. Dworkin sees some standard of equality of welfare as the most important alternative to his account. It is rejected as a standard for fixing compensation for disabled persons because it provides 'no upper bound to compensation so long as any further payment would improve the welfare of the wretched' (Dworkin 1981: 300). The theory is therefore not feasible.

is so epistemically unmanageable that it is doubtful that it can yield determinate results. There are three dimensions to this difficulty. First, the scheme is too informationally impoverished to permit accurate prediction about its outcome. A particular individual's decision to buy insurance will be affected by the sorts of plans she has for her life. Yet her life plans are likely to be influenced by her knowledge of her capacities to which, *ex hypothesi*, she is denied access. Second, we must also bear in mind the simpler point that we probably lack the imaginative resources to generate the sort of systematic and reliable information about how a whole population would respond to the broad range of insurance decisions that would determine the structure of any compensation scheme. Finally, it seems reasonable to suppose that, at least in many cases, appropriate compensation for disabled persons should be directly informed by disabled persons' own understanding of their special needs. Persons with disabilities have special intimate experiences of their disabilities and the specific disadvantages associated with them. This sort of special epistemic access can facilitate accurate identification of the crucial needs of disabled persons and can illuminate the measures which would best reduce the disadvantages faced by disabled persons. Yet the persons who make insurance decisions in Dworkin's scheme cannot directly accommodate such considerations in their deliberations. Indeed, because Dworkin assumes that participants in the market are non-disabled his theory filters out a crucial source of information about the nature and significance of disability. This suggests that the epistemic constraints imposed by Dworkin may diminish the moral significance of any answers to the insurance problem that might be generated.

It might be objected that the epistemic difficulties facing the scheme are less pronounced than I have suggested because we have a lot of information about insurance behaviour in the real world which can be used to generate answers to the hypothetical insurance problem posed by the theory. Note, however, that insurance behaviour in the real world is affected by factors that the informational constraints of the theory are supposed to neutralize. For instance, insurance in the real world often cannot be purchased for 'pre-existing conditions' and the prices of premiums for other conditions are influenced by the insurer's awareness of a person's predisposition to suffer a particular ailment. Some people who would like to buy insurance are deterred by prohibitive prices that reflect the fact that they fall into high-risk groups. Similarly, others will forgo insurance because they know they fall into a low-risk category. This means that real world insurance behaviour is unlikely to be a reliable guide to counterfactual insurance behaviour. Moreover, since most of the data we have about insurance behaviour comes from societies marked by profound economic and social inequality, such data cannot reveal much about the structure—e.g. prices of different kinds of coverage—that would arise against a background of *equal* purchasing power. The fact that some 40 million Americans have little or no health insurance surely does not indicate what their insurance behaviour would be in the egalitarian economic conditions specified by Dworkin.

Dworkin concedes that the difficulty of coming up with plausible and reliable answers to the requisite counterfactual questions presents an obstacle to the feasibility of his approach. But he thinks we can escape some of these difficulties by simplifying the basic insurance problem. He claims that we need only make estimates about the value of insurance that would be purchased against disabilities that affect a 'wide spectrum of lives' (Dworkin 1981: 299) and that we can assume that people would place roughly the same value on insurance. However, modifying the problem in this manner does not satisfactorily address the fundamental difficulty. The epistemic obstacles to effecting accurate calculations still remain. Changing the precise dimensions of the problem does not provide a more secure basis for predicting, with any confidence, even roughly the level of insurance people actually would buy under the conditions stipulated by Dworkin. It is the amount of insurance, not the fact that people might converge towards a single amount, that we must determine for the scheme to get off the ground, even as a theoretical device. The hypothetical insurance market scheme is initially attractive partly because it seems that such a strategy can produce fairly determinate results. However, the various difficulties associated with effecting calculations suggest that the scheme cannot yield such results.

The difficulties with making the requisite counterfactual judgements are even more pronounced if such judgements are portrayed as a way of helping officials design actual compensatory policies. Even if such judgements can be construed as playing a useful heuristic role within an abstract theory of justice, they would provide a much too uncertain, controversial, and difficult basis for the direct guidance of public policy. Dworkin worries that other strategies for designing actual compensatory policies are vulnerable to crass political manipulation of the sort that would result in ungenerous policies. He suggests, for instance, that a policy which predicated compensation on equality of welfare would supply little actual compensation to the persons with disabilities because it would leave 'the standard for actual compensation to the politics of selfishness broken by sympathy, politics that we know will supply less than any defensible hypothetical insurance market would offer' (Dworkin 1981: 300). However, in light of the epistemic complexities of the hypothetical insurance market scheme, it is just as likely that speculation about the outcome of the hypothetical insurance market would be heavily influenced by similarly dubious political motives. It is improbable, therefore, that speculation about how the average person would act in a hypothetical insurance market could underwrite the political legitimacy of actual compensatory policies.

There is a temptation to understand the counterfactual questions at issue here as more or less equivalent to questions about the sort coverage it would, in fact, be reasonable to provide people with or with the sort of coverage a reasonable or prudent person would purchase. Indeed, in extending the insurance scheme to the general problem of health care, Dworkin explicitly suggests that the problem is to determine how much health insurance the *prudent* person would purchase under the stipulated counterfactual conditions (Dworkin 1994: 22–3). On this interpretation of the theory, the problem of fixing levels of insurance coverage seems more tractable, as the severe epistemic difficulties posed by counterfactuals can be sidestepped. We no longer have to try to predict the likely outcome of a complex and highly artificial insurance market. Instead, the focus is directed towards what sort of compensation for disabilities or what sort of health care coverage is, in fact, reasonable or prudent. Note, however, that this interpretation actually constitutes an abandonment of the hypothetical market as a

theoretical device for gauging the demands of justice. Once the
focus shifts directly to the question of what constitutes reasonable compensation for a disability or a prudent amount of
health care, the insurance market apparatus becomes superfluous. The function of the market is to fix prices of different
packages of compensation in light of the demand for policies of
different kinds exhibited by different players in the market.
However, on the prudent insurance model, the insurance *market*
does not have any role in determining appropriate compensation. Remember that in a real insurance market, the price and
availability of insurance depends on the market decisions of
others. For instance, I will not be able to buy disability insurance
unless others are prepared to pool risks with me. If, however,
compensation is based on the sort of coverage a prudent person
would buy then the amount of compensation is determined
simply by what is prudent and not what the market will actually
supply. To be sure, the calculation of what constitutes a reasonable amount of compensation will turn on some kind of cost-
benefit analysis of what constitutes a sensible allocation of
scarce resources. However, this calculation will in no way
depend on the functioning of an insurance market.

IRRATIONALITY AND RISK

The epistemic objections to the hypothetical insurance theory of
compensation are formidable but they are probably not decisive.
There are, however, further objections to the theory. In exploring these problems, I will focus specifically on the issue of
disability compensation but the difficulties which I identify also
apply, *mutatis mutandis*, to application of the parallel theory of
just health care. So let us assume, despite the foregoing objections, that we could speculate, in a reliable manner, about the
operation of the hypothetical insurance market. The fact that
compensation for disabilities depends on the predicted behaviour of individuals is still troublesome. One problem is rooted
in the fact that most people are, as it turns out, quite bad at
assessing the significance of various kinds of statistical risk. A
large body of psychological research has identified a variety of
ways in which people make elementary mistakes and fall prey to

statistical fallacies when they are faced with even simple tasks of probabilistic reasoning (see Kahneman, Slovic, and Tversky 1982; Wason and Johnson-Laird 1972).[12] Moreover, this sort of research suggests that humans frequently behave irrationally when assessing various types of risk. This is a discovery which seems particularly significant in the context of Dworkin's theory.

On Dworkin's scheme the degree of compensation to which disabled persons are entitled is a function ultimately of both the attitudes toward and the understanding of risks displayed in decisions to buy insurance in the hypothetical market. If the purchasers of insurance are very risk averse then the level of compensation established by the insurance market will be relatively high. If they take a more cavalier attitude toward risk, the level of available compensation will be low. Similarly, insurance decisions will be affected by perceptions of relative risk—i.e. how risky one possibility is compared to another. However, whatever precise level of compensation is arrived at, the market-generated outcome will reflect the degree of irrationality of the buyers of insurance. Unfortunately, psychological research suggests that people faced with such decisions may exhibit a high degree of irrationality. Therefore, the level of just compensation will be determined partly by the irrational assessment of individuals. For instance, if average individuals underestimate the likelihood of suffering a certain disability then it seems likely that compensation for that disability will be correspondingly insufficient. If the average person mistakenly thinks that the probability of suffering a disability is infinitesimally small, then she may elect to buy no insurance against that disability. Surely it is a mistake to attach moral significance to the level of compensation generated by a mechanism so easily contaminated by common human irrationality. Once again, if we try to address

---

[12] It should be noted that there is some controversy about the purported findings of this research. L. J. Cohen, for instance, has argued that it is impossible to demonstrate human irrationality experimentally. He also claims that some findings should be rejected because they invoke mistaken norms of reasoning (Cohen 1981). It is possible that some of the conclusions about the degree to which humans fail to live up to appropriate norms of reasoning have been overstated but, in my view, the evidence amassed by Tversky, Kahneman, and others provides ample support for the claim that human irrationality in risk assessment is a real and pervasive phenomenon.

this difficulty by appealing to the insurance deliberations of prudent or otherwise idealized agents then the market component of the theory becomes redundant. In light of this, we can have no confidence that the sort of provision for disabled persons yielded by this strategy will systematically and reliably address their legitimate needs and interests. A truly adequate theory of compensation needs to address the genuine interests of persons with disabilities.

IS THE HYPOTHETICAL INSURANCE MARKET PROCEDURALLY FAIR?

A theoretically more fundamental criticism of the hypothetical insurance market challenges the notion that the scheme is procedurally fair in a way that underwrites the fairness of levels of compensation fixed by it. Perhaps the most powerful justification for the hypothetical insurance market is that it provides a mechanism that gives expression to the idea that individuals must assume responsibility for their own lives. Individuals cannot be held directly responsible for most disabilities they suffer since suffering a disability is a matter of brute bad luck.[13] However, individuals may be held responsible for the measures they take to protect themselves from the consequences of brute bad luck. The idea is that option luck may be used to mitigate the unfairness generated by brute luck.[14] The hypothetical insurance market provides individuals with an opportunity to insulate themselves, to a reasonable degree, from the effects of brute luck by offering insurance bets against suffering catastrophic, brute bad luck—e.g. having a disability. In this way individuals can, at least hypothetically, take responsibility for their own lives through decisions about what level of insurance to buy. Since insurance against disabilities is available to all in conditions of equal antecedent risk—i.e. each person is assumed to run the

[13] Some disabilities arise from reckless behaviour for which individuals may have to assume responsibility. Here, however, I will set aside the complex problems posed by voluntarily incurred risks that have catastrophic consequences.

[14] 'Option luck is a matter of how deliberate and calculated gambles turn out – whether someone gains or loses through accepting an isolated risk he or she should have anticipated and might have declined. Brute luck is a matter of how risks fall out that are not in that sense deliberate gambles' (Dworkin 1981: 281).

same risk of suffering brute bad luck—it is possible to represent any subsequent differences in the resource holdings of individuals brought about by fate as a difference of option luck. Dworkin contends that whereas differences in the opportunities individuals enjoy that reflect the effects of brute luck are unfair, those that reflect the operation of option luck may be legitimate. Of course, after insurance has been purchased, you still suffer brute bad luck if you quickly go blind while I remain sighted. But the differences between our resource holdings can be construed, as Dworkin puts it, as 'a difference in option luck against a background of equal opportunity to insure or not' (Dworkin 1981: 297).

For the purpose of making the scheme seem feasible, Dworkin suggests that we try to calculate the sort of insurance that the average person would buy. However, the ideal directs us to consider how each person can assume responsibility for the costs of bad luck through *individual* insurance decisions.[15] Theoretically then, the degree to which you are entitled to compensation for being blind will depend on how much insurance you purchased (or would have purchased) in Dworkin's special insurance market. So you are responsible, hypothetically or counterfactually, for looking out for your own interests. You cannot argue that you are entitled to more compensation than you receive under the hypothetical insurance scheme if you fail (or would have failed) to take adequate precautions against suffering some calamity. Since the market structure in which individuals make insurance decisions is procedurally fair, the compensation for disabilities yielded by the theory may be represented as fair.

This line of reasoning sounds persuasive but it is, nonetheless, open to objection on fairness grounds. The intuition Dworkin exploits here is that the insurance market presents each person with a fair gamble. Some win the insurance bet and others lose it but everyone has the same chance to buy insurance. Moreover, those whose option luck is bad cannot legitimately demand

---

[15] 'The averaging assumption is a simplifying assumption only, made to provide a result in the absence of the detailed . . . information that would enable us to decide how much each handicapped person would have purchased in the hypothetical market. If we had such full information, so that we could tailor compensation to what a particular individual in fact would have bought, the accuracy of the program would be improved' (Dworkin 1981: 298 n. 6; see also Dworkin 1993: 888).

that the payoff structure of the insurance wager (i.e. the terms of compensation for particular disabilities) be altered *post facto*. The results of the insurance market seem to resemble the outcome of a fair wager and perhaps the insurance market theory of compensation can be viewed as an instance of pure procedural justice. But appearances can be misleading.

In the first place, our conviction that individuals who gamble and lose are not entitled to compensation for their gambling losses only holds where the gamblers have the option of declining bets and avoiding risks. The option of declining a risk is not open to the person in the insurance market. Whether she purchases extensive insurance coverage or declines any coverage whatsoever, she risks suffering losses. We all face some risk of suffering a disability and we cannot choose to avoid this risk altogether. So in Dworkin's scheme we must all place bets that reflect our own attitudes to the risks associated with different disabilities. Whereas we can choose to avoid the risk involved in betting on the horses, we cannot choose to eliminate completely the risk of suffering a disability. This compulsory feature of the bet placed in the insurance market assumes greater significance in light of the fact that the sort of insurance policies that are available in the market will be determined by what most consumers are willing to buy. It is here that the potential for unfairness is introduced.

Even under the idealized economic conditions stipulated by Dworkin, the existence of insurance markets depends on the willingness of fairly large numbers of consumers to pool risks. Suppose that a large number of people in the market are not interested in purchasing insurance against suffering a serious disability. Since the supply of policies at affordable prices depends on there being sufficient demand for them, the market will not be able to supply the few sensible consumers interested in insurance coverage with adequate policies. If there is insufficient demand for pooling a certain kind of risk then insurance against that risk will not be supplied or the cost of a premium will be prohibitively high. In some case, this means there will be no compensation available even for those who suffer disabilities and who were willing to buy insurance. A situation like this, in which individuals are forced to accept serious risks without even the genuine opportunity to arrange reasonable and adequate compensation fails to satisfy the requirements of procedural fairness. We can locate the potential unfairness that arises here in the fact that persons cannot insulate themselves, in the hypothetical insurance market, from the effects of a certain type of brute luck—namely, the consequences that may arise from the attitudes towards risk that are held by others. Since the brute luck admitted by the insurance market may generate the very sort of unfairness it was initially designed to combat, it cannot be represented as a fair procedure for fixing levels of compensation owed to persons with disabilities.

Further explanation of this criticism requires a brief detour through some of the basic economic theory of insurance. The standard reason that people buy insurance is that they wish to protect themselves against the possibility of incurring a serious loss. Generally, people will only buy insurance in circumstances where the probability of loss is fairly small but the size of the possible loss is high. In entering an insurance contract a person assumes a certain financial loss, in the form a premium payment, in order to eliminate (or vastly reduce) a risk that they would otherwise face. Suppose my annual income is $20,000 and in a given year there is a 20 per cent chance that I will suffer a disability that will cause me to incur a $10,000 loss. (Admittedly, it is rather artificial to assign a precise dollar value to the cost of a disability but the exposition of the argument is facilitated by this simplifying assumption.) There is an 80 per cent probability that at the end of the year my income will be $20,000 and a 20 per cent probability that my income will be $10,000. In the absence of insurance my expected income is therefore $18,000. The expected value, in terms of income, of no insurance is arrived at by adding the dollar value of each possible outcome after each is discounted by the probability of its occurrence—($20,000 × 0.8) + ($10,000 × 0.2) = $18,000. Of course, I know that my actual income cannot be $18,000. At year end, I will have either $10,000 or $20,000. Now suppose that I am offered the opportunity to buy insurance against the risk of suffering a disability and losing $10,000. Insurance companies are in business to earn profits so they must set a premium which generates a profit after covering both the costs of expected claims and the costs of administration. Suppose the insurance company sets a premium at $2,500 for full coverage against loss due to disability. Should I purchase the insurance?

The first thing to be noticed is that insurance in a free market setting is always a financially disadvantageous investment. Without insurance my expected income is $18,000 but with insurance my income will be only $17,500. Although I fully expect to lose money on the purchase of such disability insurance, it may still be sensible for me to buy it. The economist's explanation of the rationality of insurance purchases lies in the theory of diminishing marginal utility. The rate at which income generates utility for me declines as my income rises. This means that the expected utility of insurance can exceed the expected utility of no insurance. If this is so, it is rational to purchase insurance. Let's say that the utility I derive from $10,000 is 60 utiles but due to diminishing marginal utility of income, a $20,000 income only generates 110 utiles. The expected utility of no insurance is calculated by adding the utility of $10,000, discounted by the 20 per cent chance of having this level of utility, to the utility of $20,000, discounted by the 80 per cent chance of having this income. (Expected utility of no insurance $= (60 \times 0.2) + (110 \times 0.8) = 100.$) This means that the expected utility of no insurance is 100 utiles. If insurance costs me $2,500 then the utility of having insurance is equivalent to the utility I derive from an income of $17,500 since with insurance I know with certainty what my income will be. If the utility of $17,500 is greater than 100 utiles then, according to economic theory, I should buy insurance. Let's say that $17,500 yields 101 utiles. Under these circumstances, insurance at the cost of $2,500 will be a sensible purchase. However, at a much higher premium I would be better off without insurance. From a theoretical point of view, the demand for insurance is largely attributable to the effects of diminishing marginal utility. Often we have a good reason to assume a certain loss in order to insulate ourselves from an unlikely but catastrophic occurrence, so we will be prepared to pay an insurance company to assume the risk we wish to avoid even though this entails an expected financial loss.

Dworkin's theory is fully sensitive to the foregoing features of the economic theory of insurance. He explicitly recognizes that insurance is a financially disadvantageous investment but can nonetheless be justified by appeal to considerations of expected welfare (Dworkin 1981: 318–19). However, Dworkin does not fully consider the circumstances under which a profit-seeking insurance company will be prepared to offer policies to individuals with affordable premiums. The crucial point here is that the availability of insurance depends on the capacity of an insurance company to pool together a *large number* of similar risks. Insurance companies will only be able to offer affordable policies if they can reliably predict the costs of paying out claims to insured parties who have suffered losses. The mechanism upon which insurance companies rely in securing the requisite degree of confidence about claim costs is pooling. By increasing the number of insured parties who face a given risk the insurance company increases its confidence about the costs it will face. In other words, by increasing its exposure to a given risk the insurance company increases the likelihood that expected costs will fall within a reasonable range of accuracy. Moreover, the number of exposures to risk that will be required to achieve a suitable degree of accuracy about expected costs (i.e. payment of claims) is generally very high. The explanation of the fact that insurance markets depend on pooling large numbers of similar risks lies in the mathematical and statistical properties of large numbers. Indeed, one insurance expert emphasizes that 'the foundation of insurance rests upon the law of large numbers' (Greene 1968: 33).

In circumstances in which an insurer can only pool together a small number of risks, the insurer cannot have much confidence about the actual losses that it might have to face. Consider the operation of the law of large numbers in the example cited. Suppose that 100 persons wish to buy insurance against the risk of losing $10,000. Since there is a 20 per cent risk of loss, the insurer expects that it will have to pay out 20 claims of $10,000 each. However, there is only a small probability that exactly 20 insured parties will experience a loss. It is very likely that actual losses will fall either below or above the statistical mean. Indeed, it turns out that if we assume a statistically normal (binomial) distribution of losses then the insurance company cannot be more that 68 per cent confident that actual losses will be in the range of 16–24. And it cannot be more than 95 per cent certain that actual losses will fall in the range of 12–28. This means, of course, that with only 100 insured parties the company cannot be very confident about the actual number of claims that it will have to pay out. Since there is a good chance that actual losses will deviate substantially from expected losses the insurance company cannot offer insurance to interested parties at rates that are compatible with the price at which insurance is a sensible or rational purchase. The question that naturally arises in this context concerns the degree of confidence about the actual losses an insurance company must have before it can offer insurance. No precise answer can be given because different insurance companies may adopt different attitudes towards risk. Nonetheless, much scholarship about insurance suggests that companies must be very confident—95 per cent certain—that actual losses will fall within 10 per cent of expected losses (Greene 1968: 39). With only 100 potential insured parties and with a 20 per cent chance of loss, the insurance company can only be 95 per cent certain that actual losses will fall within 40 per cent of expected losses. Hence it is unlikely that a profit-seeking insurance company would offer policies to the 100 people interested in such insurance.

So insurance theory shows that even if we accept the hypothetical and idealized assumptions under which Dworkin's insurance markets are supposed to function, economically viable insurance markets can only exist if insurance companies can exploit the risk reduction techniques that the law of large numbers permits through the pooling of similar risks. Once this point is recognized, however, the hypothetical insurance theory of compensation is vulnerable to the fundamental fairness objection. Remember that Dworkin contends that fair compensation for a disability is equivalent to the amount of insurance a person would have purchased in the hypothetical insurance market. The plausibility of the argument depends on the supposition that in the hypothetical insurance market each person has a reasonable opportunity to purchase suitable disability insurance should they desire it. Unless this condition is met then the insurance market cannot be used, even hypothetically, to transform the effects of raw brute luck into consequences that can be interpreted as arising out of differential option luck. It is, however, easy to construct counter-examples in which the hypothetical insurance market will not supply adequate opportunities to purchase insurance.

Suppose that the risks associated with a given disability correspond to those described in the example given above. Helen is a participant in the hypothetical insurance market and she decides that she would like to buy disability insurance. Moreover, let's suppose that her preference is eminently rational and not idiosyncratic. Every sensible person should desire to purchase this kind of disability insurance. As we have seen, whether Helen will be able to purchase the desired coverage depends directly on the willingness of a large number of others to purchase similar coverage. Indeed, if the insurance company is to be 95 per cent certain that actual expenses due to claims will be within 10 per cent of expected expenses, there must be at least 10,000 participants in the market who wish to buy insurance.[16] Suppose, however, that an insufficiently large number of people recognize the rationality of acquiring disability insurance. Helen and other sensible parties will be unable to buy insurance. Now suppose that Helen is unlucky. She is among the 20 per cent of the population which subsequently develop the disability. According to Dworkin's theory Helen is not entitled to any compensation because she would not have bought coverage in the hypothetical insurance market. Of course, she was unable to buy the coverage due to the irrationality of other participants in the hypothetical market. Here the procedural failing of the market is clear. It is unfair that Helen's entitlement to compensation is held hostage to the irrationality of her fellows. Yet the market permits this and therefore it does not satisfy the demands of procedural fairness. The basic objection is that even the idealized insurance market is a potentially unfair mechanism for gauging appropriate compensation standards.

COMPENSATION AND PRIVATE PROPERTY

There is one further fundamental objection to the insurance scheme I wish to consider briefly. This is the idea that Dworkin's

---

[16] Note that as the probability of a loss *decreases*, the number of exposures to the risk that an insurer requires to achieve a sufficient level of confidence *increases* dramatically. For instance, if the probability of loss is 5% then the required number of units of exposure to risk needed to achieve a 95% confidence level (i.e. such that the insurer will be 95% certain that losses will be within 10% of expected losses) is 40,000. For a full account of the mathematical basis for these and other related insurance calculations see Greene 1968: especially 37–9.

theory of compensation proceeds from a subtle but important misdiagnosis of the problem posed by disabilities. The misdiagnosis revolves around the idea that discharging obligations to disabled persons is primarily a problem about the distribution and ownership of private resources. As a consequence, Dworkin's framework is ill-suited to dealing with a problem which is arguably just if not more important—namely the nature of the broader social and institutional structures in which persons with disabilities live.

A striking feature of Dworkin's approach is that the fair accommodation of the interests of persons with disabilities consists primarily in determining the degree to which individual ownership of private property should be affected by disabilities. The sort of fair compensation for a disability generated by the insurance market always seems to take the form of individual entitlement to extra material resources. Dworkin's argument seems to license the conclusion that the demands of justice vis-à-vis disabled persons can be fully met through instituting what amounts to direct transfer payments from the non-disabled persons to disabled persons (Jacobs 1993: 111–16). Such a narrow focus on the distribution of private resources is, I believe, the inevitable result of diagnosing the unfairness associated with disabilities as arising out of an unequal distribution of personal resources. If the unfairness associated with disability is explained wholly in terms of the unfair distribution of private resources then the corresponding remedy to this unfairness lies in the redistribution of private resources. Since privately held personal resources are not to be redistributed, we need a metric for gauging the value of personal resources in the currency of privately held impersonal resources. The hypothetical insurance market can be construed as providing a means of fixing a fair exchange rate for personal and impersonal resources. If you lack a given personal resource (i.e. if you are disabled), the insurance market provides a mechanism for gauging the impersonal resources to which you are entitled by way of compensation.

The main counter-intuitive consequence of conceiving compensation solely in terms of control of private property is that it obscures the degree to which addressing the legitimate interests of disabled persons depends upon the public provision of a social environment in which disabled persons are better able to lead a good life. Concentrating on the redistribution of private resources comes at the expense of recognizing the interests disabled persons have in the social complexion of the community in which they live. In a just society, persons with disabilities should be integrated into the life of the community as full and active members. Marginalization of disabled persons cannot be eliminated merely by effecting transfers of resources. This means that the physical and social environment must be suitably hospitable to the distinctive needs of persons with disabilities. For instance, buildings must be easily accessible, barriers to satisfying employment must be eliminated, and the stigmatization of disability that is displayed in the attitudes of those who are not disabled must be combated. Providing disabled persons with extra private resources to use at their discretion is unlikely to address these dimensions of the disadvantage associated with disability. The provision of compensation in the form of transfer payments will not provide employers with incentives to offer employment to persons with disabilities or to modify the workplace environment in a way suited to the special needs of disabled workers. Moreover, even where compensation does consist in the provision of private resources, it is arguable that the hypothetical insurance market fails to distinguish adequately the kinds of resources to which disabled persons are entitled. Disabilities generate entitlements to resources that can mitigate the debilitating consequences of disabilities. But disabilities do not generate entitlements to resources that merely serve the satisfaction of desires. People with poor vision may be entitled to suitable eyeglasses but they are not obviously entitled to the cash equivalent of glasses to spend on expensive wine. Dworkin's theory, which is wholly reliant on the insurance scheme, does not provide any basis for differentiating resource entitlements in this way. The importance of such matters cannot be adequately identified or addressed within a framework that depicts compensation primarily in terms of the ownership of (undifferentiated) private resources.

I am not suggesting that Dworkin's strategy is logically inconsistent with recognition of these dimensions of the problem.[17]

---

[17] Perhaps the insurance scheme could be modified in ways that accommodate these concerns. The difficulty, however, is that the changes would appear to be ad hoc and not a natural extension of the underlying theory.

The difficulty relates rather to whether Dworkin's strategy can adequately explain why these considerations are important. We want to be able to explain why justice should be sensitive to the broader social, political, institutional, and attitudinal dimensions of the interests of disabled persons. But because of its focus on individual ownership Dworkin's theory provides too limited a framework for an adequate account of the diverse elements in an appropriate compensation scheme. A more robust egalitarian theory of disability compensation must identify the unfairness associated with disabilities as arising, not merely out of the distribution of personal resources, but also out of the way in which the interests of disabled persons are adversely affected by the complexion of the social environment in which they live.

I have argued that the hypothetical insurance theory of disability compensation is flawed for a variety of reasons. If the objections advanced here are sound then we must also be sceptical about the account of just health care that Dworkin argues can be derived from a parallel hypothetical insurance market scheme. I began this chapter with the observation that although most of us recognize that justice requires special accommodation of the interests of persons with disabilities, it is extraordinarily difficult to explain the actual requirements of fair compensation. Dworkin's theory is initially appealing because it offers the promise of a precise, principled response to this vexing problem. Yet, as we have seen, the insurance scheme fails in two crucial respects. It does not illuminate the extent or magnitude of obligation and it misidentifies the nature of appropriate compensation. Moreover, the underlying ideal of equality of resources does not provide clear guidance because the injunction to equalize resources simply cannot be met or even fully imagined in the case of disabilities. The two intertwined puzzles of how *much* compensation and *what kind* of compensation justice requires remain. Indeed, in developing the critique, I have focused almost entirely on identifying specific problems with the insurance market theory of compensation and I have not indicated what a more satisfactory theory might look like. While such a theory will not be developed here, what has been clarified are some key considerations which must shape such a theory. The principal lesson of the failure of Dworkin's theory is that a theory of disability compensation must attempt to articulate, in a concrete fashion, the different disadvantages that accrue to individuals with disabilities. The imaginative exercise of the hypothetical insurance market is unhelpful in this regard because it directs us to engage in a kind of abstract speculation that is too distant from the particular needs of disabled persons. Procedural solutions like the insurance market seem to provide an attractive approach to the problem of compensation, but I suspect they must be abandoned. Perhaps the best an egalitarian theory of disability compensation can manage is a more piecemeal but context-sensitive accommodation of the interests of disabled persons, satisfaction of which is a precondition to leading a decent life as full and equal members of the community. Appropriate forms of compensation can then be tailored to meeting these interests. From the perspective of the theory of justice, this is a disappointing conclusion since a more determinate and precise account of compensatory justice would be desirable. However, if the search for determinacy comes at the expense of fairness, it is a goal that is better not pursued.

5

Unequal Talents

IN this chapter I examine Dworkin's analysis of and proposed solution to the problem posed by natural differences in individual talent. The problem is one aspect of the issue of how we should understand the moral significance of unequal natural endowment. The general difficulty concerns the arbitrary impact that unequal endowment can have on the opportunities individuals have to lead a good life. It is largely a matter of brute luck that persons vary in the physical and mental capacities which they enjoy. Egalitarians believe that institutions should be so structured as to extinguish, as far as possible, the ill-effects of this kind of brute luck. However, as we have already seen in the case of disabilities there can be no complete or direct remedy to some of the most serious consequences of brute bad luck. It is an unfortunate fact that the life prospects of some are severely constrained by extreme physical or mental impairment for which they bear no responsibility. Yet we cannot eliminate the unfair effects of such bad luck by redistributing physical or mental capacities and thereby share equally the burdens associated with disability. Instead the challenge is to develop a strategy through which fair and appropriate compensation for the disadvantages associated with disabilities can be gauged and effected.

That the talents of individuals vary in both kind and degree generates a different problem. I believe this is because the mere fact of unequal talent need not present a significant obstacle to the achievement of the egalitarian ideal. Lacking a particular talent, unlike suffering a disability, does not constitute a direct or pervasive obstacle to leading a fulfilling life. By contrast a serious disability generally creates difficulties for the very leading of a life, irrespective of the specific projects or endeavours that constitute the life. So although the lack of a given talent may prevent a person from pursuing particular life plans, it does not systematically hinder the leading of a good life.[1] For instance, I could never compete in the Olympic decathlon because I lack the genetic make-up of an elite athlete. But this fact about my talents does not present a barrier to my leading a good life since there are many other worthwhile life plans I can pursue satisfactorily and which are not impeded by my lack of a particular talent. Serious disabilities create general and significant impediments to the implementation of virtually any worthwhile life plan. Lacking various talents merely forecloses the pursuit of options associated with particular talents. A disability makes the pursuit of *any* form of the good life more burdensome. This difference between talents and disabilities is important. It suggests that whereas suffering a disability is sufficient to entitle a person to compensation, merely lacking a talent is not sufficient to justify compensation.[2] Consequently, the problem posed by unequal talents is not the problem of determining what individuals are entitled to by way of fair compensation for lacking given talents.

THE GENERAL DIMENSIONS OF THE PROBLEM

Unequal talents assume moral significance against an institutional background in which arbitrary differences in native endowment have an unequal impact on each person's access to the benefits of social cooperation. In a market economy, for example, the distribution of resources is determined not only by the interplay of each person's choices about the goods she wishes to consume and produce but also by her ability to produce goods that are valued by others. If we assume that individuals have the prerogative of exercising the capacities they happen to have, more or less as they see fit, then differences in the income and

[1] Naturally, I am not implying that disabled persons cannot lead good lives. The point is rather that disabled persons face systematic obstacles in leading their lives that are not parallel to the ways in which lack of talent may constrain the pursuit of life plans.

[2] Sen also draws a connection between disability and entitlement. He argues that the impairment of a person's 'basic capacities' can generate an entitlement to resources. The cheerful cripple 'has needs as a cripple that should be catered to' even if, because of his cheerful disposition, he is no worse off in utility terms than others (Sen 1980: 217–18).

other advantages (e.g. status and power) derived from market activity will often track differences in talent. The voluntary exchanges of goods and services which take place in an unregulated market favour those whose capacities happen to be valued (i.e. are highly demanded) by the community. Notice the contrast between talents and disabilities that is brought out here. Whereas the significance that attaches to unequal talents is market-driven, the significance of disabilities is largely market-independent. We do not ordinarily need a market to identify disabilities that demand attention. Indeed, we might express the relevant contrast in the following terms. The advantage of possessing a talent that has a high market value is largely instrumental. A valued talent permits a person to acquire valuable resources in market transactions. The disadvantage which accrues to individuals who lack such talents is primarily a disadvantage in securing access to useful resources. If differences in talent did not adversely affect the market opportunities enjoyed by some individuals then the fact of unequal talent would not generate arbitrary disadvantage of the sort egalitarianism seeks to eliminate. By contrast, some of the disadvantages associated with serious disabilities are inherent and not merely instrumental. The general impediments to leading a good life which disabilities directly give rise to are a matter for egalitarian concern irrespective of the effect disabilities have on access to the benefits of social cooperation made available through an economic system. In this sense, some of the disadvantages associated with disabilities are inherent disadvantages.

Viewing the value of talents in terms of instrumental advantage and disadvantage does not mean that the problem of unequal talents is trivial or easy to solve. The matter is complex for, as we have seen, liberal egalitarians accept that responsible individual choice may legitimately affect entitlement to resources. Economic inequalities which only reflect different choices by responsible individuals about how to conduct their lives can be justifiable. However, liberal egalitarians reject the suggestion that the mere possession of a valued talent generates an entitlement to every advantage which can be garnered through its exercise.[3] As Rawls says, 'we seek a conception of

---

[3] Liberal egalitarians reject any strong thesis of self-ownership. A person does not own the capacities she happens to possess. The egalitarian view contrasts starkly

justice that nullifies the accidents of natural endowment and the contingencies of social circumstance as counters in the quest for political and economic advantage' (Rawls 1971: 15; see also 73–4, 101–2). So the conception of the person that lies at the heart of modern egalitarianism is one in which the personal attributes that contribute to market success are the result of a complex blend of responsible choices and circumstances beyond the control of the individual. Ultimately, this means that the sense in which we can characterize the distribution of endowments as morally arbitrary is correspondingly complex. After all, some traits that a person has will reflect the interplay between choice and natural endowment.[4] For example, two equally gifted musicians may make different choices about how many hours to devote to practice which may, in turn, have a differential impact on their earning power. These complexities, however, do not fundamentally alter the shape of the problem we face.

The task for liberal egalitarian theory is to explain how the arbitrary influence of unequal talent on distribution can be neutralized without compromising the legitimate distributive consequences of responsible individual choice. Dworkin

with the libertarian view, espoused by Gauthier (1986) and Nozick (1974), in which a very strong thesis of self-ownership is a fundamental feature of the theory of justice. Libertarianism of this sort holds that because individuals own their capacities, they are entitled to any advantage they may garner by exercising those capacities in a free market. G. A. Cohen has effectively criticized the libertarian interpretation of the thesis of self-ownership. See Cohen (1986a; 1986b) for thorough discussion of these matters, with particular emphasis on Nozick's theory.

[4] It is worth noting that the term 'natural endowment' does not simply refer to the traits of a person that are genetically determined. Indeed, Rosenberg correctly points out that none of the traits that a person has are solely a matter of genetics. 'All so-called hereditary endowments are the result of interaction between the genome and its environment' (Rosenberg 1987: 3). In light of this Rosenberg proposes a more complex taxonomy of human traits that better captures the different kinds of biological and environmental influences that shape human traits. Thus he distinguishes between hereditary, domestic, and acquired traits. The relevant feature in distinguishing these traits is the different role that human agency plays in affecting the environment that shapes the trait. In the case of acquired traits, development of a person's genetic endowment is achieved largely through the free choices of the person. In Dworkin's terms, ambition can lead to the development of talent. So strictly speaking, we cannot say that all differences in talent are morally arbitrary since some differences may be traceable mainly to choices for which individuals can assume responsibility. Nonetheless, since it is clear that a good deal of difference in talent is traceable primarily to arbitrary differences we can work with the provisional assumption that the distribution of talent amongst persons is morally arbitrary.

describes this idea as imposing the requirement that a distribution of resources be 'ambition-sensitive' but 'endowment-insensitive' (Dworkin 1981: 311). In Chapter 3 we examined the capacity of the market to track the requirement of ambition-sensitivity when we make the simplifying assumption of equal endowment. In this chapter, we examine how ambition-sensitivity can be tracked once the simplifying assumption is dropped. From an abstract theoretical perspective drawing the distinction between ambition-sensitivity and endowment insensitivity is not problematic. That is, we can make sense of the idea that people should be held responsible for their choices but should not be disadvantaged by factors beyond their control. However, in any actual institutional setting there will be difficulties in directly and accurately distinguishing the legitimate influence of choice on distribution from the illegitimate influence of endowment. We need, therefore, to identify the institutional context in which this aspect of distributive justice is to be explored.

Unsurprisingly, a market economy is the institutional background against which the problem of unequal talents is pursued by liberals. This is appropriate for a couple of reasons. First, the market mechanism displays some sensitivity to the requirement of ambition-sensitivity. Though it is by no means perfect, the price system in a well-functioning market is sometimes responsive to relevant differences in individual choice. For example, other things being equal, a person who is willing to work overtime can earn a greater income than someone in the same line of work who is unprepared to put in extra hours. Second, a market economy arguably has other virtues such as high productivity and efficiency in the allocation of resources that make it desirable. The level of material prosperity achieved in market societies is impressive and morally significant. Given the absence of any feasible alternative economic structure that can match the achievements of the market in this respect, it is appropriate to investigate how justice might be achieved in some kind of market economy. Beyond assuming that the operation of competitive markets serves to determine such things as prices, the availability of consumer goods, and the allocation of productive resources, I shall not try to identify the particular institutional arrangements that can be said to define a market economy—e.g. by specifying the kind and degree of government involvement in the management of the economy that is consistent with the market. Similarly, I wish to bracket the complex issues concerning the impact of redistributive taxation on the overall productive efficiency of a market economy. A traditional concern is that redistributive taxation undermines the incentives for personal gain that partly explain the material prosperity created in market economies. The problem of reconciling suitable incentives and justice is obviously very important. Egalitarians cannot simply assume that distributive equality is compatible with a high level of material productivity. However, these matters are not considered by Dworkin in any detail and I shall proceed with the provisional assumption that fair redistribution of market income is not inconsistent with a highly productive economy.[5]

With these stipulations about the market setting in place, the problem of unequal talents can be conceived as one of determining how the market outcomes should be adjusted so as to mitigate fairly the impact of arbitrary differences of talent on the distributions that would otherwise be secured through the market. In other words, liberal egalitarianism needs a theory of fair market adjustment if it is to be responsive to the problem of unequal talents.

OBSTACLES TO TRACKING THE DISTRIBUTIONAL SIGNIFICANCE OF CHOICE

Needless to say, the focus of this chapter is on Dworkin's distinctive contributions to the analysis and solution of the problem of fair market adjustment. Other theorists have made proposals about a suitably egalitarian theory of fair market adjustment. Yet few try to track the twin requirements of ambition-sensitivity and endowment-insensitivity. James Dick, for instance, invokes the distinction between transfer earnings— the amount that must be paid to an individual in order to prevent her from transferring to another job—and economic rent—market income that an individual receives above her transfer earnings. He suggests that we should seek to eliminate

---

[5] For discussion of the relationship between egalitarian justice and incentives see Carens (1981) and Macleod (1985).

economic inequalities that are attributable to economic rent but permit inequalities in transfer earnings (Dick 1975). More ambitiously, David Miller has recently developed a model of market socialism that attempts to harness market mechanisms in the pursuit of egalitarian objectives (Miller 1989). His theory includes a principle of contribution according to which individuals are entitled to receive the value, as determined by the market, which they have freely contributed to a product. This principle is offered as part of a choice-sensitive account of desert. And, of course, Rawls's difference principle is perhaps the most famous account of fair market adjustment. Unsurprisingly, the underlying conceptions of equality which motivate these proposals do not exactly match those identified by Dworkin. I suspect that neither Dick's rent proposal nor Miller's contribution principle speaks sufficiently to the requirement of endowment-insensitivity. And it is widely believed that the difference principle does not really address the distributive significance of individual choice. Since full consideration of these and other suggestions (e.g. Rakowski (1991)) would require a substantial digression, I shall not explore them here.

It may be useful, however, to review briefly a couple of arguments which might seem to challenge the coherency of searching for a choice-sensitive theory of fair market adjustment. First, it is worth revisiting a point raised in Chapter 2: one possible reaction to the problem is simply to deny the voluntarist thesis that motivates the ambition-sensitivity requirement in the first place. As we saw, Rawls has often been interpreted as arguing against the inclusion of considerations of desert within a theory of distributive justice on the basis that no one can take credit for the characteristics which might otherwise give rise to desert-based entitlements to resources.[6] If, as this sort of view suggests, we cannot construe any of our personal char-

---

[6] Considerations of desert-based entitlement may not always coincide with considerations of choice-based entitlement. As Robert Young notes there is 'a bewildering variety of things which are said to serve as personal desert bases' (Young 1992: 320) and only some of these putative desert bases can be considered choice-based. The amount of effort a person devotes to a project is more plausibly construed as a matter of choice than mere possession of talent, even though both can provide the ostensible basis for some desert claims. I will set aside the complexities involved in unravelling the complex notion of desert against a background of unequal talents and will focus only on the problem of the possibility of determining choice-based entitlements given unequal talents.

acteristics, including our preferences, as voluntaristic then we will be drawn to radical scepticism about the idea that individual choice can be said to give rise to entitlement to resources. Complete rejection of voluntarism would greatly simplify the theory of fair market adjustment as there would then be no need to attempt to track the influence of choice on entitlement. Short of complete rejection of voluntarism, it might be maintained that although choice does sometimes generate differential entitlement to resources, its overall significance and effect is so small as compared with other determinants of market success, as to be negligible. Notwithstanding these reservations about the distributive significance of choice, most contemporary liberals would like to predicate their theories on a more expansive notion of individual responsibility.

A different sort of challenge to the need to construct an ambition-sensitive theory of fair market adjustment is that tracking ambition is too institutionally impracticable. We should, therefore, abandon the attempt to incorporate the requirement within the theory of justice. Joseph Carens, for example, argues that the articulation of ideals of distributive justice should be constrained by a realistic appraisal of the possibility of designing feasible social institutions through which ideals can be implemented. There is, in short, no point in insisting on a requirement like ambition-sensitivity if it is impossible to design social institutions that could, even imperfectly, track this requirement. Indeed, Carens argues that this sort of dimension of distributive justice 'cannot be adequately articulated without reference to ·a particular model of how that ideal should be institutionalized' (Carens 1985: 46). So although Carens acknowledges that the liberal impulse to develop a choice-sensitive theory of fair incomes is based on powerful intuitions, he is sceptical about the possibility of designing feasible institutions through which the abstract philosophical convictions might be realized.

An important presupposition of a liberal egalitarian theory of fair market adjustment is that some market-generated inequalities in income are fair. Nonetheless, Carens believes that in light of the difficulties of actually implementing a genuinely choice-sensitive incomes policy, we would come closer to fulfilling the egalitarian ideal by equalizing incomes. The sophisticated systems of redistributive taxation needed to give effect to the ideal of ambition-sensitivity against a background of unequal talents would be impossibly complex. Carens's argument is not directed specifically against Dworkin's proposal but it does pose an interesting challenge.

However, I think that Dworkin's theory is less vulnerable to the problem highlighted by Carens than other possible approaches. Dworkin does not think that the taxation system should attempt to track ambition-sensitivity directly. Rather we rely upon a theory of market adjustment to identify a level of income that can serve as a social minimum to which every person is entitled. Since the provision of a minimum income through the income tax system does not involve any obviously unrealistic assumptions about the design of social institutions, Dworkin's theory is less open to the charge that the articulated ideal of justice is not realizable. Admittedly, this means, on Dworkin's approach, that the income system can only crudely approximate the demands of egalitarian justice. This is a concession to Carens's point, but Carens's suggestion that equalizing incomes is the best we can do may be premature. The issue is not whether we should pursue an unattainable ideal of justice but how close we can come to realizing it, given suitable sensitivity to the limits of feasible institutional design. Equal incomes may be closer to the ideal than a minimum income. But we can only adjudicate between different options if we have a clearer sense of how the ideal is to be understood in the first place.

TWO DIMENSIONS OF DWORKIN'S THEORY

In the previous chapter, we investigated and found wanting the hypothetical insurance scheme which Dworkin uses to solve the problem of unequal natural endowment in the case of disabilities. His theory of fair market adjustment is provided by a more complex variant of this hypothetical insurance market approach. Dworkin believes this approach can identify and justify a fair system of redistributive taxation which is suitable for application in actual liberal societies.

In what follows, I explore the theoretical underpinnings of the hypothetical insurance market approach and I consider the adequacy of the system of redistribution it supports. The arguments considered here are complex and I should make clear that there are two distinct foci of criticism in this chapter. The first concerns Dworkin's treatment of the difference between talents and disabilities. I briefly mentioned this issue in the last chapter but I postponed discussion of it for this chapter. The second cluster of issues concerns the details of the theory of fair market adjustment supplied by the hypothetical insurance market. Though the issues are related, my more detailed criticisms of Dworkin's theory of fair market adjustment do not depend directly on the discussion of the distinction between talents and disabilities.

The rest of this chapter has the following shape. I begin by examining the distinction Dworkin draws between talents and disabilities. Dworkin argues that the problems of disabilities and talents require theoretically independent solutions. I agree with this conclusion. However, I believe that his analysis of the distinction between talents and disabilities is flawed. It does not provide the appropriate rationale for the contention that the problems posed by disabilities and unequal talents are distinct. Second, I explain the details of the elaborate hypothetical insurance market scheme which supplies Dworkin's theory of fair market adjustment. I argue that the characteristics and implications of such a scheme are significantly different from what Dworkin supposes. This lays the groundwork for two important objections to basing the theory of fair market adjustment on the operation of a hypothetical insurance market. Finally, I consider and criticize Dworkin's contention that the hypothetical insurance market argument can explain how substantial inequalities of income and wealth in actual liberal societies may be acceptable from an egalitarian perspective.

THE INDEPENDENCE VIEW

I have suggested that human disabilities and unequal talents pose distinct problems which require independent theoretical solutions. I will call this the *independence view*. Dworkin shares the independence view: the hypothetical insurance market scheme that provides his theory of fair market adjustment is

importantly different from, and independent of, the insurance
market scheme he employs to determine fair compensation for
suffering a disability. I believe the best reason for accepting the
independence view is that suffering a disability is fundamentally
different from lacking a talent. That there is a fundamental
difference here seems confirmed by, among other things, the
intuition that whereas suffering a disability is sufficient to entitle
a person to compensation, merely lacking a talent is not sufficient to justify compensation. Dworkin's understanding of these
matters is interesting because acceptance of the independence
view is not predicated on the supposition that disability and lack
of talent are fundamentally different. Indeed, Dworkin rejects
that supposition. He offers a different interpretation of the
distinction between talent and disability and thus provides a
different rationale for the independence view. Both these aspects
of Dworkin's theory are, however, problematic.

In ordinary discourse it is natural to distinguish different
dimensions of natural endowment. Some people are born severely disabled and others are blessed with exceptional talents.
Most people are neither disabled nor exceptionally gifted. They
enjoy what can be termed the normal range of basic human
capacities. Prima facie, a satisfactory analysis of natural endowment should be able to preserve and explain these distinctions.
That is, it should be able to offer an account of the difference
and relationship between: (1) suffering a disability; (2) enjoying
a special talent; (3) having a basic human capacity. Persons who
lack special talents and suffer no impairment of a basic capacity
are not disabled. They are ordinary in the sense that they have
basic capacities which function in the normal range for healthy
humans. Dworkin's theory is in some sense revisionist since
it denies that our intuitions about these familiar distinctions
are well founded. Of course, our initial convictions about the
soundness of these distinctions might prove mistaken. But it
is reasonable to suppose that the burden of proof lies with the
revisionist critic who wishes to challenge our initial intuitions.
Dworkin's account of the difference between talents and disabilities is interesting in its own right and it also plays a crucial
role in his overall theory because it underlies his adoption of a
modified hypothetical insurance market scheme. I shall suggest,
however, that Dworkin is mistaken when he denies there is a

fundamental difference between talent and disability. His arguments do not provide the appropriate rationale for distinguishing the problems raised by disabilities and talents. Hence his insistence that a different hypothetical insurance market scheme must be used to generate a theory of fair market adjustment is not sufficiently justified.

There are two components to Dworkin's treatment of the distinction between talents and disabilities. First, he insists that the difference between talents and disabilities is only a matter of degree. On this view, there is no fundamental difference between lacking a talent and suffering a disability. Second, talents and disabilities may nonetheless be differentiated for the purpose of addressing issues of distributive justice because they stand in different relationships to individual ambition. I will call these claims the *difference of degree thesis* and the *ambition thesis* respectively. The difference of degree thesis represents Dworkin's understanding of the distinction between talent and disability. The ambition thesis grounds his rationale for employing two different hypothetical insurance schemes in his theory. It explains, in other words, his commitment to the independence view.

THE DIFFERENCE OF DEGREE THESIS

Let us first consider the difference of degree thesis. Does it provide an adequate explanation of the intuitively different dimensions of natural endowment? The suggestion is that the distinction between talents and disabilities should be conceived as a matter of degree. Unfortunately, this important claim is not elaborated in any detail. Dworkin says only: 'Though skills are different from handicaps, the difference can be understood as one of degree: we may say that someone who cannot play basketball like Wilt Chamberlain, paint like Piero, or make money like Geneen, suffers from (an especially common) handicap' (Dworkin 1981: 314–15). The natural interpretation of this remark is that a skill (or talent) can be defined as the presence of any human power or capacity. Correspondingly, a handicap (or disability) can be defined as the absence of any human power or capacity. We may suppose, in other words, that there is a wide range of mental and physical capacities which individuals may potentially possess. To 'suffer' a disability is simply to lack at least one of these powers. To have a talent is simply to enjoy at least one of these capacities. This account is consistent with Dworkin's idea of 'personal resources' (noted in the previous chapter) as 'qualities of the mind and body that affect people's success in achieving their plans and projects: physical and mental health, strength and talent' (Dworkin 1991: 37). Brute genetic luck distributes 'personal resources' unequally. A person who is untalented in a given respect lacks a personal resource enjoyed by others. Similarly, a disabled person lacks a personal resource enjoyed by others. Construed in these terms, there is no deep difference between being disabled and being untalented. Both conditions merely consist in some kind of personal resource deficit.

So the claim that the difference between disabilities and skills is a matter of degree boils down to the idea that disability is a simple function of the absence of some realizable human capacity. No distinction is drawn between the *character* of different capacities or personal resources. Lacking the capacity to walk is not fundamentally different from lacking the capacity to run 100 metres in ten seconds. On this view, disability is a matter of degree in the sense that the more capacities or personal resources a person lacks, the more disabled she is. Presumably, if one lacks enough capacities one is considered disabled and not merely untalented but ultimately the difference of degree thesis admits no fundamental distinction between disability and mere lack of talent.

Dworkin's view may seem initially plausible because it proceeds from an accurate and important observation. It is unquestionably true that talents and disabilities represent ways in which individuals differ in the sorts of powers they are in a position to exercise. This is the important kernel of truth in the difference of degree thesis. However, Dworkin's analysis is problematic because it obscures the significance of certain differences among the powers or capacities which humans can have or lack. It entails rejection of the idea that a distinction may be drawn between 'basic human capacities' and 'special capacities'. By basic capacities I mean, roughly, the species-typical physiological and psychological traits of healthy human beings. Special capacities (or talents) are capacities that are developed beyond usual human parameters. For instance, unassisted physical mobility (e.g. being able to walk) is a basic human capacity while being able to run 100 metres in ten seconds is a special capacity.

Because it rejects this distinction Dworkin's view cannot accommodate the possibility that only the absence or serious impairment of a 'basic capacity' constitutes a genuine disability. Indeed, the principal difficulty with the difference of degree thesis is that it leads to a conflation of disability with the mere absence of capacity—absence of capacity of any sort. This has counter-intuitive consequences. First, it implies that everyone is, in some sense, disabled since no one enjoys the entire repertoire of possible human capacities. I think this distorts and trivializes the significance of suffering a disability. *Pace* Dworkin, it is surely a mistake to suppose that my inability to paint masterpieces should be construed in any way as even a very common disability. Moreover, because Dworkin's position measures disability only in degrees, it can yield strange judgements of relative disability. For instance, if we make judgements of relative disability based only on a comparison of the undifferentiated capacities individuals have and lack then we arrive at peculiar conclusions. It would be odd to say that Anna who cannot walk is less disabled than able-bodied Brian because Anna has more highly developed artistic, musical, and intellectual capacities than Brian. Finally, this approach seems to entail that it is appropriate, at least in principle, to compensate individuals merely because they lack particular skills. Since lacking talent on Dworkin's view is a disability, and since it is appropriate to compensate individuals because they are disabled, compensation for the mere absence of talent must also be contemplated. But as I have already noted, mere lack of talent does not plausibly generate entitlement to compensation. Mere lack of talent does not represent a direct obstacle to the leading of a good life.

A more satisfactory explanation of the distinction between talent and disability is needed. An obvious alternative is the view hinted at in the foregoing criticisms. It identifies disabilities and talents by reference to an account of basic human capacities.[7]

---

[7] This approach follows the lead of Amartya Sen, who has argued that a satisfactory theory of political morality must recognize the importance of some account of human 'capabilities' and 'functionings' (Sen 1980; 1985*a*; 1985*b*). Needless to say,

The point of departure for such an account is the idea that a disability results from the absence or serious impairment of a basic human capacity. A talent exists when the functioning of a basic capacity surpasses a normal or ordinary level of functioning for a human. (A talent, so understood, does not necessarily have a high market value.) Disabilities are rooted in some kind of malfunction of basic capacities. Dworkin explicitly rejects this approach. He finds dubious the assumption that there is a repertoire of physical and mental (cognitive and non-cognitive) capacities which can provide the requisite standards for assessing the functioning of basic human capacities. Indeed, he rejects the idea that there can be a non-arbitrary standard of basic human capacities. His argument rests on the premiss that any standard of normal human powers must be drawn from the particular capacities instantiated in a specific representative individual. Since individuals vary in the capacities they enjoy, the selection of any one representative individual will be arbitrary and hence any standard of basic capacities or normal human powers will be arbitrary.[8]

This line of reasoning is unpersuasive. The idea that a standard of normal powers or basic capacities must be identical with the specific capacities of a single representative person is mistaken. In fact, the relevant standard can be drawn from our scientific understanding of the biological and psychological traits which are common to humans. Knowledge of the sort needed here is not predicated on the study of a single representa-

---

my description of this approach is very rough and incomplete. My aim is not to develop a worked-out theory of the relationship between basic capacities, talents, and disabilities. Rather I want to suggest that an approach along the line I sketch is a plausible alternative to the position adopted by Dworkin. Similarly, I do not want to suggest that this approach is normatively neutral. After all, it seems to embrace the assumption that, in general, properly functioning basic capacities contribute positively to the leading of a good life and that impairments to the normal capacities encumber the leading of a good life. This assumption is not uncontroversial. Theorists such as Tremain (1996), who holds that disadvantages which accrue to persons with different capacities are never inherent but rather the product of discriminatory social reaction to 'different forms of life', will presumably object to my tripartite division between disabilities, basic capacities, and talents.

[8] Dworkin does not articulate this objection explicitly. But it is clearly implied by the rhetorical question he poses in the context of discussing a standard of normal powers. In rejecting the idea of a benchmark of normal powers he says: 'But whose powers should be taken as normal for this purpose?' (Dworkin 1981: 300).

tive individual. After all, an account of basic human capacities should reflect the capacities generally displayed by the human species. Reliance on suitable scientific data in constructing such an account is neither arbitrary nor inconsistent with other basic commitments of egalitarian liberalism. I am not suggesting that the identification of basic human capacities along with standards of normal functioning provides a definitive and uncontroversial distinction between disabilities and talents. Nevertheless, even a simplified understanding of the species-typical characteristics of humans allows us to appreciate the plausibility of this approach. There are evident complexities in the full development of this view for there will be difficulties identifying the normal range of human capacities in any precise way. Nonetheless, there are many contexts in which we seem able to identify appropriate standards of normalcy. For instance, vision, hearing, and physical mobility and the capacity to use and understand language can all be considered basic human capacities. With respect to these capacities we seem able to identify reasonable parameters of normal functioning. Of course, what constitutes normalcy may, in some instances, be difficult to ascertain. But presumably we can treat this, at least partly, as a statistical problem. Normal parameters are fixed partly by reference to statistically average capacities. Standards of normal vision and hearing upon which we currently rely are not obviously arbitrary. They seem to provide a reasonable way of identifying both disabilities (e.g. blindness) and special talents (e.g. perfect pitch). In light of the feasibility of this approach, Dworkin's rejection of a basic capacities strategy for the differentiation of talents and disabilities is unjustified.[9]

THE AMBITION THESIS

Notice that, taken on its own, the difference of degree thesis implies that the independence view is mistaken. For if there is no fundamental difference between suffering a disability and

---

[9] Something like the approach I have sketched seems presupposed by the *International Classification of Impairments, Disabilities and Handicaps*. As Bickenbach notes, the ICIDH proceeds from the 'assumption of the biomedical grounding of disablement' (Bickenbach 1993: 25).

lacking a talent, then it would seem appropriate not to view these aspects of unequal natural endowment as giving rise to distinct problems of distributive justice or as requiring independent solutions. My rejection of the difference of degree thesis suggests that there is a basis for the independence view that is rooted in the fact that disabilities and talents are fundamentally different. Given his adoption of the difference of degree thesis, Dworkin must justify his commitment to the independence view in some other way. This brings us to the second dimension of the contrast Dworkin draws between talents and disabilities, which concerns the different relationship in which they supposedly stand to individual ambition. (Recall that ambition is to be understood here in the special sense stipulated by Dworkin. It refers roughly to the aims, projects, and preferences voluntarily adopted by a person.) I call this the *ambition thesis*.

The ambition thesis provides Dworkin's rationale for acceptance of the independence view. Two components of the ambition thesis can be distinguished (Dworkin 1981: 313–14; 316). First, it is asserted that there is a closer, more intimate relationship between talent and ambition than between disability and ambition. Second, it is claimed that talents and ambition are closely related in a special way. Whereas the connection between talent and ambition is reciprocal, the connection between disability and ambition operates only in one direction. The idea here is that ambition can be shaped by talent and ambition can shape talent. For example, someone with skill in mathematical computation might be influenced by that fact to pursue a scientific career and someone with political ambition might develop skills in public speaking. However, this reciprocal relationship does not hold, it is claimed, between disabilities and ambition. While a person's life plan may be influenced by her disabilities, that plan cannot affect a person's disabilities. As we shall see, these features of the relationship between talent and ambition are supposed to make counterfactual calculations of the sort which the insurance market for disabilities relies upon impossible to effect in the case of unequal talents. Thus Dworkin's adoption of the independence view is predicated on the ambition thesis. However, before turning to this purported upshot of the ambition thesis, it is worth evaluating the two claims that comprise the thesis itself.

The first claim is problematic. To begin with, it simply is not clear exactly how the closeness of the relationship between skills, disabilities, and ambition is to be conceived or gauged. Dworkin never fully explains what closeness of connection in this context consists in. Nevertheless, we may suppose it concerns the sort of impact or influence ambition can have on talent and disability and vice versa. If this is the correct interpretation then there is reason to doubt that the wide range of complex relationships between talent, disability, and ambition are accurately reflected in the generalization that ambition and talent are more closely related than ambition and disability. There are many cases in which disability has an obvious and profound influence on ambition. The influence may be negative. A person may be discouraged from adopting worthwhile projects because her disability presents an obstacle to the pursuit of such plans. But the influence may have a positive dimension. Facing a disability may spur a person to pursue enriching and challenging goals. There is no obvious metric with which to measure the closeness of the relationship between ambition and disability and talent. There is also no obvious reason to suppose that ambition is more closely intertwined with one's talents than one's disabilities. Dworkin's claim about there being a specially close relationship between talent and ambition seems too vague and speculative to carry any real theoretical weight.

The second claim, about the unique reciprocal relationship between talent and ambition, is more difficult to assess.[10] There is, of course, a trivial sense in which it is true. If disabilities are conceived as the absence of powers then ambition cannot affect disability because there is no object for ambition to act upon. But this is an uninteresting observation without any real significance. Interpreted in a different way the claim seems more interesting but is still open to question. Unpacking the reciprocal relationship component of the ambition thesis, we can

---

[10] One might interpret Dworkin as claiming that the special closeness of the relationship between talent and ambition which I have disputed actually consists only in the unique reciprocal relationship. Certainly, Dworkin suggests that the reciprocal relationship is one way in which the closeness of the relationship between talent and ambition is exhibited. But since the general claim of closeness of relationship can be distinguished from the claim of reciprocity, it is worth examining the claims separately.

distinguish four possible connections between ambition, talent, and disability:

(1) A person's natural talent can affect her choices about how to lead her life.

(2) A person's choices about how to lead her life can affect the talents she develops.

(3) A person's disabilities can affect her choices about how to lead her life.

(4) A person's choices about how to lead her life can affect the disabilities she has.

For the reciprocal relationship component of the ambition thesis to be plausible either (3) or (4) must be false. Since the connection between disability and ambition captured by (3) is surely plausible, acceptance of the ambition thesis would seem to depend on the falsity of (4). Yet it is by no means clear that (4) is false. After all, decisions about how to lead one's life can certainly result in the loss of capacities a person would otherwise enjoy. There is, for instance, the possibility that the influence of ambition may lead to the development of a disability. This can occur indirectly, as when the pursuit of an ambition carries with it unintended (but foreseeable) impairment. For example, pursuing a boxing career may result in severe brain damage. But it is also possible for ambition to lead directly to disability. On Dworkin's account of disability as the mere absence of a capacity it is obvious that a person may lose some capacity in the pursuit of life plans. Many people deliberately destroy their capacity to conceive children through voluntary sterilization.[11] In face of these kinds of examples, Dworkin's claim concerning the unique reciprocal connection between talent and ambition is insufficiently supported.

---

[11] Even if we adopt a more demanding conception of disability it is possible, though perhaps not probable, for ambition to lead directly to serious disability. Although it would have to be for rather unusual reasons, a person could decide to cultivate a severe disability. For example, the philosopher Franz Brentano believed the blindness he suffered in later life actually helped him in his work. He did not destroy his eyesight deliberately but it is conceivable that he might have disabled himself had he recognized how blindness could contribute to the projects he cared most about. Les Jacobs brought this example to my attention.

THE INDETERMINACY ARGUMENT

I have suggested that there is room for dispute about the soundness of both the specific claims which comprise the ambition thesis. But even if the claims upon which the ambition thesis is predicated are questionable, it is worth examining the role the ambition thesis plays in the rest of Dworkin's theory. Why does Dworkin need the controversial ambition thesis? The most important upshot for Dworkin of the specially close relationship there is said to be between ambition and talent is that the hypothetical insurance market scheme that he employs to solve the problem of providing fair compensation for disabilities cannot be used to solve the parallel problem posed by unequal talents. The sort of compensation to which individuals who are disabled are entitled is determined by asking what sort of insurance individuals who do not know whether or not they are disabled would buy if everyone faced an equal risk of suffering from any given disability. If the hypothetical insurance model could be applied to the problem of unequal talents, it would serve to determine the sort of compensation to which persons lacking various skills are entitled. However, although Dworkin believes this type of insurance market scheme can be applied successfully in the case of disabilities, he argues that the attempt to apply it to the problem of talents must collapse. And it is the ambition thesis that provides the basis for what I will call the indeterminacy argument.

We noticed in considering the hypothetical insurance market for handicaps the following difficulty. There is a certain indeterminacy in the issue of what ambitions and tastes someone who is handicapped would have if he were not, and this indeterminacy infects the question of how much of what insurance he would then buy. The indeterminacy is manageable in the case of ordinary handicaps because generalizations are nevertheless possible. But it would not be manageable in the case of skills, because if we suppose that no one has any idea what talents he has, we have stipulated away too much of his personality to leave any intelligible base for speculation about his ambitions, even in a general or average way. The connection between talents and ambitions, which I described earlier, is much closer than that between ambitions and handicaps—it is, for one thing reciprocal—and much too close to permit that sort of counterfactual speculation. (Dworkin 1981: 316)

This argument invites a number of comments. First, notice how the indeterminacy argument depends on the success of the ambition thesis. The requisite insurance calculations cannot be made because of the confounding consequences of the special relationship between talent and ambition. We can acknowledge that Dworkin is right to think that the epistemic constraints imposed on the hypothetical insurance market for disabilities generate indeterminacy about the kind of insurance individuals would purchase. However, the difficulties I detected with the ambition thesis give us reason to doubt that indeterminacy is really a greater problem in the case of talents than in the case of disabilities. The point is not that counterfactual speculation of the sort required by the insurance scheme can be reliably effected in the case of both disabilities and talents. Rather my suggestion is that the supposedly more pronounced problem of indeterminacy faced by extending the insurance market theory of disability compensation to the problem of unequal talents depends on a mistaken premiss about the uniqueness of the relationship between talent and ambition. The conclusion that accurate counterfactual speculation is more difficult in the case of talents than in the case of disabilities remains unsubstantiated. This objection presents Dworkin's theory with a dilemma. Either the problems of unequal talents and disability may be handled by the same hypothetical insurance market or the hypothetical insurance market must be abandoned altogether because it cannot yield determinate results with regard to either unequal talents or disabilities.

A second observation points to a different difficulty. The indeterminacy argument arises in the context of the assumption that we can contemplate using the hypothetical insurance market for disabilities to solve the problem posed by unequal talents. The suggestion considered by Dworkin is whether we can extend the insurance market theory of disability compensation to the problem of unequal talents. This is puzzling for it is arguable that viewing the problems of disabilities and unequal talents as distinct does not really make sense within Dworkin's theoretical framework. Given Dworkin's conception of disability as the absence of any capacity, it would seem as though the hypothetical insurance market for disabilities already provides coverage against lacking skills. Insurance for lacking a talent is, *ex hypothesi*, already available in the market for disability insurance because lacking a talent is simply one kind of disability. In setting the indeterminacy argument up in this way Dworkin seems to be smuggling in a different understanding of talents and disabilities from the one implied by the difference of degree thesis. The indeterminacy argument only makes sense if we assume that the hypothetical insurance market for disabilities provides coverage only against the possibility of lacking certain kinds of capacities—those, specifically, which result in genuine disability. Otherwise the problem of unequal talents would have already been solved by the insurance market theory of disability compensation. We must suppose, in other words, that a more fundamental distinction can be drawn between suffering a disability and lacking a talent. But as we have seen Dworkin rejects the possibility of drawing this kind of distinction.

The foregoing considerations show, I believe, that Dworkin is wrong in thinking that a hypothetical insurance market for talents faces a special problem of indeterminacy—i.e. one which is much more insurmountable than the problem of indeterminacy faced by the hypothetical insurance market for disabilities. However, this should not be interpreted as lending support to use of the device of a hypothetical insurance market in developing a theory of fair adjustment. In the next two sections I will show why even a modified hypothetical insurance market cannot supply a theory of fair market adjustment.

A brief review of the argument thus far may be helpful. I have criticized Dworkin's handling of the problem of unequal natural endowment on two main grounds. First, I argued that his explanation of the nature of the distinction between talents and disabilities is unsuccessful. The difference of degree thesis is not persuasive. Second, I showed that his rationale for treating the problems of disabilities and talents as distinct is unpersuasive, given the framework in which he situates these issues. The independence view is correct but the ambition thesis and the indeterminacy argument do not provide the right kind of support for it. Finally, in developing these criticisms, I sketched an alternative approach to understanding the distinction between disabilities and talents. This approach holds, *pace* Dworkin, that a non-arbitrary standard of basic human capacities can be identified and employed to distinguish mere lack of talent from disability.

Together these arguments raise doubts about the adequacy of the theoretical framework upon which Dworkin's theory of fair market adjustment is based. If the claims upon which Dworkin's use of the hypothetical insurance market is predicated are flawed then there is reason to doubt that the insurance market scheme can yield a satisfactory theory of fair market adjustment. Given the internal logic of equality of resources, Dworkin has failed to supply a persuasive rationale for treating the problem of fair market adjustment as distinct from the problem of disability compensation. We might think that further examination of Dworkin's solution to the problem of unequal talents is not warranted. However, the modified insurance scheme that Dworkin thinks provides the best theory of fair market adjustment is sufficiently interesting and important to warrant independent investigation. Consequently, I will now explore the details of the hypothetical insurance market scheme with a view to determining whether, despite criticisms directed at what seem to be its foundations, it could provide an adequate way of tracking the requirements of ambition-sensitivity and endowment-insensitivity.

THE HYPOTHETICAL INSURANCE MARKET THEORY OF FAIR MARKET ADJUSTMENT

The hypothetical insurance market scheme for talents is perhaps the most technically complex element in Dworkin's account of liberal equality. Once again, Dworkin asks us to imagine the operation of an idealized insurance market. This time, however, the market operates with different background assumptions in place. First, individuals are aware of the talents they enjoy but they have no way of knowing what income they can derive from exercising their talents in a market setting without income tax. (They are even unaware whether they will be able to earn any income.) Second, each person has an equal initial share of the impersonal resources that are available before market activity begins (i.e. before anyone engages in the production and exchange of new resources). Third, information about each person's 'tastes, ambitions, talents and attitudes towards risk' (Dworkin 1981: 316) is supplied to a (super!) computer which predicts the projected income structure—'the number of people earning each level of income' (Dworkin 1981: 317) that would be found in a market economy without income tax.[12] Fourth, each person assumes that 'he has the same chance as anyone else of occupying any particular level of income in the economy' (Dworkin 1981: 317). Fifth, (competitive) insurance firms offer policies that provide coverage against failing to have the opportunity to earn a named level of income in the projected income structure. Sixth, the cost of premiums varies with the level of coverage selected and the cost of a premium at any given level is the same for everyone. Finally, premiums are paid at fixed periods from the income each person derives from market activity.

Given this background the computer is asked to determine what level of insurance coverage individuals would, on average, purchase.[13] The average level of coverage that the computer predicts would be purchased by people in these circumstances provides a way of identifying a minimum level of income to which individuals are entitled.[14] A system of redistributive taxation to be

[12] Notice that the computer is supplied with just the sort of information that would seem to obviate the need to use insurance markets in developing a theory of fair market adjustment. The computer is given information about everyone's talents and ambitions and asked to determine how these factors (along with others) will influence the distribution of income. To effect the requisite calculation the computer would seem to have to distinguish the influence of talent and ambition on the distribution of income. But it is supposedly because we are unable to distinguish reliably between the influence of talent and ambition that we need a second best theory that can imperfectly satisfy the requirement of ambition-sensitivity and endowment-insensitivity. Rakowski raises some other puzzles about the dependence of the insurance scheme on such a computer and such a data base (Rakowski 1991: 132–3).

[13] As with the case of disabilities, a truly ideal insurance market should provide individualized coverage: insurance coverage should be tailored to each person's insurance preferences. The simplifying assumption that incomes should be adjusted on the basis of the average amount of insurance that would be purchased is made partly because the necessary calculations for an individualized scheme are impossibly complex and partly because an individualized scheme could not be translated into any practicable income tax policy.

[14] Dworkin develops a very complex argument that purports to show that this scheme is most compatible with a progressive income tax system (Dworkin 1981: 324–6).

administered by the state can then be designed to ensure that everyone receives at least the minimum income. Dworkin contends that the adjustments to market-determined distributions effected by this scheme provide a reasonable and practicable—though admittedly imperfect—way of tracking the requirements of ambition-sensitivity and endowment-insensitivity. There are, however, at least two reasons why the insurance scheme does not track, even imperfectly, the requirement of ambition-sensitivity and why, therefore, it does not supply an appropriate theory of fair market adjustment. Both these difficulties can be identified by examining Dworkin's speculation about the probable results of his hypothetical insurance scheme.

EQUAL INCOMES, INSURANCE, AND AMBITION-SENSITIVITY

The first problem is that it is extremely likely, for reasons I shall presently explain, that the level of coverage which would be purchased in the insurance market would result in an equal distribution of income. An equal distribution of income would only be consistent with ambition-sensitivity if there were no relevant differences in individual ambition—i.e. differences which can affect individual entitlement to resources. But the supposition which provides the motivation for employing the insurance market in the first place is that there are likely to be differences in ambition of the sort that can justify differential entitlement to resources. Since ambition-sensitivity is a requirement of a fair distribution of resources, the redistribution sanctioned by the insurance market will be unfair if it simply eliminates inequalities traceable to choices rather than endowment. Indeed, the problem of unequal talents would not be vexing for the egalitarian if we could assume that the legitimate distributional effects of choice are negligible.

Something like this first objection is anticipated by Dworkin. He notes that it might seem that individuals would 'leap at the chance to buy a policy that would protect them against not having the very highest income projected for the economy, and would pay them, if they do not, the difference between the great income and what they actually earn' (Dworkin 1981: 319). If everyone opted for such a policy then everyone would wind up with the same post-income tax income: a result which, as I have indicated, is inconsistent with the requirement of ambition-sensitivity. But Dworkin thinks the prediction about the outcome of the insurance scheme upon which the objection depends is mistaken. He argues that it would be irrational to purchase such a high level of insurance.

The argument that individuals would not purchase coverage against the opportunity to earn the highest projected income hinges on the idea that buying such a policy would be a 'financially disadvantageous bet' that cannot, like some other types of financially disadvantageous bets, be justified on expected welfare grounds. Dworkin defines a financially advantageous bet as 'as a bet such that the cost of the bet is less than the amount of the return if "successful"—if the covered risk eventuates or if the bet is won—discounted by the improbability of success' (Dworkin 1981: 318). A financially disadvantageous bet is a bet in which 'the cost of the bet exceeds the expected return, so calculated' (Dworkin 1981: 318).

(a) Is hypothetical income insurance financially disadvantageous?

The insurance policies offered by commercial insurance companies are financially disadvantageous bets. A company that offered financially advantageous bets would quickly go out of business as its costs would exceed its revenues. This does not imply, however, that purchasing insurance is always irrational. Recall that the justification of insurance lies in the expected utility of insurance in face of the diminishing marginal utility of income. Roughly, it will be rational to purchase an insurance policy if the utility loss associated with buying the policy is less than the utility loss associated with the uninsured risk eventuating, discounted by the probability of the risk eventuating. The diminishing marginal utility of income explains this possibility. As income increases, the contribution of each extra dollar of income to utility gets smaller and this means that losses of income do not affect utility uniformly. Thus a person may find that accepting a certain $6,000 loss (in the form of an insurance premium) may have a higher expected utility than accepting a

10 per cent chance of the loss of $50,000, even though accepting the certain loss is financially disadvantageous.

It is against this backdrop that Dworkin argues that it would be irrational for individuals to purchase insurance coverage against having the opportunity to earn the highest income. There are two components to the argument. First, top income insurance is a financially disadvantageous bet. Second, it is not the sort of financially disadvantageous bet that can be justified on grounds of expected utility.

Dworkin arrives at the conclusion that buying top income insurance is a financially disadvantageous bet simply by assuming that the hypothetical insurance market must operate under the same constraints as commercial insurance. Commercial insurance companies can only offer financially disadvantageous bets. Thus Dworkin thinks 'we can take it as a given that insurance at that level would be a financially disadvantageous bet. Otherwise, it would not be offered by the insurance firm' (Dworkin 1981: 319). This seems a reasonable assumption but it is, in fact, mistaken. Dworkin has made the seemingly plausible inference that because an insurance firm cannot operate at a loss, it can only offer its clients financially disadvantageous bets. Yet an insurance firm can offer financially advantageous bets to some of its clients, without losing money, provided the loss is compensated by profit derived from other clients who accept financially disadvantageous bets. This actually happens in certain government-run universal health insurance systems. Healthy individuals with substantial incomes must pay financially disadvantageous premiums that subsidize the health care costs of the poor and infirm. This means that in a universal health care system the payment of a premium by the poor and infirm can be a financially advantageous bet. Of course, such systems work by forcing some people to accept bets that are inconsistent with pursuit of their self-interest. Competitive insurance firms in a free market cannot extract premiums from their clients in this way and thus cannot offer some people financially advantageous bets which are subsidized by the financially disadvantageous bets of others. The reason is simple. Individuals will buy policies which provide the desired level of coverage on the least financially disadvantageous terms. Firms offering financially advantageous policies for some will lose the clients who pay the financially disadvantageous premiums to firms which do not subsidize clients. Dworkin thinks the insurance offered in his hypothetical insurance market must be financially disadvantageous because he assumes that the consequences of market forces will be the same in his market as it is in the real market.

There is, however, a crucial difference between the two markets that Dworkin seems not to have sufficiently appreciated. In the real world, individuals interested in purchasing insurance can gauge the financial cost of any bet they are offered. A person cannot accept a bet which exceeds the financial resources available to her. (You cannot gamble with money you do not have.) So insurance in the real world offers individuals a way of protecting something they already have (e.g. property) against the risk of losing it (e.g. to theft). If the risk eventuates (e.g. property is stolen), insurance provides compensation for the loss. Real world gambles offer individuals a chance to augment what they already have at the risk of losing what they already have. In the real world, paying a premium involves a financial loss but each person can gauge the size of loss relative to her total income and calculate whether the expenditure is worth the security it offers.

The circumstances in which the hypothetical insurance market operates are very different. Crucially, no one knows what her income will actually be and in these conditions of uncertainty it is far from obvious that top income insurance would be financially disadvantageous or even whether it makes sense to conceive of the problem in these terms. Consider the application of Dworkin's insurance scheme to the following case. Suppose, for simplicity's sake, that there are five participants in the economy and that the computer-projected income structure is as depicted in Table 2.[15]

Dworkin's first premiss is that it must be financially disadvantageous for individuals who do not know what income they will have to buy coverage against not earning the highest income in this economy. Is this premiss sound? Since the highest income is

---

[15] I have not selected these figures at random. They correspond to the actual pattern of income distribution, expressed in quintiles, for US families in 1977 (Leftwich and Sharp 1980: 239). Thus in 1977 41.5% of household income went to the top fifth of the population while the poorest fifth of the population received only 5.2% of available income.

TABLE 2. *Income distribution*

	Income ($)
A	415,000
B	242,000
C	175,000
D	116,000
E	52,000

$415,000 and since 80 per cent of the population will be unable to earn that sum, the price of a policy that would top up the incomes of those unable to earn $415,000 would be $215,000 (on the assumption that everyone bought the same policy, paid the same premium, and the insurance company operated cost free and made no profit).[16] This might seem peculiar. The price of the premium actually exceeds the predicted income of 60 per cent of the population. It means that participants whose incomes turn out to fall below $215,000 must pay their premium partly out of the money from the policy which brings their post-insurance income up to $415,000. Of course, this means that no one can really have an income of $415,000 if everyone buys top

[16] Dworkin assumes that the insurance companies must operate at a profit (Dworkin 1981: 318) but this is a very strange assumption. The practical realization of any income insurance scheme would consist of a redistributive taxation system administered by the government. While such a system would have operating costs there is no reason to suppose that it would have to operate at a profit. Government-run health insurance plans do not aim at generating a profit. Since the insurance companies in Dworkin's scheme are merely hypothetical and since the earning of profits is not necessary to the provision of insurance, there is no good reason for Dworkin to suppose that insurance companies seek profits. Given the simplifying assumptions made here, the price of the premium of top income insurance is calculated by adding together the amount of income each person needs to raise their income to the top level and dividing this figure by the number of individuals buying insurance. In our example, E needs an additional $363,000; D needs $299,000; C needs $240,000; B needs $173,000 and A needs no additional income. Therefore, the insurance company must collect $1,075,000 in order to provide each person with the requisite income supplements. Since we assume that everyone buys the same top income insurance policy, the premium each person must pay is $215,000 ($1,075,000/5 = $215,000). Note that in analysing the hypothetical insurance market I am setting aside problems discussed in the previous chapter about the significance of the size of the population seeking insurance to the availability of insurance.

income insurance. By purchasing such a policy each person would end up with exactly the same income—$200,000. For 60 per cent of the population $200,000 represents a substantial increase in income over what they would get without insurance. The other 40 per cent do financially better without any insurance. Income insurance is merely redistributive; it cannot create extra income *ex nihilo*.

The question whether top income insurance is a financially disadvantageous bet now seems a little obscure. Since the policy results in a net financial gain for C, D, and E, one is inclined to say that from the vantage of the individuals who will occupy those positions the policy *is* a financially advantageous bet. (From the vantage of these individuals, it is a bet which they have no chance of losing. And it is not clear whether that is a bet.) The opposite applies to A and B. But, of course, no one knows what position they will, in fact, occupy so no one has any antecedent reason for assessing the financial impact of the policy any differently from anyone else. Ultimately, it is difficult to view the problem posed in the hypothetical insurance market as a choice between different bets which have distinct costs for distinct individuals. There is no clear sense in which the selection of a policy has a cost for the individuals involved. We might think that the cost of the insurance policy is just the price of the premium—$215,000. But this would be misleading since policy holders who collect can pay for the premium from the proceeds of the policy and thus it cannot represent a true cost for them.

(b) The presumptive case for top income insurance

In order to assess the rationality of purchasing top income insurance we must reframe the problem. A better way of modelling the problem posed in the hypothetical insurance market is to view competing policies as offering individuals a choice between different lotteries. Insurance policies can be represented as lotteries in the sense that each policy provides a prize structure (i.e. the projected post-insurance income) along with the odds each person has of winning the prize (i.e. the probability that any person will end up with a given post-insurance income.) A policy of top income insurance buys each person the certainty of receiving the average income.[17] Foregoing any sort of insurance, in the example above, gives each person a 20 per cent chance of collecting the highest income but also a 20 per cent chance of collecting the lowest income. So rational selection of an insurance policy depends on the application of principles of rational choice to different lotteries. There is controversy about what principles should inform the deliberations of rational agents in conditions of uncertainty. For instance, our assessment of the rationality of different attitudes towards risk will influence our judgement about what sort of policy should be purchased. If we assume that, in the circumstances, people are risk-averse, then it is likely that top income insurance would be purchased. By contrast, if we assume that rational agents are very risk-tolerant, then it is quite possible that little or no insurance would be purchased.

Despite possible controversy over the rationality of different degrees of risk tolerance, there are two powerful arguments which support the purchase of top income insurance. First, if we make the reasonable assumption that individuals are risk-averse and would view the prospect of having a low income as very grave, then it might be appropriate to appeal to a maximin principle to solve the insurance problem (cf. Rawls 1971: 154–5). On the lottery interpretation of the insurance problem, maximin would clearly endorse selection of top income insurance. Second, and more significantly, the principle of maximizing expected utility also recommends purchase of top income insurance. Assuming there is diminishing marginal utility of income, an expected utility maximizer will *always* prefer a certain outcome to any lottery which has an equivalent expected monetary value. For instance, given a choice between a certain $200,000 (i.e. top income insurance) and a lottery that gives a person an 80 per cent chance of $150,000 and a 20 per cent chance of receiving $400,000, an expected utility maximizer will prefer the former option.[18] The different possible configurations of insurance policies available in Dworkin's insurance

---

[17] In effect, each person whose pre-tax income fell below the average income would receive an income supplement which would be derived from taxing the income of those who earn above the average.

[18] There is a mathematical theorem—known as Jensen's inequality—that establishes the truth of this generalization.

market all have the same expected monetary value—$200,000 in our example. Thus a utility maximizer would always opt for the certain income supplied by top income insurance. This result is particularly important because Dworkin assumes that rational agents would base their insurance decisions on considerations of expected utility. There is, therefore, a very powerful presumptive case for the rationality of top income insurance.

The presumptive case for top income insurance paves the way for the first objection to the insurance market theory of fair market adjustment. If the outcome of the insurance market is an equal distribution of income—the upshot of universal purchase of top income insurance—then we have little reason to believe that the insurance market scheme can track, even imperfectly, the requirement of ambition-sensitivity. It is only because we think it is likely that differential ambition will lead to justifiable differences in income that we need a theory about how the relevant differences can be gauged in practice. Thus a theory that proposes to gauge approximately these differences and yet yields (or is extremely likely to yield) an equal post-tax income outcome cannot be correct given the parameters of the problem stipulated by Dworkin.

(c) Possible rejoinder: the talent enslavement objection

If Dworkin is to resist this damaging conclusion he must give us reason to believe that there is some special disutility associated with top income insurance which is sufficient to render the purchases of such insurance unjustifiable. There is an interesting argument in which Dworkin insists that top income insurance carries with it special risks of diminished utility. His argument is a kind of disaster avoidance argument. The idea is that although top income insurance carries a high probability of a small gain in welfare, it also carries with it the small chance of a disastrous outcome, which makes top income insurance an irrational purchase. If, as is very likely, it turns out that you earn less than the top income, top income insurance will boost your income and welfare over what they would have been under a regime of no insurance. Dworkin suggests, however, that because of the diminishing marginal utility of income and the high cost of the premium the gain in welfare, though very likely, will not be substantial. If, however, it turns out that you are able to earn the highest income, the policy will not supplement your income or increase your welfare from what it would have been without insurance. Dworkin contends that this outcome would likely be so bad that it would be worth avoiding the small possibility of it eventuating, even if avoiding it involved forsaking an almost certain gain. According to Dworkin, the person with top income insurance who is able to earn the highest income is in a bad position because 'he must now work at close to his top earning capacity just to pay the high premium for his insurance on which he collected nothing—just, that is, to break even. He will be a slave to his maximum earning power' (Dworkin 1981: 320). It is not obvious exactly why this is such a dreadful prospect but the concern seems to be that a person in this position might be forced to pursue a career she hated.[19]

However, these considerations do not provide a good argument against top income insurance. There are two difficulties with the argument. To begin with, there is no reason to accept Dworkin's contention that top income insurance can only yield the high probability of only a small welfare benefit. Speaking of top income insurance Dworkin says: 'someone who buys this insurance faces an extremely high chance of gaining very little' (Dworkin 1981: 320). As I have already explained, it is misleading to think of the merits of different levels of insurance coverage in terms of prospective gains and losses. There is, after all, no fixed baseline from which to measure the expected gains or losses of different policies. Preferences between different policies based on considerations of expected welfare must be predicated on the relative level of expected welfare associated with each policy. The calculation of the expected welfare of each policy will, of course, be sensitive to how the probability of different outcomes affects expected welfare. We can compare the ex-

---

[19] That this is the possibility that worries Dworkin seems to be confirmed by the example of Deborah and Ernest that Dworkin discusses. 'Suppose two people, Deborah and Ernest, both purchase insurance at the sixtieth percentile level. Deborah is beautiful and could in fact earn at the ninetieth percentile as a movie star. They have otherwise the same talents and interests, and these other talents would not earn at the sixtieth level. Ernest recovers under his policy, but Deborah does not. She is faced with the choice of a movie career which she detests, or trying to pay the premium and the other expenses of her life from whatever salary she could earn at jobs she and Ernest both prefer. . . . Deborah is, as it turns out, enslaved by her singular talent' (Dworkin 1981: 323).

pected value of different policies simply by comparing their overall utility scores. On that basis we might conclude that top income insurance did not yield the highest expected utility but we could not say that such coverage carried with it the high probability of a small welfare gain. Note that this is different from saying that top income insurance could carry with it a high probability of achieving a given level of welfare. That sort of statement would make sense. So Dworkin confuses the issue when he claims that the probable welfare gains of top income insurance would be small. The real issue is whether there is any reason to think that top income insurance would, because of special risks it might entail, have a lower expected welfare than lower levels of insurance coverage.

So what about the possibility of 'being a slave to one's maximum earning power'? Could that possibility have a sufficient impact on expected utility calculations to render top income insurance unpalatable? In this context, however, the notion of talent enslavement is a red herring. First, the income structure that is predicted by the computer reflects the pre-tax income individuals would have if they pursued the type of employment they desire. Presumably, individuals with high pre-tax incomes will have chosen to pursue certain careers and we have no reason to suppose that they would choose careers they loathed. Thus individuals who enjoy high earning potential are unlikely to find themselves with careers they detest. Such individuals may be disappointed to learn that their hypothetical insurance decision does not permit them to keep all of their high pre-tax income. But post-tax disappointment is not the same as talent enslavement. Second, the talent enslavement objection to top income insurance only gets off the ground if we are able to distinguish reliably between what individuals are able to do and what they are unwilling to do. That is, it supposes that we can distinguish the impact of talent and ambition on income. But the whole motivation for the insurance market in the first place is that this distinction cannot be accurately drawn in practical settings (Dworkin 1981: 313–14).

This second point may not be obvious at first sight, so let me explain the way in which the talent enslavement objection depends on distinguishing the impact of talent and ambition on income. The talent enslavement objection holds that under a regime of top income insurance a person with the talent to earn the top income must engage in the work that will net her the top income even if she actually prefers employment that generates a lower income. She must earn the top income in order to pay the high premium of top income insurance. But consider the situation from the perspective of the insurance company. Suppose Alice accepts employment at a low income—an income, let us say, which would entitle her, other things being equal, to an income supplement that would raise her income to the top level. Since her income is below the level at which income insurance would kick in, she files a claim with the insurance company for an income supplement. The insurance company denies the claim and insists further that Alice pay the full cost of the premium because it claims to know that Alice is, in fact, able to earn the top income. Here Alice would suffer the disutility associated with top income insurance if the high-income career which is available to her is a career she hates. But the company cannot know that Alice has the talent that would permit her to earn the top income and that her ambition is preventing her from earning it unless it can identify the respective contributions of talent and ambition to her income earning potential. And given the epistemic obstacles which Dworkin argues surround judgements about the impact of talent, as distinct from ambition, on income, the company will not have access to the relevant information. After all, if it were possible to make accurate and reliable judgements distinguishing the influence of choice and endowment on income then we would not need to rely on a scheme like Dworkin's to track the requirements of ambition-sensitivity and endowment-insensitivity.[20]

Interestingly, Dworkin does suggest two strategies insurance companies could rely upon in the attempt to ascertain the true earning potential of would-be claimants. If these strategies for detection of true earning power were sufficiently accurate then the talent enslavement objection might seem applicable after all.

[20] This contrasts with the situation in the disability insurance scheme. In the case of disabilities we need some way of determining how much we should compensate disabled persons because, especially in the case of serious disabilities, there is no way to completely eliminate disability related disadvantages and thereby secure equal life chances for disabled persons. In the case of unequal talents we could, in principle, make resource distribution endowment-insensitive if we had the relevant information about the impact of talent on income.

First, insurance companies often seek to reduce moral hazard problems[21] through the device of co-insurance. Co-insurance reduces moral hazard by requiring that the beneficiary of a policy assume responsibility for paying the first part of the claim. Second, Dworkin suggests that companies could place the burden of proof on claimants to establish that they are unable to earn the insured level of income. Companies might insist, for instance, that claimants demonstrate they have made a good faith effort to find employment that provides income above the insured level. Both these devices discourage claimants from misrepresenting their true earning potential to insurance companies and indirectly reveal some information about the earning potential of customers. Insofar as individuals have information about their true earning potential, these devices increase the confidence that companies can have in the veracity of the actual earning potential that individuals claim to have. The incorporation of these devices into the hypothetical insurance scheme suggests that an individual's talent-based earning potential is not as opaque as Dworkin's earlier arguments implied. It can be conceded that companies will sometimes be able detect a divergence between the earning potential claimed by an individual and her true earning potential. Yet unless we attribute unrealistically sensitive powers of detection to companies it is probable that, for the most part, they would have to pay off on the basis of earned income and not of perceived potential earnings.[22]

A tension in Dworkin's argument seems to be revealed here. The talent enslavement objection only has prima-facie credibility if insurance firms can establish the talent-based earning potential of each person. Otherwise no one could face the prospect of being required to pursue a high-paying but odious career. Yet accurate identification of talent-based earning potential obviates the need to rely upon the hypothetical

[21] Moral hazard is the phenomenon whereby the very existence of insurance increases the likelihood that an insured-against outcome will occur. For example, drivers may drive less cautiously if they know that insurance will cover damages caused by an accident.

[22] Curiously, Dworkin acknowledges that the best real world approximation of the insurance market by a system of redistributive taxation would probably tie 'redistribution to actual earnings rather than ability to earn' (Dworkin 1981: 327). The rationale given here is that the devices needed to discover ability to earn might be 'offensive to privacy, or too expensive in administrative costs, or too inefficient in other ways' (Dworkin 1981: 327).

insurance market in the first place. For instance, if we can determine that Alice is earning the maximum income, given her particular talents, that she is in a position to earn, then she should be entitled to the highest income available in the economy. In such a case, we would know that it is only her lack of talent and not her choices that explain her low income.

Setting this difficulty aside, we may still want to assess the force of the talent enslavement objection to top income insurance on the assumption that insurance companies can identify talents in a way that leaves open the possibility that purchasing such coverage would be a 'silly bet'. Would it be antecedently irrational for Alice to purchase top income insurance given the possibility that she could be enslaved to her maximum earning power? If Alice is an expected utility maximizer she will have to estimate the disutility of being a slave to her maximum earning power along with the likelihood that she will find herself in this unfortunate position. Even if the disutility of suffering talent enslavement is very high, it is an extremely remote possibility— very few people will have maximum-earning-power talents and of this small group only a small number will find the prospect of exercising those talents highly unattractive. Consequently, the disutility effect of talent enslavement will be small. Note also that if expected utility calculations about prospective income insurance policies are to be made sensitive to welfare losses associated with being trapped by one's talents then rational consumers should also factor in the less remote possibility that they will have talents that only permit them to pursue dreary, alienating, low-paying jobs. If the work that most people perform is not intrinsically satisfying then most people will have a strong reason to ensure that their income is as high as possible. So people who purchase only a low level of income insurance, as Dworkin recommends, may find themselves suffering the disutility of a boring, alienating career. It is quite possible that the disutility of being confined by one's talents associated with lower levels of income insurance would counterbalance any disutility of talent enslavement associated with top income insurance. All things considered, it seems likely that factoring in the disutility of talent enslavement would have a negligible negative effect on the expected utility of top income insurance. From her position of ignorance about the earning power of her talents, Alice's decision to purchase top income insurance is not irrational. Even under favourable assumptions, the talent enslavement objection provides an ineffectual objection to the rationality of purchasing top income insurance. At any rate, Dworkin's argument does not provide us with sufficient reason to reject the presumptive rationality of top income insurance established in the previous section. Hence the first general objection to the hypothetical insurance model of fair market adjustment has been sustained. The equal distribution of income that, *pace* Dworkin, is the likely upshot of the hypothetical insurance market shows that the scheme is at odds with the requirement of ambition-sensitivity.

HOW HYPOTHETICAL INSURANCE CALCULATIONS ARE AMBITION-INSENSITIVE

The second general deficiency of the hypothetical insurance market model of market adjustment concerns the relationship of the insurance scheme to the requirement of ambition-sensitivity. This problem is much simpler and easier to diagnose than the previous one. The objection is simply that the insurance decision faced by individuals in the insurance market has no direct connection with the requirement of ambition-sensitivity nor does it indirectly track it. The insurance scheme must be defended on the ground that it is a reasonable surrogate for directly linking ambition and entitlement to resources. But no such construal is plausible. Dworkin inadvertently draws attention to this point in the course of explaining how the argument from the hypothetical insurance scheme putatively replicates a world in which talents are not unequal.

It contrasts two worlds. In the first those who are relatively disadvantaged by the tastes and ambitions of others, vis-à-vis their own talents to produce, are known in advance and bear the full consequences of that disadvantage. In the second the same pattern of relative disadvantage holds, but everyone has subjectively an equal antecedent chance of suffering it, and so everyone has an equal opportunity of mitigating the disadvantage by insuring against it. The argument assumes that equality prefers the second world, because it is a world in which the resources of talent are in one important sense more evenly divided. (Dworkin 1981: 331)

In this passage the requirement of ambition-sensitivity has dropped out of the picture. The insurance market is depicted as providing nothing but a way in which the disadvantages associated with unequal talent can be mitigated. Is it possible that Dworkin believes that rough ambition-sensitivity is a corollary of the putative endowment insensitivity secured by the insurance market? Surely this would be a mistake. In fact, the insurance market simply ignores the legitimate distributive consequences of differences in ambition. This objection holds true independently of my earlier speculation about the likely outcome of the insurance market.

Although it is difficult to gauge precisely the relative distributional significance of talent and ambition, it does seem possible to provide a rough answer to the question: How much of the difference in people's income is attributable to the influence of talent and other arbitrary factors and how much is attributable to the influence of ambition? If the insurance market is represented as a mechanism that can track ambition-sensitivity even imperfectly then the level of income insurance it recommends should correspond, at least roughly, to our general understanding of the relative impact of talent, and ambition on income distribution. Suppose Dworkin is right about the level of insurance that would be purchased and that only a very low level of income insurance would be purchased on average. Call that level L. Now suppose according to our current understanding of the relationship between ambition, talent, and income differentials, that there is a very low (but admittedly imprecise) correlation between differences in ambition and differences in income and a very high (but admittedly imprecise) correlation between differences in talent and differences in income. Surely this information would be relevant to determining appropriate income policies and assessing the success of the hypothetical insurance market scheme. A low correlation between income differentials and differences in ambition suggests that a high level of income insurance—well above level L—would more faithfully track ambition-sensitivity. But the calculations internal to Dworkin's insurance scheme which result in level L simply do not display any sensitivity to general claims concerning the relative impact of ambition and talent on the distribution of income. Even imprecise estimates of the relative impact of talent and ambition on income cannot affect calculations about the level of income insurance that would be purchased. This shows that the hypothetical insurance market does not address the question of ambition-sensitivity, even indirectly. The insurance problem it sets as a substitute for direct tracking of ambition-sensitivity is not an appropriate surrogate. The theory cannot, therefore, provide the basis for an appropriate theory of fair market adjustment. Ultimately, this is unsurprising: the hypothetical insurance market is a device that attempts to harness rational prudence to track a moral concept of ambition-sensitivity. The epistemic constraints Dworkin invokes to secure some measure of impartiality do not eliminate entirely the divergence that often exists between the demands of morality and the dictates of rational prudence.

The foregoing criticisms of the account of fair market adjustment provided by the hypothetical insurance market centre specifically on the ways that Dworkin's strategy fails to come to terms with ambition-sensitivity. However, it is worth noting that some of the objections to reliance on a hypothetical insurance market developed in the previous chapter may be reprised here. We can, for instance, argue that the scheme makes lavish assumptions about the sorts of complex counterfactual problems it is possible, even in principle, to solve. The account of fair market adjustment yielded by Dworkin's strategy may also be problematic because the insurance process may be infected by the possibly irrational beliefs of the individuals who ultimately set the level of coverage. The idea here is that the level of insurance coverage is supposed to be determined by the actual choices individuals would make—choices which may be irrational. This means that market-determined income insurance is potentially unfair because the sort of coverage that is available depends partly on the insurance decisions of parties who cannot be relied upon to make rational insurance decisions. As I have already discussed these general difficulties with relying on the device of the hypothetical insurance market, I will not pursue them any further here. All told, the problems with Dworkin's approach seem insurmountable. Egalitarians must look elsewhere for a theory of fair market adjustment.

THE CONSERVATIVE INTERPRETATION OF
FAIR MARKET ADJUSTMENT

I wish to drive home my reservations about Dworkin's theory by examining briefly the surprising practical conclusions Dworkin seems prepared to draw from his hypothetical insurance market argument. Prima facie, the theory of equality of resources would seem to have very radical consequences for the distribution of wealth and income in contemporary liberal societies. Dramatic differences in wealth and income of the sort that presently exist in liberal societies seem difficult to reconcile with a theory that requires that equal resources be devoted to the life of each person. Surely equality of resources must, at least in principle, call for a massive redistribution of resources in contemporary societies.[23] Dworkin does claim that even though the minimum level of income to which individuals would be entitled on his theory is relatively low, it would be 'well above the level of income presently used to trigger transfer payments for unemployment or minimum wage levels in either Britain of the United States' (Dworkin 1981: 321). So his theory cannot be construed simply as a rationalization of existing inequalities. However, Dworkin sees the insurance market argument as providing justification for substantial inequalities in income and wealth and as portraying such inequalities as consistent—albeit imperfectly consistent—with the abstract demands of egalitarian distributive justice. This feature of Dworkin's interpretation of the implications of his theory is best disclosed in his discussion of Nozick's famous Wilt Chamberlain example (Nozick 1974: 161–3).

Nozick supposes an equal distribution of wealth, followed by uncoerced trades to mutual advantage in which each of many people pays a small sum to watch Chamberlain play basketball, after which he grows rich and wealth is no longer equal. Equality of resources would not denounce that result, considered in itself. Chamberlain's wealth reflects the value to others of his leading his life as he does. His greater wealth at the end of the process, is of course traceable mainly to his greater talent, and only in small part, we may assume, to the fact that he is willing to lead a life that others would not be. But almost no one

---

[23] Presumably, the redistribution required would be even more radical if the principles applied globally and not just within existing liberal societies.

would have purchased, in the hypothetical insurance market we described, insurance against not having talents that would provide such wealth. That insurance would be, for almost everyone, a strikingly irrational investment. So our discussion would not justify taxing any of Chamberlain's wealth for redistribution to others not so fortunate, if we attend only to the fact, as Nozick does, that others have much less wealth than he does. (Dworkin 1981: 336–7)

I have already argued that Dworkin is mistaken about the level of insurance that would be purchased in his insurance market so I do not think he is right in maintaining that the sort of redistribution licensed by the insurance market would leave Chamberlain's wealth intact. But what is really remarkable about this passage is that it implicitly suggests that Chamberlain is not really entitled to most of the wealth he derives from playing basketball, irrespective of the outcome of the insurance market. After all, Dworkin says that most of Chamberlain's wealth is traceable to his talent and not to his ambition. That Dworkin is prepared to accept as just the distribution of wealth in the Chamberlain case suggests that the logical structure of equality of resources has somehow been inverted. As it is initially presented the hypothetical insurance market is portrayed as the best device through which the requirements of ambition-sensitivity and endowment insensitivity can be tracked. Presumably, this means that the defensibility of the insurance scheme depends on its capacity, in practice, to track these complex requirements. But in the Chamberlain example it seems as though the insurance market scheme has become theoretically more important than the requirement it was initially supposed to track. Redistribution is *not* justified, in the Chamberlain case, because the insurance market argument supposedly would not justify it. Dworkin does not interpret this as a case where there is an imperfect match between an abstract requirement of justice and the device which is designed to give the abstract requirement more determinate content. Rather the hypothetical insurance market argument is represented as a fundamental component of the theory of equality of resources. By so elevating the theoretical importance of the hypothetical insurance market, Dworkin encourages us to believe that genuine egalitarian justice only requires fairly modest liberal reforms to income distribution. Yet this surprisingly conservative conclusion is

more the result of a misplaced faith on the market as an interpretive device for the demands of equality than of a direct
reading of the egalitarian conception of justice with which
Dworkin begins. From the perspective of the latter we surely
cannot endorse the inequalities which are represented as legitimate on Dworkin's interpretation of the insurance market
scheme.

POSSIBLE DIRECTIONS FOR EGALITARIANISM

In order to justify its adoption, the insurance scheme must track
the requirements of ambition-sensitivity and endowment-
insensitivity at least as well as, and hopefully better than, other
alternatives. The Chamberlain case confirms the suspicion that
the insurance scheme falls well short of closely tracking these
requirements. Even as an imperfect solution to the problem of
unequal talents Dworkin's theory is unsatisfactory. Nonetheless, we should consider what can be learned from the failure of
the hypothetical insurance market approach about the construction of a more adequate theory.

We must, I think, acknowledge that any satisfactory solution
to the problem of unequal talents will necessarily be imperfect.
This is partly due to the limits of institutional design. Any
feasible system of redistributive taxation will inevitably require
reliance on simplifying assumptions and rough rules of thumb
which represent a departure from perfect justice. This is an
uncontroversial constraint on the construction of a theory.
Beyond this point there are, I think, three general directions
egalitarian theorizing on this issue might take. First, we might
try to tinker with the details of the hypothetical insurance market scheme in order to eliminate the various defects it currently
faces. Similarly, we might try to come up with some other device
capable of generating reasonable criteria of fair market adjustment. This sort of strategy is not, in my view, very promising.
The inevitable difficulty which is faced by devices like the hypothetical insurance market that seek to track the distributive
significance of choice indirectly is that in practice they lie at too
great a distance from the moral ideal which is supposed to
animate them. As a consequence the account of fair market

adjustment recommended by an indirect, device-driven strategy does not serve as a practical surrogate for the original ideal. Instead, criteria for fair market adjustment which are in tension with the moral ideal are substituted for the ideal.

As we have seen, the motivation for adopting an indirect strategy for the tracking of the distributive significance of choice against the backdrop of unequal talents is that it is simply too difficult to track this requirement accurately in any direct way. Given the difficulty of devising a suitable indirect approach, there is a second, more pessimistic, direction in which egalitarian theory might move. Perhaps egalitarian theory should give up the attempt to track the distributional significance of choice in any systematic way. Carens's suggestion that the closest feasible approximation to a choice-sensitive distribution is an equal distribution of income has some merit. Justice might be better served by more focus on the problem of designing feasible institutional mechanisms for the realization of a flatter but more manageable account of fair market adjustment. Given the deep, pervasive, and arbitrary inequalities that are characteristic of contemporary societies, a move towards income equalization would represent substantial progress. Yet at both a theoretical and a practical level, abandonment of a choice-sensitive ideal of distributive equality would constitute a major setback for egalitarianism. The notion of individual responsibility that underwrites the requirement of ambition-sensitivity is compelling. Moreover, critics of egalitarian reform have scored political points by emphasizing how egalitarian proposals effectively deny that individuals must often assume a measure of responsibility for their own lives. The liberal egalitarian commitment to individual autonomy will seem hollow if the exercise of agency is ignored when it comes to dealing with practical distributive questions. One need not accept the inflated and exaggerated accounts of the distributional significance of choice commonly found in libertarian political rhetoric to think that the significance of choice is more than merely theoretical. The hazard of a proposal like Carens's is that egalitarian concerns about distributive justice will be further marginalized.

The only remaining option for egalitarian theory, I believe, is the development of criteria of fair market adjustment that speak more directly to the substantive demand of ambition-sensitivity.

I think that Dworkin and others have been unduly sceptical about this possibility. Perfect ambition-sensitivity is an impossible goal but it is premature to abandon a direct approach altogether. The initial motivation for the hypothetical insurance market is only that it is *difficult* to track reliably the relative influence of talent and ambition on the distribution of income. But as we have seen, the insurance market scheme ultimately embraces the more extreme position that it is impossible, not merely difficult, to make any meaningful observations about the relative impact of talent and ambition on income. It simply gives up on the attempt to track ambition-sensitivity and endowment-insensitivity more directly. Dworkin gives up the attempt to track this requirement directly essentially because we cannot 'find some way of identifying, in any person's wealth, at any particular time, the component traceable to differential talents as distinguished from differential ambitions' (Dworkin 1981: 313). This means we cannot 'fix the rates of our income tax so as to redistribute exactly that part of each person's income that is attributable to his talents as distinguished from his ambitions' (Dworkin 1981: 314).

Notice that in Dworkin's argument the conclusion (we should not make any attempt to track ambition-sensitivity and endowment-insensitivity directly) is inferred from the premiss (we have no hope of tracking ambition-sensitivity and endowment-insensitivity perfectly, on a person by person basis). I think that the Chamberlain example gives us a reason to reject this inference. We cannot determine exactly what portion of his greater wealth is attributable to talent and what portion is attributable to ambition but we can make some reasonable estimates about the relative impact of ambition and talent on income distribution. This leaves open the possibility of more direct, albeit less precise, approaches to the problem of fair market adjustment.

The assumption that we can make the requisite generalizations in a practical form is controversial but not implausible. After all, the very identification of the problem of fair market adjustment depends on making some crude generalizations about the relative contribution of volitional and non-volitional factors to market success. We take the problem seriously because we are confident that a rather substantial portion of market success is attributable to our circumstances and not to our choices. We should explore, more thoroughly, the epistemic basis for our convictions in this regard to determine whether less intuitive, and more accurate, generalizations of the requisite sort are possible. Given the shortcomings of the other general strategies as responses to the problem of fair market adjustment, I think the direct strategy is worth considering seriously. Certainly its rejection by Dworkin is premature.

It is disappointing to have to conclude by noting that the problem of fair market adjustment probably admits of nothing better than an imperfect solution. No doubt we set our sights too high if we aim for a solution that is both extremely accurate and institutionally realistic. However, I think we pay only lip service to the powerful and radical egalitarian impulse that Dworkin locates at the heart of liberalism if we conclude that the best theory of equality only requires, for its realization, a somewhat more generous welfare state that leaves largely intact the huge disparities in income, opportunity, and power characteristic of contemporary liberal societies.

6

The Place of Liberty

DWORKIN'S commitment to equality as the animating principle of a liberal theory of political morality sets him apart from many other liberals who maintain that liberalism's most fundamental commitment is to a conception of liberty. Dworkin has consistently rejected any strategy for the defence of the particular individual liberties typically prized by liberals which proceeds from the assumption that liberty itself is the paramount ideal.[1] Yet liberty and equality are frequently depicted as competing and potentially inconsistent ideals. It is often maintained that egalitarian distributive objectives cannot be pursued without some valuable loss of individual liberty (Nozick 1974: 160–4). To the degree that this characterization of liberty and equality as deeply conflicting ideals is accurate, Dworkin's effort to articulate a systematic theory of egalitarian liberalism may prove to be theoretically infeasible. After all, Dworkin wants to defend an egalitarian account of distributive justice while maintaining liberalism's traditional commitment to the protection of extensive rights to individual liberty. In the previous chapters, we have explored Dworkin's understanding of the distributive implications of embracing an abstract ideal of equality. In this chapter, we focus on the place of liberty within egalitarianism. The general problem to be addressed is whether a fundamentally egalitarian conception of political morality can adequately accommodate liberalism's characteristic commitment to the protection of individual liberty. More specifically, we will investigate the success of Dworkin's attempt to locate a commitment to liberty within the very structure of equality of resources. Equality of resources is said to encompass an attractive conception of liberty in a unique and powerful way. Dworkin argues

---

[1] For example, Dworkin rejects the idea that there could be any general right to liberty that could be invoked to explain the particular individual liberties that should be protected by the state (Dworkin 1977: 266–72).

that the special connection he detects between liberty and equality of resources permits liberals to affirm the traditional commitment to the protection of individual liberty without compromising equality. I share Dworkin's conviction that it is possible to provide a secure place for individual liberty within egalitarianism. However, Dworkin's claim that adoption of equality of resources provides the most promising basis for comfortably accommodating liberty within an egalitarian theory of political morality is mistaken. I shall argue that equality of resources offers no special advantages for explaining the status of liberty. Indeed, Dworkin's insistence that the market—in the form of the hypothetical auction of resources—must play a central theoretical role within liberal theory distorts our understanding of the place of liberty in equality. We begin with a brief examination of the popular view that equality and liberty can be conflicting ideals.

FRAMING THE PUTATIVE CONFLICT BETWEEN EQUALITY AND LIBERTY

Dworkin believes that there is a sense in which it is possible to manufacture a sharp conflict between liberty and equality. He distinguishes flat and normative descriptions of equality and liberty. Liberty in the flat sense is equivalent to the absence of constraint. This is liberty as licence. Equality in the flat sense is simply used to 'indicate sameness or identity along some specified or understood dimension' (Dworkin 1987: 5) In the flat senses of these terms, we can identify conflicts between liberty and equality. It will inevitably be the case that establishing equality along a specified dimension will involve the imposition of some constraint on how individuals may act. However, the conflict between liberty and equality in this flat sense is not significant because neither liberty as licence nor equality as mere sameness is an attractive or defensible ideal. As Dworkin notes, the legal prohibition on murder imposes a constraint on individual action and thus might be thought to diminish liberty. Yet we do not think that this constraint and the resulting reduction of liberty is normatively significant. The attraction which liberty holds as a political virtue depends on the articulation of a normative conception of liberty which specifies a set of discrete liberty rights which have special value. Similarly, the force of the political ideal of equality is not reflected in mere sameness but rather in the specification of a particular normative conception of equality which picks out the respects in which individuals should be equal (e.g. in resources, or welfare, etc.). Once this distinction is in place, we can see that liberty is only diminished by equality if the particular valued liberties which constitute the most attractive normative conception of liberty are threatened by the best specification of a normative conception of equality.

The problem, as Dworkin sees it, then, is to determine whether there is a deep tension between liberty and equality understood as normative conceptions. There will, of course, be controversy about the precise contours of normative conceptions of liberty and equality. Liberals, for instance, are united in believing that individuals should not be constrained from expressing their political convictions, even though individuals are not free to slander others. Yet there is substantial debate about whether protected free speech includes hate propaganda which may undermine the equal standing of citizens. The fact that there are such disputes about the bounds of liberty suggests that we need some justificatory framework from which we can adjudicate such conflicts. Ultimately, one of Dworkin's aims is to identify just such a framework, one which links an attractive conception of equality to an attractive conception of liberty in a way that helps resolve disputes about the appropriate components of a normative conception of liberty.[2] However, Dworkin's more immediate objective is to demonstrate that a defensible normative conception of equality is compatible with a recognizably liberal conception of liberty. So for the purpose of establishing the compatibility of liberty and equality understood as normative ideals, Dworkin claims that an acceptable conception of liberty must incorporate a set of discrete liberty rights. 'These rights will include, at a minimum, rights to freedom of conscience, commitment, speech and religion, and to

[2] The three specific examples which Dworkin discusses are: (1) whether political liberty is infringed by the imposition of spending limits in political campaigns; (2) whether freedom of choice in medical care is threatened by the elimination of a private sector in health care; and (3) whether minimum wage legislation unfairly restricts freedom of contract (Dworkin 1987: 4–5).

freedom of choice in matters touching central or important aspects of an agent's personal life, like employment, family arrangements, sexual privacy and medical treatment' (Dworkin 1987: 7). Henceforth, I shall refer to this package of discrete liberties as basic liberties or the liberal conception of liberty.

The familiar liberty rights which make up this conception of liberty provide a basis for testing the compatibility of liberty and equality. Liberty and equality will be in competition only if these liberty rights or some subset of them prove incompatible with the best understanding of the demands of equality. For instance, equality and liberty would collide in a troubling fashion if the promotion of distributive equality required the imposition of constraints on political speech. However, Dworkin emphasizes the normative primacy of equality: 'Any genuine conflict between liberty and equality—any conflict between liberty and the requirements of the best conception of the abstract egalitarian principle—is a contest that liberty must lose' (Dworkin 1987: 9). So the task Dworkin sets for himself is to explain how equality of resources furnishes a secure place for the standard liberal conception of liberty. We can test the success of his argument in two ways. First, we can consider how Dworkin's special argument compares with other possible egalitarian strategies for the defence of liberty rights. Second, we can consider whether the proposed accommodation of liberty within the structure of equality of resources is plausible in itself. In other words, we can assess both the comparative and intrinsic merits of Dworkin's position. I will begin by explaining a strategy for the defence of liberty from the point of view of equality which Dworkin rejects as inadequate. This will set the stage for the comparative assessment of Dworkin's argument. I will then turn to the details of Dworkin's favoured approach and assess both whether it succeeds on its own terms and whether it is superior to the competing theory.

THE INTEREST STRATEGY

How can an attractive conception of liberty be defended from an egalitarian perspective? Dworkin identifies one important approach which he dubs the interest strategy (Dworkin 1987:

13). The structure of the interest strategy is quite simple. It makes no commitment to equality of resources as the best interpretation of equality; rather it links the defence of liberty rights to the way in which human interests are served by the provision of liberty. In its most general form, it has two basic steps. It starts by stipulating 'a particular account of how people's interests are to be identified and what function of different people's interests an ideal distribution aims to satisfy' (Dworkin 1987: 13). At the second step 'it argues that, as things fall out, certain liberties are instrumentally connected to the satisfaction of interests so that protecting interests in the right proportion or according to the right formula requires establishing and respecting rights to these liberties' (Dworkin 1987: 13).

In my view, some version of this strategy provides the most plausible defence of liberty from the egalitarian perspective. Dworkin notes that there are different variations of this strategy and he rejects them all quickly. Since none of the particular versions of this strategy which Dworkin rehearses are especially attractive, I will not examine them here.[3] I will, however, describe a way of developing the interest strategy which is plausible and which meets Dworkin's general objections to predicating an egalitarian defence of liberty on an account of human interests. My version of the interest strategy proceeds from two important ideas that Dworkin frequently emphasizes. These are that our highest order interest is in leading a good life, a life that is in fact good, and that our current beliefs about what the good life consists in may be mistaken (Dworkin 1983: 25–7). If we accept these claims, as I think we should, then we have

---

[3] Dworkin briefly discusses and rejects three possible versions of the interest strategy. There is a utilitarian version in which the defence of liberty rights is linked to the maximization of welfare. On this view 'protecting freedom of choice and defending rights to free speech and other fundamental liberties is the best available means of achieving the greatest possible welfare' (Dworkin 1987: 13). The crude contractarian version of the interest strategy defence of liberty requires 'demonstrating that everyone would in fact agree to principles of justice protecting liberty, or would agree to such principles after proper reflection' (Dworkin 1987: 14). (Rawls is credited with a more sophisticated defence of liberty that only partially relies on a type of interest strategy (Dworkin 1987: 16–17)). Finally, Dworkin considers whether the interest strategy could be combined with equality of resources by treating liberty as a resource for which people in the auction can bid (Dworkin 1987: 19–22).

very good grounds for defending fairly extensive liberty rights over matters of great personal concern.

We start by arguing that the interests which individuals have a legitimate stake in having recognized are those which significantly contribute to the possibility of leading a good life. An ideal distribution of resources would aim at equally satisfying every individual's interest in securing the conditions necessary to the possibility of leading a good life. The securing of liberty of various kinds turns out to be a very important condition of leading a decent life. This is not because liberty itself is intrinsically valuable.[4] We need not assume, for instance, that any constraint on action is a normative loss. Rather we can proceed by emphasizing the instrumental contribution certain kinds of liberty make to the possibility of leading a good life. Specifically, certain forms of liberty allow us to explore and pursue effectively those things which are intrinsically valuable. Our interest in securing certain types of liberty, while extremely important, is nonetheless instrumental.

It does not take much by way of argument to establish how the provision of freedom is related to our legitimate interests. Indeed, there is an important strain in liberal thought which tries to illuminate the connection between liberty and our interests. J. S. Mill, for instance, famously argued that liberty of speech was particularly conducive to the discovery of truth and the growth of knowledge. The interest strategy follows the lead of Mill by linking the defence of certain liberties to the satisfaction of basic human interests, such as the discovery of knowledge.

The basic liberty rights defended by liberals—e.g. liberty of thought, expression, association, etc.—are very important to our learning about valuable ways of life and revising our mistaken views about what is valuable. We need room to experiment in order to discover what sort of life is in fact valuable. We may also benefit from learning from others through exposure to their ideas, practices, and ways of life. If, as seems likely, many basic liberties stand in this relation to our interest in leading a good life, then it would seem as though we have good grounds

---

[4] Kymlicka provides a convincing refutation of the position that freedom is inherently valuable (1988*a*: 186–9).

for supposing that equality requires the requisite liberties to be made available to all on an equal basis. Equality instructs us to protect the liberty of individuals because the provision of equal liberty rights responds to impartial concern for each person's interest in leading a good life. Of course, people also need other resources if they are to learn about and pursue the good life and egalitarians must also be concerned about adequate provision and fair distribution of these resources. There may be cases in which the provision of certain liberties conflicts with the provision of other resources important to the securing of the conditions for the leading of a good life. In these cases, any conflict should be resolved—although arriving at the appropriate resolution may prove difficult and controversial—by determining which sorts of resources make the most important contribution to providing the conditions for leading a good life. The supposition on which this strategy depends is that basic liberties play an indispensable role in permitting individuals to realize their most fundamental interest in leading a good life. I do not think it is dogmatic to suppose that many familiar liberal liberties could be successfully defended on this basis. One important feature of this approach is that it permits us to assess the relative importance of different liberties and thus discriminate between the liberties which we typically believe merit protection and those which do not. Whereas freedom of political speech plays an important role in facilitating deliberation about matters of great importance, the liberty to slander does not speak to an important human interest. If a compelling argument can be advanced that the protection of some liberty, such as freedom to slander, does not contribute importantly to the possibility of leading a good life and moreover threatens harm, then we have good grounds for restricting the liberty. What would be the point of protecting a type of liberty which did not contribute the possibility of leading a satisfactory life? That sort of liberty would seem valueless and potentially destructive.

These remarks about how the interest strategy might successfully be employed in an egalitarian defence of liberty can be supplemented by appeal to the endorsement constraint which we encountered in Chapter 2. As Kymlicka says 'no life goes better by being led from the outside according to values the person doesn't endorse. My life only goes better if I'm leading it from the inside, according to my beliefs about value' (Kymlicka 1988*a*: 183). If it is a necessary condition of leading a good life that one must freely adopt and pursue one's own goals then we have an additional interest-based reason for favouring provision of extensive liberty in matters of great personal concern. The requisite endorsement of goals and life plans will only be possible in circumstances congenial to freedom of choice. Note that the sort of egalitarian interest-based argument suggested here in no way depends on acceptance of equality of resources or a model of market interaction for the establishment of its conclusions. This version of the interest strategy aims at defending individual liberty by providing a direct interpretation of the abstract egalitarian thesis.

OBJECTIONS TO THE INTEREST STRATEGY

Although many of the resources for developing a compelling interest-based egalitarian defence of liberty are to be found in Dworkin's work, he explicitly rejects reliance on any such strategy. What are his general objections to employing any version of the interest-based strategy in defending liberty? There are two basic objections that Dworkin stresses. They both try to exploit the idea that interest-based arguments provide too fragile a basis for an adequate defence of liberty. In my view, however, neither is convincing.

(a) A threat to basic political liberty?

The first objection claims that because most people would be willing to trade away certain important liberties (e.g. liberty to participate in public political demonstrations) in exchange for other goods which they might prefer (e.g. more crime prevention), appeals to individual interest cannot adequately ground appropriate protections of liberty. The interest-based strategy is held hostage, according to this objection, to the de facto preferences of the (majority of the) public. Dworkin thinks, for instance, that most Americans would believe it to be in their interest to trade away some of their civil liberties in exchange for other goods they prefer. If this is an accurate estimation of public preferences (and Dworkin is surprisingly confident that it is) then, according to Dworkin, the interest strategy requires that we satisfy the preferences of the majority by making trades which diminish basic liberty, provided that such trades are favoured by a majority (Dworkin 1987: 15–16). The interest strategy, therefore, is not compatible with a liberal conception of liberty in which free political speech is sacrosanct. However, the suggestion that an interest-based strategy must, in matters of political liberty, capitulate to the preferences of the majority hardly represents the most plausible interpretation of this strategy.

There are three replies to Dworkin's interpretation and criticism of the interest strategy. First, there is a puzzle concerning the source of the objection. Strictly speaking the complaint, as it is presented, is difficult to represent as an equality-based objection. After all, it does not purport to show that the lesser political liberty putatively licensed by a preference rendering of the interest strategy violates the fundamental requirement of equal concern and respect. It is most naturally understood as an argument which appeals to pre-theoretical convictions about the importance of preserving political liberty. The egalitarian interest strategy can be rejected, it seems, simply if it fails to yield the desired liberal liberty rights. But this sounds like an appeal to some independent principle of liberty, one that might even call the authority of the egalitarian thesis into question. Equality is important, the argument might go, but it must be interpreted in a way consistent with our (independent) commitment to individual liberty. Since Dworkin generally seeks to avoid direct appeals to the independent value of liberty in political theory it is odd that his objection to the interest strategy should appear to be predicated on some such appeal. It might, all things considered, be an unattractive consequence of egalitarianism that it cannot securely accommodate certain liberty rights. But this, if true, should move us away from acceptance of the uniquely fundamental role played by equality considerations—a move which Dworkin certainly does not want to make.

Second, and more significantly, it is wrong to suppose that a sensible version of the interest strategy would license the liberty-diminishing trades Dworkin is worried about. It may be true, as Dworkin speculates, that many people would *prefer* such trades but the interest strategy need not be responsive to the de facto preferences of individuals. After all, de facto preferences need not and often do not correspond to genuine interests. A plausible rendering of the interest strategy should attend to actual individual interests. The demonstration that many individuals would prefer liberty-diminishing trades only undermines the interest-based justification of liberty if de facto preferences serve as accurate indicators of genuine individual interests. But this is a dubious supposition, one which is undermined by Dworkin's own claims about the fallibility of our beliefs about the good life.

The real issue is whether it is plausible to suppose that the trading away of political liberty would really be in the interest of many people. Dworkin thinks that it is difficult to deny that such trades are indeed in the interest of most people. He asks, 'why is it irrational for someone who knows his political convictions are conventional to trade off the general liberty of political demonstration for whatever advantages he believes this would bring him?' (Dworkin 1987: 17). I have already indicated some of the reasons, having to do with the fallibility of our convictions, why such a trade would be irrational. A sensible person with conventional views should realize that her views may be mistaken and should not take lightly measures which make it more difficult for these views to be examined critically. The opportunity for critical examination afforded by exposure to different views is very important. Moreover, the sensible person should also recognize that her views may not always be conventional. She would suffer a great loss were she to find herself in a minority which was unable to voice its position effectively. For these reasons I think, *pace* Dworkin, that it is not 'a whistling-in-the-dark act of faith' (Dworkin 1987: 17) to suppose that there are good reasons why it would be irrational for a sensible person to accept many trades which diminished political liberty.

Third, even if it were true that some liberty-diminishing trades are in the interest of a majority, this would not be enough to establish that the interest strategy is bound to endorse reduction of political liberty. For the interest strategy to justify a reduction in political liberty it would be necessary to establish not only that there was in fact some powerful majority interest in reducing political liberty but also that such a general reduction of liberty would not violate the requirement that each person be accorded equal concern and respect. We may assume that a proper interpretation of treating individuals with equal concern and respect requires that every individual be secured an equal opportunity to lead a decent life. If securing certain political liberties is a necessary condition of individuals in a minority having a fair chance to lead a decent life and if reduction of political liberty is in the interest of a majority but is not a necessary condition of enjoying an opportunity to lead a decent life, then the interest-based strategy will not justify accommodating the genuine but non-essential interest of the majority. Some interests are simply more urgent and fundamental than others. It is reasonable for priority to be given to the satisfaction of such interests when they conflict with less crucial interests.

(b) Too controversial?

Dworkin's second objection to the interest strategy focuses on what might be called the marketability of the interest strategy. Adoption of the interest strategy means that 'the place of liberty in justice remains hostage to disputes about what those interests actually require' (Dworkin 1987: 16–17). Dworkin speculates that the interest-based defence of liberty may be vulnerable to certain communitarian theories about the necessary conditions of leading a good life. He notes that 'some philosophers and sociologists insist that people are much more likely to think that their lives have value, and that they have been successful in realizing their powers for justice and conviction, in a society with a settled and relatively unquestioned common theory of the good life, on which they can draw for confirmation and reinforcement' (Dworkin 1987: 16–17).[5]

If the communitarian view of the conditions of leading a good life were true then quite substantial restrictions on liberty might be justified by the interest strategy. In the extreme it might, for instance, justify restrictions on religious and political liberties and the establishment of a state religion. Dworkin seems to

[5] Dworkin does not explicitly identify the views he is concerned with as 'communitarian' but I think it is clear that it is communitarian arguments which motivate the objection he considers. There is a clear parallel between the position Dworkin identifies and the arguments of contemporary communitarians (MacIntyre 1981; Sandel 1982, 1984; Taylor 1985).

think it is an objection to reliance on the interest strategy that employing it is just too controversial given the seeming popularity of communitarian accounts of the conditions most conducive to the realization of our most fundamental interests. Yet Dworkin nowhere indicates that he thinks the communitarian account is, in fact, correct and in other work he (like other liberals) has been extremely critical of it (e.g. Dworkin 1989; Gutmann 1985; Kymlicka 1989a). Since any worked-out theory of political morality must broach controversial issues, it hardly constitutes an objection to reliance on the interest strategy that it raises potentially controversial empirical and philosophical issues about the good life. I might add that I think there are decisive objections to the communitarian thesis at issue here, so I do not think it really threatens the defence of liberty. Of course, if it really could be established that provision of certain civil liberties is inconsistent with, or even antithetical to, provision of the conditions necessary to leading a good life, then we would have to reconsider the suggestion that such liberties ought to be restricted. If, for instance, the absence of a state religion providing authoritative moral instruction left people aimless, confused, and generally unable to pursue a decent life, then it would be reasonable to reopen the case for establishment of a state religion. However, as things stand, we reject the necessity of such institutional arrangements partly because we reject the contention that a state religion would really contribute to the possibility of individuals leading good lives.

The virtue of the interest strategy is its structural simplicity. It provides a natural way for egalitarians to defend a robust conception of liberty and it permits us to assess the normative significance of different liberties. It is true that in any fully developed version of the interest strategy, it would be necessary to make complex and potentially controversial judgements both about how human interests are served by the provision of given liberties and about how different kinds of human interests should be weighed and compared. But that is surely an inescapable feature of moral and political discourse.

I have now explained my reservations about Dworkin's rejection of an interest-based argument for the defence of individual liberty. To be fair, Dworkin does not think he has knockdown arguments against the interest strategy. Rather he hopes to indicate that it may provide a rather fragile and thus unsatisfying account—unsatisfying, that is, at least to liberals—of the place of liberty within egalitarianism. He claims that there is a superior strategy, one by means of which liberals can confidently embrace equality as their fundamental principle without jeopardizing the central place of basic liberty within the liberal tradition. The extremely complex argument which Dworkin develops is designed to give liberty an invulnerable and non-contingent place in the egalitarian ideal. The aim is to show that an important and powerful liberty principle is partly constitutive of the egalitarian ideal itself. We must now examine this approach to the problem of locating the place of liberty within equality.

OVERVIEW: THE ROLE OF LIBERTY WITHIN EQUALITY OF RESOURCES

In order to understand Dworkin's attempt to explain how the accommodation of liberty within an egalitarian framework is possible, we must return to the auction device (i.e. the ideal market) that the theory of equality of resources is predicated upon. The crucial claim Dworkin wishes to make with regard to the reconciliation of liberty and equality is that we should not regard liberty and equality as distinct ideals. Indeed, he argues that the very articulation of the theory of liberal equality depends on exploiting a principle of liberty that is an intrinsic part of the auction. In other words, Dworkin's commitment to liberty is not independently derived from an egalitarian account of justice. Rather a conception of liberty plays a direct and fundamental role in the very definition of distributive equality supplied by equality of resources.

The market can only be relied upon as a device for defining equality of resources if it can be supposed to yield, at least in principle, some determinate outcome. However, the outcome of the auction envisioned by Dworkin can only be determinate if there is a specification of the sort of liberty each participant in the auction enjoys. Thus, we need to specify a conception of liberty *before* we can actually define equality of resources. Initially, this suggestion seems to run against the grain of

Dworkin's commitment to equality as fundamental and his rejection of the theoretical priority of liberty. However, Dworkin argues that there is no real difficulty in supposing that equality of resources depends on a conception of liberty. Liberty should be construed simply as 'an aspect of equality . . . rather than an independent political ideal potentially in conflict with it' (Dworkin 1987: 1). The abstract principle of equal concern remains the fundamental ideal but a conception of liberty is an essential part of the conception of distributive equality. Hence in equality of resources, liberty becomes an aspect of equality.

Let us examine this idea more closely. The auction upon which equality of resources depends only makes sense if there is some baseline stipulation of what one may and may not do with the resources one acquires in the auction. Every auction needs a baseline liberty/constraint system. Without such a system a person could not sensibly make a bid on a resource since she would not know how she would be allowed to use it. Similarly, the sorts of bids people will make in an auction may be radically different depending on what baseline liberty/constraint system is in place. Different baselines will yield different distributions of resources because the envy test will be affected by what one is allowed to do with the resources one has (Dworkin 1987: 21). This point can be easily illustrated. Dworkin gives the example of how restrictions of freedom of expression can affect the auction. 'If the baseline stipulates that though a party can use clay for any other purpose he likes, he cannot use it to make a politically satirical sculpture, someone will want clay much less than he would without that background constraint, and so bid a much lower price for it' (Dworkin 1987: 21). The reason that the particular version of what constitutes an equal division of resources falls out of Dworkin's version of the auction is that the baseline liberty/constraint system gives individuals extensive freedom to determine how they shall use the resources they acquire.[6] The traditional liberal commitment to extensive individual liberty thus can be depicted as part and parcel of equality

[6] It should be noted that when Dworkin initially presented the market as a device crucial to the interpretation of distributive equality he did not give any explicit recognition to the need to identify the baseline liberty/constraint system presupposed by the auction. Instead, he presupposed a liberal baseline—one in which individuals are free to use the resources they acquire in the auction as they see fit.

of resources. Equality of resources is partly defined by a particular baseline which delineates the sorts of liberty that individuals are permitted to exercise. Specifically, equality of resources supposes a baseline which secures a good deal of so-called negative liberty; it leaves individuals unencumbered by significant legal constraint (Dworkin 1987: 1). Subject to some fairly minimal constraints, individuals may use the resources they acquire in pursuit of their idea of a good life. Recognizing the role of the baseline in defining equality of resources points to another way of harmonizing equality and liberty—we can view liberty as constitutive of a conception of equality. We may pursue a 'constitutive strategy'.

DOGMATIC CONSTITUTIVE STRATEGIES VS. THE CONSTITUTIVE BRIDGE STRATEGY

There are, according to Dworkin, different versions of the 'constitutive strategy' for the joint accommodation of liberty and equality. Some of them he rejects out of hand as dogmatic and unsatisfactory. The dogmatic versions of the constitutive strategy simply 'define an egalitarian distribution so that liberty is already present in the very definition of equality' (Dworkin 1987: 25). For example, a libertarian seeking to reconcile liberty and equality could provide a stipulative definition of equality as consisting in the equal provision to each person of rights to private property and familiar market freedoms. On this account, equality and liberty cannot conflict because any action which violated one of the protected liberties would, *ex hypothesi*, violate the proposed definition of equality. Dworkin thinks finding a place for liberty within equality by definitional fiat is unsatisfactory. I agree, and this means that equality of resources cannot be represented as accommodating individual liberty simply through the specification of a liberal baseline. The selection of a particular baseline must be justified.

Dworkin attempts, therefore, to employ a version of the constitutive strategy which provides a justification for the conception of liberty which is built into the idea of equality of resources. The argument thus depends on explaining how the baseline incorporated in equality of resources is necessary to the best interpretation of the egalitarian thesis. He must show, in other words, why the particular baseline which is presupposed by equality of resources—one that accommodates the liberties most cherished by liberals—provides the best interpretation of abstract equality. Towards this end Dworkin develops a complex argumentative strategy that he believes provides the requisite link between the abstract egalitarian thesis and equality of resources as defined by the (liberal) baseline. He calls this argument the constitutive bridge strategy because it attempts to provide a link between the abstract demand that a 'community treat its members with equal concern' and 'equality of resources, which proposes that an auction under certain conditions, realizes equal concern' (Dworkin 1987: 25).[7] If successful, the constitutive bridge strategy may explain how a deep and distinctive commitment to individual liberty is entailed by adoption of equality of resources. It is not dogmatic since it aims at providing a compelling justification of the liberty-accommodating baseline which defines equality of resources.

OUTLINE OF THE CONSTITUTIVE BRIDGE STRATEGY

The constitutive bridge strategy is extremely elaborate. It has the following basic structure and components. We hold two ideas in place: (1) the abstract egalitarian principle, which demands equal concern, and (2) equality of resources, which proposes that an auction under certain conditions realizes equal concern. We select the baseline system, from among those we consider, that builds the best bridge between those two ideas. That is, we select the baseline system that gives most plausibility to the claim that an auction from that baseline treats people with equal concern (Dworkin 1987: 25).

The complexity of this strategy is easy to detect. Aside from the unusual metaphor of a bridging argument, the complete

[7] Dworkin does not make any attempt to link this argument for the accommodation of liberty within an egalitarian framework (which first appeared in 1987) with his previous discussion of such matters (e.g. Dworkin 1977: 240–58, 266–78; 1985: 293–303). Indeed he explicitly says that he makes no effort 'to discover how far my argument qualifies or expands' earlier contributions to the subject (Dworkin 1987: 13). I shall also make no attempt to explore possible connections between these different arguments.

version of the constitutive bridge strategy invokes no less than five separate substantive principles. These principles are meant to operate in concert and any force they command seems to rest principally on their intuitive plausibility.

Briefly, here are the principles Dworkin invokes along with a summary explanation of the role they play in fixing the baseline. First and most importantly, there is *the principle of abstraction*. It fixes the form in which goods are to be sold in the auction and establishes a strong presumption in favour of individual freedom of choice. Second, *the principle of security* places the constraints on individual liberty necessary to provide people with basic security of person and property. This principle justifies 'legal constraints forbidding physical assault, theft, deliberate damage to property and trespass of the sort that are common to the criminal and civil laws of all developed legal systems' (Dworkin 1987: 26). Third, *the principle of correction* provides a way of dealing with externalities which might be introduced into the auction. This principle justifies the introduction of the constraints on freedom (e.g. zoning laws or prohibitions on pollution) that are necessary to mitigate the effects of externalities that would otherwise distort the objective of achieving an equal distribution of true opportunity costs.[8] Fourth, *the principle of authenticity* ensures that the conditions governing the formation of the personalities and preferences of participants in the auction are rich enough to enable participants to be fully aware of the range of possible goals and their likely consequences. Before individuals can make sensible and appropriate bids in the auction they have to have had the opportunity to explore their convictions and develop goals, etc. According to Dworkin, this means that the principle of authenticity must afford 'special protection to freedom of religious commitment, freedom of expression, access to the widest literature and other

---

[8] The sort of externalities that Dworkin is concerned about here are those which would arise because parties to the auction may lack perfect knowledge about how the resources acquired in the auction will be used. If one knew that a resource purchased by one party would be used in a pollution-generating way then one could outbid the would-be polluter for the resource. However, since we cannot reliably know how individuals will use the resources they acquire we cannot eliminate the possibility of externalities arising after the auction. The principle of correction adjusts the rules governing the legitimate uses of resources by imposing restrictions on the use of resources which anticipate and counter externalities (like pollution) which would otherwise emerge.

forms of art, freedom of personal, social and intimate association, and also freedom of nonexpression in the form of freedom from surveillance' (Dworkin 1987: 35). In the absence of wide-ranging opportunities to develop and explore one's personality, the auction (since it relies on individual's preferences) could not provide a compelling interpretation of abstract equality. Fifth, *the principle of independence* guards individuals against the effects of prejudice that might otherwise be a result of the auction. It renders illegitimate, and provides justification for adjusting, auction outcomes which reflect the contempt or hatred of one group towards another. Racist preferences which might otherwise be satisfied through the auction (e.g. for white-only neighbourhoods) are not to be given weight in the determination of what constitutes an equal distribution of true opportunity costs.

This is only a skeletal account of the principles invoked in Dworkin's argument but I think it is sufficient to provide some indication of its sheer complexity. Whatever original appeal the market has as a simple device for defining equality and supplying liberalism with secure foundations must surely be mitigated by the numerous and variegated principles that must be relied upon in establishing a special connection between liberty and equality. The purported natural links between liberty and equality of resources are difficult to detect. However, while the complexity of Dworkin's strategy may legitimately provoke us to query its plausibility, there are more specific criticisms of it which will justify our rejection of it. I now turn to these.

Instead of commenting extensively on each of the steps in Dworkin's argument, I will focus my comments on the most important (and problematic) features of it. The principle of abstraction plays a fundamental role in defining an adequate baseline and it provides an important grounding for liberty by establishing a 'strong presumption in favour of freedom of choice'. 'It insists that an ideal distribution is possible only when people are legally free to act as they wish except so far as constraints on their freedom are necessary to protect security of person and property or to correct certain imperfections in markets (or other auction-like distributive mechanisms)' (Dworkin 1987: 25). Other modifications to the baseline are supplied by the other principles that I have outlined above. They have the effect of qualifying, to some degree, the liberty-generating impact of the principle of abstraction.

The basic idea behind the principle of abstraction is that resources must be made available to individuals in a way that is as sensitive as possible to their possible life plans. Since there is a wide diversity of possible life plans, resources should be made available in their most abstract (but feasible) form. For example, iron ore should be auctioned instead of steel. Greater abstraction in the form in which resources are made available allows people greater flexibility in designing and pursuing projects. Sensitivity to the possible life plans of individuals is also achieved by providing individuals with extensive freedom to determine how resources will be used. Dworkin argues that resources can only be employed in people's projects if they can count on controlling, to some reasonable degree, the resources they own. Hence the principle of security—which places 'constraints on liberty necessary to provide people with physical security and enough control over their own property to allow them to make and carry out plans and projects'—is required (Dworkin 1987: 26). However, aside from constraints required by considerations of security 'the principle of abstraction insists that people should in principle be left free, under the baseline system, to use the resources they acquire, including the leisure they provide and protect through their bidding program, in what way they wish' (Dworkin 1987: 29). The foregoing gives the basic shape of the argument of the bridge strategy. At first glance, the constitutive bridge strategy turns mainly on how the principle of abstraction provides grounds for the claim that the baseline presupposed by equality of resources embodies a liberal conception of liberty. The supplementary principles help refine the baseline but the main argument for a liberal baseline is supposed to be given by the principle of abstraction.

INTERPRETING THE CONSTITUTIVE BRIDGE STRATEGY

In assessing the adequacy of this argument, it is appropriate to begin by considering a structural peculiarity of the bridge strategy which arises on one interpretation of it. The principle of abstraction is billed as providing a natural link between the abstract egalitarian ideal and equality of resources. It speaks to the abstract demands of equality by insisting that resources be made available to individuals in a form compatible with our basic interest in leading a good life. Similarly, it speaks to the design of the auction by delineating a baseline without which no meaningful auction would be possible. In constructing the bridge strategy, Dworkin asks that we accept equality of resources as the best interpretation of the abstract egalitarian ideal. He asks that we hold the abstract egalitarian ideal and equality of resources constant. But this seems to suppose that equality of resources as a conception of equality is identifiable independently of specification of the baseline. It is not clear, however, how this is possible. Dworkin emphasizes that different specifications of the baseline will generate different distributions of resources, some of which will be plainly unsatisfactory from the point of view of justice. Each baseline will affect the way the envy test is satisfied and thus different baselines will generate different versions of equality of resources. Indeed, it is arguable that the appeal of the resource auction modelled by equality of resources is entirely dependent on the specification of the baseline. Some baselines will make it seem an attractive theory of equality, others will make it look most unattractive. The structural problem is this: it does not seem possible to hold the idea of equality of resources constant or accept it as the best interpretation of the abstract ideal of equality without already knowing what the baseline is. If this is right then there is something problematic about the design of the bridge version of the constitutive strategy. It asks us to hold an idea constant while developing a theory (e.g. through adoption of the principle of abstraction) which seems to give content to the very idea we have been asked to hold constant. If equality of resources does not have any determinate content until the baseline liberty/constraint system has been specified then it makes no sense to speak of building a (liberty-accommodating) bridge between the abstract egalitarian plateau and equality of resources. The constitutive bridge strategy is, on this interpretation, incoherent.

TRUE OPPORTUNITY COSTS

The natural response to this initial criticism is to claim that the core idea of equality of resources which is to be kept constant

has been misidentified. Dworkin suggests that we need only hold
constant the idea that some form of auction in which everyone
has equal bidding power is the best mechanism for fairly measuring the costs of each person's projects to the projects of others.
As we have noted before, the idea of equality of resources is that
'true opportunity costs' should be equalized. Its aim is that 'each
person have an equal share of resources measured by the cost of
the choices he makes reflecting his own plans and preferences, to
the plans and projects of others' (Dworkin 1987: 27). We cannot tell whether resources are justly distributed unless we can
accurately measure these costs and an auction that incorporates
the appropriate version of the envy test is the best measuring
device. On this interpretation of the bridge strategy, we hold
constant only the abstract core idea of equality of resources. We
need not have knowledge of the structure of any particular
version of the auction to be confident in asserting that some
version of the auction—a version to be determined by the bridge
strategy—provides the best way of calculating the crucial notion
of true opportunity costs. Instead, we give theoretical promin-
ence to the more abstract claim that application of an envy test
under formal conditions of equality (i.e. with everyone having
equal bidding power in an auction) can fairly measure true
opportunity costs provided it is applied from the appropriate
baseline liberty/constraint system. In other words, we suppose
that the envy test is sensitive to basic considerations of equity in
a way that transcends the particular baseline which defines a
specific auction. And it is that idea we must hold constant in
constructing a bridge from the abstract egalitarian ideal. We
seek a justification for selecting the baseline which provides the
most accurate measurement of true opportunity costs. On this
construal, the envy test provides only a 'necessary condition for
an ideal distribution' (Dworkin 1987: 23). But it is a necessary
condition that may be employed in illuminating an egalitarian
conception of liberty. We rely on the principle of abstraction to
delineate the baseline which best measures true opportunity
costs and thereby links abstract equality to the envy test. This
interpretation of the bridge strategy seems structurally coherent.
However, there are difficulties with the proposal.

To begin with, it is unclear why we should suppose that
the envy test stripped from any particular baseline should be

thought to have special egalitarian credentials. In previous chapters, I have identified various reasons for thinking that satisfaction of the envy test, even when applied from Dworkin's favoured baseline, should not be construed as a necessary condition for an ideal distribution. So we might simply dispute the premiss of the bridge strategy that requires us to attribute special egalitarian virtues to the envy test. But I will not press that objection here. Instead, I will argue that even provisional acceptance of the envy test and the allied notion of opportunity costs does not rehabilitate the strategy.

There are two different lines of criticism which can be raised against this interpretation of the constitutive bridge strategy. The first focuses on problems concerning the putative links between the principle of abstraction, a liberal conception of liberty, and the notion of true opportunity costs. The second challenges the suggestion that a functional version of the constitutive bridge strategy can be distinguished, in substance, from the main idea of the interest strategy.

THE PRINCIPLE OF ABSTRACTION AND A LIBERAL CONCEPTION OF LIBERTY

For the refined interpretation of the constitutive bridge strategy to succeed, Dworkin must demonstrate that there is a justification for the selection of a baseline which embraces a liberal conception of liberty. More specifically, there must be a way to distinguish different baselines with respect to the degree to which they measure true opportunity costs, and the baseline which measures true opportunity costs must reflect a liberal conception of liberty. So the initial task is to determine which form of an auction of resources tracks true opportunity costs. How do we do this? Dworkin suggests that we have an intuitive sense of the fairness of different auctions which gives us guidance in tracking the notion of true opportunity costs. For instance, an auction with a baseline which prohibited individuals using their resources to express unpopular political opinions might seem to distort the opportunity costs of various resources. Dworkin, of course, thinks that an auction which proceeds from a liberal baseline best measures true opportunity costs. And if this claim can be made good then equality of resources can be depicted as providing a secure foundation for liberty. The favoured liberal baseline cannot, however, simply be nominated on an ad hoc basis. A principle is, therefore, needed to justify our conviction that some auctions are fairer than others and that an auction with a liberal baseline best tracks true opportunity costs. The principle of abstraction is the needed principle. True opportunity costs are measured by an auction in which resources are auctioned in their most abstract form because an auction is fairer when 'it offers more discriminating choices and is thus more sensitive to the discrete plans and preferences people in fact have' (Dworkin 1987: 27–8). The principle of abstraction provides the key to securing an attractive conception of liberty within equality of resources because it grounds our convictions about true opportunity costs while at the same time establishing a basis for a liberal conception of liberty. As we have seen, the principle of abstraction seems to establish a presumption of freedom of choice. People should be free to use the resources they acquire in whatever way they see fit, subject to the limits imposed by the principle of security. The liberal conception of liberty built into equality of resources does not appear ad hoc or dogmatic because it can grounded in the principle of abstraction.

If this argument is to succeed, at least two conditions must be satisfied. More specifically, Dworkin must show: (*a*) that there is a way to distinguish different baselines with respect to the degree which they measure true opportunity costs; and (*b*) that the baseline which measures true opportunity costs reflects a liberal conception of liberty. For the sake of argument, let us assume that the principle of abstraction is intuitively plausible. We can test the success of the constitutive bridge strategy by determining whether the principle of abstraction, on closer inspection, provides a unique basis for selecting a liberal baseline over baselines which are clearly not liberal. If the principle of abstraction is indeterminate between liberal and non-liberal baselines or if it leads to baselines which are hostile to a liberal conception of liberty then the constitutive bridge strategy is problematic.

The full specification of an auction baseline would be extremely complex but we need only focus on elements of the baseline which would clearly distinguish liberal baseline from other baselines. Let us focus, therefore, on the case of free speech since it allows us to distinguish liberal baselines from other baselines in an uncontentious way. We can distinguish three different baselines with respect to free speech. First, it seems reasonable to suppose that a *liberal baseline* must permit individuals to use the resources they acquire in the auction to express their political views publicly. However, a liberal baseline presumably does not extend to individuals the right to use resources in order to slander other individuals. Second, we can imagine a plainly *illiberal baseline*, one in which individuals are forbidden to use their resources to engage in public political demonstrations. We will assume that the illiberal baseline also forbids slander and libel. Third, consider what might be called a *non-liberal baseline*. This is a baseline in which public political demonstrations are permitted but which also permits individuals to use their resources to slander and libel others. The question is whether the principle of abstraction provides a basis for selecting the liberal baseline over the illiberal and non-liberal baselines.

Remember that Dworkin thinks that most Americans would prefer to restrict the liberty to engage in public political protests in order to have more resources devoted to projects which they care more about (e.g. more crime prevention). Suppose that Dworkin is right about this but that in addition to the majority there are some people who wish to engage in political protest and still others who would like to be able to slander people they do not like. We have, in other words, a population with quite different plans and preferences and we have to determine what kind of auction will best measure true opportunity costs. On Dworkin's argument, we select the baseline which best measures true opportunity costs by appealing to the principle of abstraction. 'The principle recognizes that the true opportunity cost of any transferable resource is the price others would pay for it in an auction whose resources were offered in as abstract form as possible, that is, in the form that permits the greatest possible flexibility in fine-tuning bids to plans and preferences' (Dworkin 1987: 28).

Dworkin would have us believe that the principle of abstraction favours the liberal baseline and that the liberal baseline provides the best measure of true opportunity costs. Yet application of the principle of abstraction to this case yields ambiguous results. Consider how the different baselines affect the cost of resources and the degree to which resources are available in a way which is 'sensitive to the discrete plans and preferences people in fact have' (Dworkin 1987: 28). For example, which baseline—liberal, illiberal, or non-liberal—measures the true opportunity costs of placards? Placards, we can suppose, can be inscribed with political slogans (e.g. 'Workers of the world unite!'), phrases indicating support for professional sports teams (e.g. 'Go Leafs! Go!'), or slanderous remarks (e.g. 'Macleod is a scoundrel!'). Obviously, the selection of baselines will affect the price of placards in an auction. For instance, in an auction with an illiberal baseline the price of placards is likely to be lower than in an auction with a liberal baseline because political protesters and people who wish to engage in slander will not bother expending resources on placards which they cannot use as they would like. Similarly, an auction with a non-liberal baseline will likely place a higher price on placards than an auction from either a liberal or non-liberal baseline since there will be greater overall demand for placards.

Which baseline does the principle of abstraction recommend? The attempt to answer this question reveals the indeterminacy of the principle. First, it might seem that the principle of abstraction favours the illiberal baseline. If the appropriate baseline is one which is as sensitive as possible to the de facto preferences and plans of individuals, then, since most people are not interested in political protest, the illiberal baseline seems best. After all, it is most sensitive to the preferences of the majority. Of course, the rejoinder might be made that the illiberal baseline is less sensitive to the preferences of political activists and slanderers. This is true but it is equally true that a liberal baseline is less sensitive to the plans of the majority than an illiberal baseline. The principle of abstraction seems therefore to be indeterminate as between a liberal and illiberal baseline. Or at least it is indeterminate if we interpret the sensitivity to preferences required by the principle to mean 'supportive of preferences'. In this sense of sensitivity, a baseline is more sensitive to given preferences if it makes it easier to implement those preferences than other baselines. This is a natural interpretation of the requirement of sensitivity but perhaps Dworkin has a different sense in mind.

He might contend that sensitivity should be understood as 'responsive to preferences'. A baseline would be more sensitive to preferences in this sense if it permitted all preferences to play a role in influencing the price of goods in the auction. On this construal of sensitivity, the principle of abstraction would rule out the illiberal baseline on the ground that some preferences, namely preferences to engage in political protest, are denied an equal role in influencing the price of placards. An auction which measures true opportunity costs, it might be argued, should be sensitive to the discrete plans and preferences of everyone. This rejoinder does not, however, solve the indeterminacy problem in a way that helps Dworkin. Consider the non-liberal baseline which permits slander. This baseline is arguably more responsive to the preferences of the population than the liberal baseline precisely because it permits every person's preferences, including the preferences of slanderers, to influence the price of placards. This suggests that the principle of abstraction does not uniquely favour a liberal baseline. Either the principle of abstraction, on the 'responsive' construal of sensitivity, is indeterminate between the liberal and non-liberal baselines or it actually favours the non-liberal baseline. In the former case, the constitutive bridge strategy fails because it does not adequately discriminate between liberal and non-liberal baselines. In the latter case, the constitutive bridge strategy fails because it does not provide a basis for inclusion of the constraints (e.g. constraints against slander) which are part of a recognizably liberal conception of liberty. If true opportunity costs are measured by an auction which permits individuals to use their resources to slander one another then equality of resources comes closer to embracing a conception of liberty as licence and hence is unattractive.

The indeterminacy of the principle of abstraction is an embarrassment for the constitutive bridge strategy. In order to eliminate the troublesome indeterminacy, it is necessary either to add more substantive content to the principle of abstraction itself or to invoke supplementary considerations via other principles which forestall the awkward conclusion we have reached. The supplementary principles (e.g. the principles of independence, security, and authenticity) which are part of the full version of the constitutive bridge strategy may bring us closer to a suitably liberal baseline. However, Dworkin cannot appeal to these principles without compromising the integrity of the constitutive bridge. As we shall now see, the supplementary principles only add needed substantive content because they are predicated upon generalizations about the character of human interests of the very sort which are officially eschewed by the constitutive bridge strategy. In effect, any workable version of the constitutive bridge strategy reduces to a version of the interest strategy.

THE HIDDEN INTEREST STRATEGY IN THE CONSTITUTIVE BRIDGE STRATEGY

The commitment to liberty exhibited in the constitutive bridge strategy is purportedly not predicated on an account of how certain 'liberties are instrumentally connected to the satisfaction of interests' (Dworkin 1987: 13). Indeed, the bridge strategy is supposedly distinguished from the interest strategy precisely because the former, unlike the latter, does not make a commitment to individual liberty dependent on disputes about how human interests are best served by liberty. Dworkin's claim that equality of resources provides a unique accommodation of liberty within the ideal of equality depends on establishing the success and distinctiveness of the bridge argument. With this in mind, we now turn to the second general objection to Dworkin's attempt to find a place for liberty within equality of resources. This is that any conception of liberty embraced by equality of resources is, in fact, traceable to some kind of account of how particular liberties serve fundamental human interests. No particular conception of liberty can be associated with the envy test. In effect, this means that to the degree that the constitutive bridge strategy can be made to function, it depends on considerations which are not substantively distinct from the interest strategy. The uniqueness of the constitutive bridge strategy is thus brought into question. We can explore this claim by considering more closely the character of some of the principles upon which the bridge strategy depends.

We have seen how the conception of sensitivity embedded in the principle of abstraction is not sufficient to ground a liberal conception of liberty. At best, it gets us part way to a liberal baseline. This would be an impressive achievement if the plausibility of the principle is independent of generalizations about the connection between liberty and human interests. Yet the commitment to liberty expressed in even the principle of abstraction is naturally understood as reflecting assumptions about people's most fundamental interests. For instance, making resources available to individuals in their most abstract form only makes sense if we assume that most people are able to make productive use of resources in that form. We assume, for instance, that individuals will be better able to lead genuinely good lives if they are free to tailor resources to their own plans and projects. It seems a good idea to make resources sensitive to the discrete plans of individuals because it is plausible to suppose that such sensitivity is conducive to leading a good life. In this respect, the principle of abstraction reflects the supposition that most individuals are best able to make decisions about what plans they should pursue and thus should be free to determine how to lead their personal life. In other words, extensive liberty over matters of great personal concern advances our interest in leading a good life. Note, however, that there is an important range of cases in which this supposition about the interest we have in personal liberty does not hold. For instance, the plausibility of the principle of abstraction diminishes when it is applied to the situation of very young children. Whereas it is plausible to suppose that adults will generally fare better if they are at liberty to determine their own bedtime, young children's interests are not served by extending the same liberty to them. The principle of abstraction is less attractive in the case of children precisely because the implicit assumptions about how human interests are served by sensitivity to the discrete plans of individuals do not hold in that case. All this suggests, however, that the extension to individuals of extensive liberty in matters of great personal concern secured by the principle of abstraction presupposes the instrumental connection between liberty and our interest in leading a good life. So even in the principle of abstraction, we can detect elements of the interest strategy.

The possibility of distinguishing a successful version of the constitutive bridge strategy from the interest strategy becomes even more remote when we consider some of the other principles that help define the baseline. Consider, for example, the rationales behind the principle of security and the principle of authenticity. Dworkin says that the principle of security places limits on individual liberty that are 'necessary to provide people with enough physical security and enough control over their property to allow them to make and carry out plans and projects' (Dworkin 1987: 26). This reflects a view about how human interests are served by constraints on action. Individuals are denied the freedom to engage in theft and assault because such liberty is detrimental to the possibility of others leading good lives. Moreover, being free to assault someone cannot be characterized as instrumentally important in leading a good life. Limiting liberty by prohibiting such behaviour is consistent with showing concern for each person's interest in leading a good life. A similar analysis applies to the rationale for the principle of authenticity. This principle adds to the conception of liberty the requirement that individuals enjoy 'freedom to engage in activities crucial to forming and reviewing the convictions, commitments, associations, projects and tastes that they bring to the auction' (Dworkin 1987: 35). The importance that attaches to the provision of these liberties is clearly traceable to the instrumental role they play in ensuring that individuals are able to lead a good life. Protecting these liberties is justified because our present convictions about the good may be mistaken and thus we have an interest in securing the conditions most conducive to rational revision of our convictions. The principle of authenticity makes sense because it responds to assumptions about our interests—e.g. that we have an interest in leading a life which is, in fact, good and our convictions about the good are fallible.

Similar remarks apply to the principle of independence which is invoked to explain, in part, how certain constraints on liberty form part of a liberal baseline. Dworkin says that the principle of independence 'checks the principle of abstraction by endorsing baseline constraints necessary to protect people who are the objects of systematic prejudice from suffering any serious or pervasive disadvantage from that prejudice' (Dworkin 1987: 36–7). This principle, or something like it, might provide the basis for solving the problem described above about the principle of abstraction furnishing a possible warrant for the endorsement of a non-liberal baseline. The principle of independence might be invoked in order to justify a prohibition on slander. The auction will be fairer, perhaps, if individuals are protected from the disadvantages which some would suffer if slander were permitted. But on what basis can we accept such a claim? Surely the most natural rationale involves distinguishing between the different kinds of human interests which are served by different kinds of speech. For example, we accept constraints against slander but not against free political speech because we suppose that whereas crucial human interests are better served by free political discourse than by political censorship, the liberty to slander serves, at best, a trivial interest of the slanderer while threatening to undermine a fundamental interest we have in not being slandered.

The principles of security, authenticity, and independence might help to reduce the fatal indeterminacy of the principle of abstraction. Perhaps these principles can together provide the justification for selection of a liberal baseline for equality of resources. Yet when we reflect on the considerations which make acceptance of these principles plausible, we find that we must appeal to generalizations about the relative importance of different liberties to various human interests. This interpretation of the principles of the constitutive bridge strategy is also consistent with the, perhaps unguarded, characterization of the value of liberty with which Dworkin begins his discussion of the place of liberty: 'liberty seems valuable to us only because of the consequences we think it does have for people: we think lives led under circumstances of liberty are better lives just for that reason' (Dworkin 1987: 2). Of course if, as I have suggested, the principles that Dworkin uses to fix the baseline of equality of resources derive their plausibility from the instrumental relationship of different liberties to individual interests, then the bridge strategy cannot offer a deeper defence of a conception of liberty than other egalitarian theories. On my analysis then, Dworkin's constitutive bridge strategy is caught on the horns of a dilemma. Either the strategy fails in its own right because the principle of abstraction does not provide a sound bridge to a liberal conception of liberty. Or the strategy cannot be distinguished in any substantive way from the interest strategy because the only way to identify the liberties that individuals should enjoy in the auction setting is through an appeal to the instrumental importance of certain liberties. In either case, we have no reason to believe that equality of resources supplies a special basis for affirming the importance of the protection of basic liberties from an egalitarian perspective.

It is true that some conception of liberty must be built into the auction which defines equality of resources. However, this does not mean that basic liberties are best defended by acceptance of equality of resources. Indeed, if the argument of this chapter is correct then egalitarians derive no special advantages in securing a place for liberty within equality by adopting equality of resources. As we have seen, even if it can be made to work, the constitutive bridge strategy is extraordinarily complex and cumbersome. As such, it does not compare favourably with a suitably developed version of the interest strategy. The latter provides a much more natural and elegant accommodation of liberty rights than the former. The appeal of the constitutive bridge strategy is that it purports to provide a way of securing a place for liberty within equality without directly broaching controversial claims about the relationship between human interests and liberty. In fact, however, the bridge strategy provides a needlessly circuitous route for defending liberties and it cannot be divorced from the potentially thorny issues surrounding the connection between human interests and liberty. Hiding this connection in a series of supplementary principles does not make it go away. The interest strategy is both simpler and, in a sense, more honest, because it addresses these issues directly. This does not jeopardize the place of liberty within equality. Egalitarians can confidently defend important liberty rights but they must be prepared to broach problems about the relationship between liberty and human interests.

7

Neutrality or Tolerance?

A CHARACTERISTIC feature of modern liberalism is that the state must exhibit a kind of impartiality towards different conceptions of the good. It must neither seek to promote directly or to favour systematically any comprehensive ideal of the good life nor should it adopt policies which have as their aim the elimination or discouragement of lifestyles which are, according to popular sentiment, deviant or degenerate. Instead, the state must respect the fact that its citizens have chosen to adopt and pursue diverse conceptions of the good.[1] In contemporary discussions, this ideal is generally identified as liberal neutrality. The idea that the state must be neutral with respect to the conceptions of the good held by its citizens is often linked to liberalism's traditional commitment to tolerance. Indeed, the terms tolerance and neutrality are sometimes used interchangeably (Waldron 1993: 144). I shall argue, however, that an important distinction can be drawn between liberal neutrality and liberal tolerance. Both ideals reflect certain anti-perfectionist impulses in liberalism. But tolerance is less comprehensively anti-perfectionist and it better fits the egalitarian foundations of modern liberalism than neutrality.

Perfectionism[2] is the view that the distribution of resources and opportunities in a community can properly be influenced by judgements made by the state about the value of different

---

[1] There is an important caveat to this claim. It is the legitimate prerogative of the state to prohibit or discourage conceptions of the good which are inconsistent with the principles of justice accepted by the state. For instance, a liberal egalitarian state may seek to eradicate racist conceptions of the good which treat some races with contempt. The conceptions of the good to which the state adopts a stance of neutrality or toleration must be consistent with justice (Dworkin 1991: 112; Rawls 1993: 195–6).

[2] Here I am a treating perfectionism only as a principle of political morality and not as a comprehensive moral theory. For an attempt to construct and defend a wholly perfectionist moral theory see Hurka (1993).

conceptions of the good.[3] Liberalism is frequently portrayed as hostile to perfectionism because perfectionism seems inconsistent with allowing individuals to decide for themselves what kind of life is worth leading. Individuals should be free to develop and pursue their own convictions without the participation of the state in the evaluation, enforcement, or advocacy of particular ideals about what constitutes human excellence. Moreover, liberals usually associate perfectionism with intolerance and the coercive repression of the practices deemed by popular sentiment to be deviant or offensive to the values of the community. Some familiar examples of perfectionism which lead to the association of perfectionism and intolerance include legal prohibition of homosexual activity, legally mandated school prayer in public schools, and moralistically inspired censorship of pornography.[4] Measures like these usually depend for their justification on a claim (often a dubious one) about the ethical character and worth of different practices. Thus homosexuality is reviled as a degenerate and defective way of life that is inconsistent with widely held community values. Prayer, by contrast, is depicted as a virtuous activity that helps to foster the ethical integrity of the community.

In recent years, liberals have sought to bolster their opposition to measures aimed at the enforcement of 'personal morality' by appeal to neutrality. Neutrality seems to provide a principled objection to such policies because it imposes a general prohibition on appealing to perfectionist considerations as a

[3] Conceptions of the good are views about the nature and constitutive elements of a valuable life. Conceptions of the good may be comprehensive or partial. A comprehensive conception of the good attempts to delineate a complete account of the sources and nature of a good life. A partial conception of the good merely identifies particular activities or projects that contribute to the realization of human excellence. Commitment to a religion can constitute a comprehensive conception of the good since adoption of a faith is sometimes viewed as grounding the meaning of a person's entire life. The idea that the appreciation of fine music is a valuable human activity is likely to constitute only a partial conception of the good. Aesthetic appreciation is a possible component in a good life but it does not constitute a full account of the good life.

[4] Liberals can consistently support some restrictions on pornography on other grounds. Most liberals are prepared to accept restrictions on pornography, including censorship, if it can be established that pornography leads to demonstrable harm (e.g. in the form of violence against women). Similarly, as Rae Langton (Langton 1990) argues, liberals must also take seriously the idea that restriction of pornography might be justified on the ground that the presence of pornography in the community undermines the equality rights of women.

legitimate basis for legislation. The ideal of neutrality thus seems attractive because it can provide a principled rationale for some of liberalism's most distinctive commitments. Embracing neutrality has, however, generated significant tensions within liberal theory. First, neutrality is an implausible principle if billed as the fundamental principle upon which liberalism is predicated. It is more credibly viewed as a derivative and perhaps contingent commitment (Kymlicka 1989b: 903). Yet many of the attempts to justify liberalism's commitment to neutrality seem unsatisfactory. Thus although neutrality may serve some liberal purposes well, it is an ideal with elusive theoretical foundations. Second, adoption of neutrality seems inconsistent with other important liberal commitments. A lot of state activity that liberals have traditionally endorsed is difficult to reconcile with neutrality. Specifically, it seems difficult to justify government policies and programmes which aim at preserving and enriching the artistic and cultural character of communities without appeal to perfectionist considerations of the sort forbidden by neutrality.

In this chapter, I examine Dworkin's influential contributions to this debate. I believe that elements of Dworkin's theory can be developed to construct an account of the appropriate relationship of the state to the good. As it stands, however, Dworkin conflates two distinct ideals. Specifically, he equivocates between an ideal of liberal neutrality and an ideal of liberal tolerance.[5]

The argument of the chapter is developed in stages. First, I substantiate the claim that Dworkin's theory exhibits a tension between two conflicting conceptions of the appropriate stance of the state vis-à-vis different views of the good. I clarify the sense in which an ideal of neutrality can be attributed to Dworkin and I distinguish different varieties of perfectionism in order to explain the ideal of liberal tolerance more adequately.

[5] In describing the liberal view of the appropriate relationship of the state to different conceptions of the good, Dworkin sometimes speaks of liberalism's commitment to neutrality (e.g. Dworkin 1985: 191–3, 205; 1987: 30; 1991: 41, 110–11, 118), sometimes of liberalism's commitment to tolerance (e.g. Dworkin 1985: 185–7, 205; 1989: 479–85, 487, 491; 1991: 10, 41, 113–17), and sometimes to liberalism's opposition to the enforcement of personal morality (e.g. Dworkin 1985: 206, 347–9; 1987: 29–31). The ideals of neutrality and tolerance are different but both oppose the enforcement of personal morality. So there is no distinct third ideal which might be attributed to Dworkin.

Second, I consider the connection between the egalitarianism upon which Dworkin's liberalism is predicated and the ideals of neutrality and tolerance I have distinguished. Dworkin's egalitarian framework is, prima facie, compatible with the justification of a wide array of perfectionist policies. This compatibility affects the sorts of arguments Dworkin can marshal in support of neutrality or tolerance. Specifically, it means that he must argue indirectly for neutrality or tolerance by arguing against perfectionism. Third, I explain and evaluate the three principal anti-perfectionist arguments that Dworkin uses to defend his ambiguous liberal position. These arguments provide the key both to understanding how the perfectionist tendencies of egalitarianism can be resisted and to assessing the relative merits of tolerance and neutrality. Ultimately, I argue that the best reconstruction of Dworkin's liberalism is one which rejects the comprehensively anti-perfectionist ideal of liberal neutrality. Liberal tolerance is a more attractive ideal and is more compatible with the egalitarianism that animates much modern liberalism.

LIBERAL NEUTRALITY

Many critics of liberalism assume that liberalism's most fundamental commitment must be to a principle of neutrality. While some liberal theorists have explicitly embraced this position (e.g. Ackerman 1980; Lamore 1987), Dworkin's endorsement of neutrality is contingent on its compatibility with equality.[6] This is not to suggest that Dworkin views neutrality as an unimportant element of liberal doctrine. Rather, it means that neutrality derives its importance from its putative connection to and compatibility with the best interpretation of fundamental equality. Dworkin's theory is therefore not vulnerable to the charge that it assigns axiomatic status to a principle of neutrality and is somehow incoherent or implausible on that account. But what

[6] In some of his work—e.g. in his influential essay 'Liberalism' (Dworkin 1985: 181–204)—Dworkin himself may have been guilty of encouraging the interpretation of liberalism that treats neutrality as the basic premiss of liberal political morality. In that essay there was a tendency to conflate equality and neutrality but in other work Dworkin (Dworkin 1985: 205–13) has refined and revised his view of the place of neutrality in liberalism.

exactly does Dworkin's conception of liberal neutrality consist in?

Kymlicka has distinguished two versions of the ideal of liberal neutrality and this distinction provides a useful framework for illuminating Dworkin's interpretation of neutrality (Kymlicka 1989b: 883–4; see also Rawls 1993: 191–4; Raz 1986: 111–62; Waldron 1993: 149–51). First, neutrality might be understood as imposing the requirement that government action must have an equal impact on all conceptions of the good. That is, the consequences of state activity must be the same for all conceptions of the good. Kymlicka labels this 'consequential neutrality'. Second, neutrality can be understood as imposing a restriction on the kind of rationale the state may employ in the justification of policies. Specifically, the state is prohibited from justifying policies by appeal to any kind of perfectionist judgements. It must refrain from taking a stand on the comparative value of different conceptions of the good when formulating public policy and determining the allocation of resources. Kymlicka calls this 'justificatory neutrality'.

Dworkin does not endorse consequential neutrality. Consequential neutrality is inconsistent with the principles of individual responsibility and fairness found at the heart of Dworkin's egalitarianism. A state that embraced consequential neutrality would have to aim at making each person's conception of the good equally easy to implement, irrespective of the costs to others that this might entail. This 'equally easy' form of neutrality is inconsistent with Dworkin's interpretation of equality because it may require the unfair subsidization of expensive tastes. As we have seen, equality of resources insists that responsible individuals pay the full price of the lives they choose to lead. Consequently, it aims at a form of neutrality in which 'the resources people have available, with which to pursue their plans or projects or way of life, be fixed by the costs of their having these to others, rather than by any collective judgement about the comparative importance of people or comparative worth of projects or personal moralities' (Dworkin 1987: 30; see also 1989: 481–3; and 1991: 117). Dworkin believes that a market, operating from a position of equal initial purchasing power, provides the best way of fairly measuring the relevant costs. The state must, therefore, leave the assessment of different conceptions of the good entirely to the economic and cultural market place. A state policy in which the success or failure of different views of the good depends completely on the choices individuals make in the market place will not have the same impact on all conceptions of the good. Some conceptions will gain adherents and others will lose; some projects will be easy to pursue; others will be impossibly expensive. All this indicates that the form of neutrality endorsed by Dworkin cannot be consequential neutrality.

The foregoing considerations indicate that one important strand of Dworkin's interpretation of equality commits him to acceptance of a form of justificatory neutrality. We can label this the market model of neutrality. The state is explicitly prohibited from implementing policies that stem from perfectionist judgements. Perfectionist-inspired polices are objectionable partly because they distort the true costs of conceptions of the good and provide some individuals, in effect, with an unfair share of resources. In a state in which resource allocation is guided by perfectionist judgements those whose conceptions of the good are favoured by the state will have a greater than equal share of resources devoted to their lives. Moreover, because the market can be relied upon to determine accurately and fairly the degree of support that different elements of a culture can lay claim to, there is no need for any state support of culture. On the market model of neutrality, the success or failure of different elements of society's culture should depend entirely on how different elements fare in free competition in non-state forums.

STATE SUPPORT FOR ART AND CULTURE

There is another dimension of Dworkin's work which leads to a different conclusion about the adequacy of the market model of neutrality. The roots of this interpretation lie in Dworkin's contention that the liberal state may provide support for cultural institutions, the arts, and other cultural projects when the market fails to support such valuable elements of a community's life adequately. In arguing for the legitimacy of state support of the arts, Dworkin's strategy involves emphasizing the importance of preserving a rich, innovative, and diverse cultural structure through which citizens can formulate, revise, and critically examine their own conceptions of the good. On this view, a rich cultural structure is portrayed as part and parcel of the language citizens employ in articulating and developing a conception of the good. Having secure access to the benefits of a genuinely rich culture can contribute significantly to the possibility of leading a good life. Since the market may not always succeed in establishing or maintaining a vibrant culture, the state may legitimately employ its resources to subsidize valuable elements of culture which the market does not sustain. The precise rationale for this support is complex, and underdeveloped. It derives partly from a direct demand of justice for the protection of the interests that future generations have in their cultural heritage. 'We inherited a cultural structure, and we have some duty, out of simple justice, to leave that structure at least as rich as we found it' (Dworkin 1985: 233). But Dworkin also makes clear that citizens in existing communities have a compelling interest in the protection and provision of a rich and vibrant cultural environment. This view of the state's responsibility for the social and cultural environment fits better with what I will call an ideal of 'liberal tolerance'—which I explain below—rather than a view of neutrality.

Dworkin's recognition of the legitimacy of state support of culture cannot be squared with the market model of neutrality. There are two reasons for this. First, and most obviously, state subsidy of elements of culture involves tampering with the market-derived cultural framework. The aspects of culture identified by the state as worthy of support receive resources that the market, left to its own devices, will not furnish. This is at odds with the conception of neutrality which holds that unfettered market mechanisms can be relied upon to determine fairly the character of a community's culture. It might be thought that the sort of subsidization of culture viewed as legitimate by Dworkin could, in fact, be justified on grounds internal to the market model of neutrality by invoking the economic theory of market failure. For instance, it might be suggested that because the provision of culture through the market faces problems of free riding, exclusive reliance on market mechanisms may lead to an economically sub-optimal provision of culture. The suggestion here is that we can view subsidized elements of the culture as some variety of public good that is under-supplied by the ordinary operation of the market. If the state can accurately calculate the 'true market demand' for various elements of culture then it may subsidize the arts without recourse to perfectionist judgements. In this way we can view state support of the arts as a 'merely tactical solution to a technical problem' (Dworkin 1985: 225).

Yet Dworkin explicitly rejects this market-friendly solution for a number of reasons.[7] The most fundamental obstacle to this approach is that it depends on an incoherent assumption, namely that we can identify the market demand there might be for a culture with a certain character independently of the influence that culture has in shaping the demand. 'The intellectual culture of a community exerts such a profound influence over the preferences and values of its members that the question of whether and how much they would prefer a different culture to the one they currently have becomes at best deeply mysterious' (Dworkin 1985: 227). So because the cultural structure within which our deliberations about what is valuable take place can have a dramatic impact on those deliberations, we cannot expect a meaningful answer to the technical economic question posed by the public goods approach about what sort of culture the community really wants.

The second reason that Dworkin's endorsement of cultural subsidies marks a retreat from the market model of neutrality is that any state engaged in the support of culture along the lines envisioned by Dworkin will have to make judgements about which types of cultural pursuits and enterprises are worthy of support and which are not. This entails making judgements about the comparative worth of the different projects and cul-

---

[7] In addition to the incoherence problem that I discuss, Dworkin identifies two other but less crucial difficulties with the public goods argument. First, there is a problem of 'time lag'. Unlike many other public goods, it may take a very long time before the benefits of the supply of culture are realized by the public. Consequently, Dworkin thinks we 'cannot be confident that those who will pay the cost will reap the benefit' (Dworkin 1985: 226). Second, there is a problem of 'indeterminacy' that compounds the time lag problem. The difficulty is that our judgements about how support of culture will affect the lives of members of the community are too indeterminate. 'If we cannot predict what impact a public program will have on people's lives in the future, how can we justify that program as helping to give them what they really want?' (Dworkin 1985: 226).

tural enterprises for which the state might provide some kind of support. It is important to emphasize here that Dworkin does not think that state subsidy should be aimed merely at preserving the cultural status quo no matter what its character. Rather the objective of state action is to preserve and promote a '*rich* cultural structure, one that multiplies distinct possibilities or opportunities of *value*' (Dworkin 1985: 229, my emphasis). A rich cultural structure presents options that are 'innovative' and 'diverse' and display 'complexity and depth' (Dworkin 1985: 229). Determining which elements of culture present genuine opportunities of value in this sense implicates the state in judgements about what constitutes 'human excellence in various forms of culture' (Rawls 1971: 25).

Consider, for instance, a community in which two different elements of the culture—roller derby and opera—cannot survive without government assistance. Roller derby fans believe that roller derby is entertaining and exciting. Moreover, they think that opera is boring and pretentious. They regret that the market cannot sustain what they view as a valuable element of the culture but they are not concerned about the possible loss of opera. (Perhaps roller derby fans believe that the pleasures afforded by their sport are superior to the inaccessible aesthetic challenges posed by opera.) Opera fans, by contrast, think that roller derby is a shallow, meaningless diversion. For them, opera, not roller derby, is the valuable feature of the culture threatened by the market. The government in this community faces the question of whether it can justify furnishing a subsidy to either opera or roller derby. Assume that it cannot afford to support both. If the government is to employ Dworkin's strategy in this instance, then it must make some judgement about the depth, complexity, and innovative qualities displayed respectively by roller derby and opera. If it concludes, as Dworkin implies that it can, that a subsidy to opera is warranted because of its contribution to the richness of the cultural structure then the state will have made a judgement, along some publicly disputed dimension of value, about the comparative worth of opera and roller derby. The state is saying, in effect, that opera contributes more to the richness of the cultural structure than does roller derby or that opera provides a distinct opportunity of value whereas roller derby does not. Such judgements clearly are not neutral with respect to different conceptions of cultural excellence.

This shows that the implementation of Dworkin's strategy must be predicated on accepting the legitimacy of at least a limited range of perfectionist considerations. If this were not so the injunction to identify and support 'distinct opportunities of value' would be pointless. Why should the state look for *valuable* opportunities unless the relative value of opportunities is actually relevant to determining how state resources should be allocated? So if, as Dworkin clearly maintains, a legitimate aim of state policy is the maintenance of a rich and diverse cultural environment then the state will have to try determine which projects etc. are actually likely to contribute to realization of this aim. Yet the making and implementation of such judgements by the state is precisely what is prohibited by the market model of neutrality.[8] In discharging its responsibility to ensure that citizens have a sufficiently rich repertoire of genuinely valuable options in deciding how to lead their lives, the state must be prepared to assess the adequacy of the options supplied by the market. And it will have to make judgements about the relative value of the different options it might choose to support. In more recent work, Dworkin seems more prepared to accept this point directly. He notes that fixing the parameters within which individuals decide how to lead their lives may require 'collective decisions about which lives to promote or recommend as better, particularly when popular culture presses the other way and so provides too few examples of these lives' (Dworkin 1991: 85 n. 44).[9]

---

[8] In one passage, Dworkin makes a proposal that might seem to mitigate the apparent tension between his commitment to the market and his commitment to support of the arts. He suggests a scheme for providing support to the arts in which individuals are entitled to tax exemptions for the contributions they make to cultural projects. In this way, individual citizens and not the state determine how much support various projects receive (Dworkin 1985: 233; see also Kymlicka 1989a: 81). But even if such a strategy succeeded in realizing the goal of securing a rich and diverse cultural structure—and Dworkin explicitly concedes that it may not be sufficient—the state would still be implicated in market-tampering perfectionist judgements. The state would have to decide which kinds of projects (e.g. opera but not roller derby) qualified for the programme of tax exemptions. And such decisions will, if they are to be guided by the criteria of Dworkin's strategy, be predicated on judgements about the value of different options.

[9] There are a number of very complex questions about the procedures a state may

It should now be clear how Dworkin's position on the relationship between the state and the good is ambiguous. On the
one hand, he argues that state policies which depend on state
judgements about the relative merit of different conceptions of
the good and result in intervention in the market-derived culture
must be rejected. On the other hand, he thinks a liberal state can
be justified in supporting the arts and other valuable elements of
a culture even though such support inevitably implicates the
state in perfectionist judgements and interference in the cultural
market place. That there are two conceptions of the appropriate
relationship between the state and the good exhibited in
Dworkin's theory reflects the general tension in liberal theory I
noted above. The first conception leaves all judgements about
the good to the market place. It can be unproblematically identified with the market model of neutrality. The second conception is a little more difficult to characterize precisely. It clearly
holds that some perfectionist activity by the state may be
legitimate. But it would be a gross misrepresentation of
Dworkin's views to suggest that under this conception the state
is at liberty to pursue any form of perfectionism which it believes will improve the social and cultural environment of the
community. This second conception, once it is further clarified,
may be identified as incorporating an ideal of liberal tolerance.
This is a controversial claim since it implies that the apparently
conflicting ideals of toleration and perfectionism can be recon-
ciled. In my view, however, the supposed conflict between perfectionism and toleration is somewhat illusory. In order to
substantiate this suggestion it is necessary to examine the idea of
perfectionism more closely.

employ in rendering these decisions which go to the heart of democratic theory. For
instance, what role should democratic majorities and elites have in making such
judgements? What procedures should be employed in determining how funds are
allocated to the arts? Dworkin does not explore these issues in any detail beyond
insisting that the majority cannot simply use the state to create the ethical or cultural
environment it prefers. After all, part of the rationale for state support of the arts is
that valuable options are not sufficiently supported by the majority in the first place.
Nonetheless, Dworkin does not suggest that elites should have a free hand in these
matters. I will not investigate any of the questions relating to the specific design of
the procedures appropriate to limited state perfectionism. Instead, I will focus on the
theoretically prior question of whether any form of state perfectionism is compatible
with egalitarian justice.

VARIETIES OF PERFECTIONISM

So far, I have employed only a general characterization of perfectionism. However, a number of distinct types of perfectionism can be identified. First, *prohibitive perfectionism* employs the coercive apparatus of the state to punish, through the application of legal sanctions, individuals who engage in activities which are inconsistent with the views of the good endorsed or deemed acceptable by the state. The legal prohibition of homosexual activity is a good example of prohibitive perfectionism. Second, *mandatory perfectionism* uses the coercive apparatus of the state to require individuals to participate actively in practices associated with a conception of the good favoured by the state. A policy of mandatory school prayer is an example of mandatory perfectionism. Third, *educative perfectionism* uses state resources in the non-coercive support of activities or practices which the state deems valuable and in the non-coercive discouragement of activities or practices which the state believes lack value. Government subsidy of the arts is a possible example of educative perfectionism as is government advertising about the dangers of smoking.

Two different varieties of educative perfectionism may further be identified. One focuses narrowly on the direct promotion of specific conceptions of the good. The other focuses more generally on the provision of an environment conducive to effective rational reflection on the worth of a variety of ends. *Sectarian educative perfectionism* seeks to secure the success of particular views of the good. The direct purpose of sectarian educative perfectionism is to win adherents to a particular view of the good championed by the state. A state that tried to convert its citizens to Christianity by heavily subsidizing the televising of Christian evangelists would be engaged in sectarian educative perfectionism. (Similarly, a state that tried to convert its citizens into dedicated devotees of opera by subsidizing opera heavily would be engaged in sectarian educative perfectionism.) By contrast, *pluralistic educative perfectionism* has a different rationale and objective.[10] It aims at securing an environment conducive to

---

[10] The contrast between pluralistic educative perfectionism and sectarian educative perfectionism corresponds roughly to a distinction drawn but not fully elaborated by Dworkin between the structural aspects of culture and the particular content

independent deliberation about the good partly by ensuring that the deliberative context includes a rich repertoire of genuinely valuable options. Diversity is promoted not for diversity's sake nor in the hope that a particular view of the good will be embraced by citizens but because a rich intellectual and cultural environment plays an indispensable role in facilitating effective deliberation about the good. It is important to stress, however, that pluralistic educative perfectionism is not indifferent to the actual value of the options it identifies as worthy of support. It is a genuine, albeit mild, form of perfectionism because it does permit the state to make judgements about the value of different options—e.g. that some options contribute the richness of the culture because they are appropriately deep, complex, and innovative.[11] However, the rationale for support of these options lies principally in the instrumental role their provision plays in

of culture (Dworkin 1985: 229). Dworkin argues that the state should focus its efforts broadly on promoting the general richness of the cultural structure and should endeavour to avoid narrowly partisan attention to particular projects or institutions. (This does not mean, of course, that specific institutions and projects cannot obtain government support.) Sectarian educative perfectionism does aim at securing a culture with a particular content. It is similar in aim to both mandatory and prohibitive perfectionism because the state's explicit objective is to authoritatively fix a particular conception of the good. However, whereas mandatory and prohibitive perfectionism rely on coercion, sectarian educative perfectionism seeks to authoritatively fix ends through a form of persuasion. Pluralistic educative perfectionism, by contrast, is concerned with the broader, structural features of culture such as the depth and variety of valuable options that a community's culture has to offer.

[11] Notice that the value judgements permitted by pluralistic educative perfectionism will not be endorsed by all citizens of the community. For instance, many members of the Old Order of Amish probably reject the contention that a rich cultural structure is one that 'multiplies distinct possibilities or opportunities of value' (Dworkin 1985: 229). After all, the conception of the good espoused by the Amish suggests that we should insulate ourselves from the very diversity that Dworkin believes the state should promote. This confirms my claim that Dworkin's argument for support of the arts is not compatible with neutrality. Note also that pluralistic educative perfectionism does make certain assumptions about the nature of deliberation about the good. The basic idea is that effective deliberation cannot take place in the absence of a reasonable degree of pluralism. We are in a better position to deliberate about the sort of life that is worth leading by individuals if we have access and exposure to a variety of potentially valuable activities and practices through a living culture. We learn about how we might lead our lives well partly by exploring the opportunities of value presented by our culture. This understanding of the social context of deliberation is accepted by a wide range of theorists. For instance, Kymlicka relies heavily upon it in defending his theory of minority rights and he notes that Taylor, Raz and Rawls all share a similar view (Kymlicka 1989a: 79–82).

securing the sort of cultural structure that is most conducive to individuals making well-informed, autonomous choices about the sorts of lives they wish to lead. Government subsidy of public libraries is plausibly construed as an instance of pluralistic educative perfectionism.

LIBERAL TOLERANCE

With these distinctions in mind, we can now return to the ideal of liberal tolerance which I claim can be detected in Dworkin's work.[12] Liberal tolerance can be defined in a way parallel to the definition of liberal neutrality. Liberal tolerance places restrictions on the rationale that can be employed to justify state policy and on the means available to the state in pursuit of its aims. Specifically, it prohibits reliance on all the forms of perfectionism I have identified except pluralistic educative perfectionism. However, unlike the market model of neutrality, the ideal of tolerance is sensitive to the fact that market forces may not always work to produce the circumstances most conducive to rational deliberation about the good. Where the cultural market place fails to supply a sufficiently rich or distortion-free context of deliberation, liberal tolerance allows the state to engage in pluralistic educative perfectionism. That is, it may choose to support valuable projects and institutions that are likely to contribute positively to the social and cultural context in which individuals develop and revise their views of the good. Note that this ideal of liberal tolerance only recognizes the possible legitimacy of limited state perfectionism. It does not suppose that the context of deliberation secured in the absence of state activity is necessarily defective. The degree to which the state should exercise its prerogative to influence and augment the circumstances

---

[12] I do not believe that the view of liberal tolerance which I attribute to Dworkin is a feature only of his recent writings. It is true that in recent work (Dworkin 1991) Dworkin seems more directly sympathetic to some mild form of perfectionism. However, I believe this perfectionist streak is consistent with his views on the legitimacy of state support of the arts which were articulated much earlier (Dworkin 1981). Similarly, Dworkin continues to endorse a market-driven conception of distributive justice (equality of resources) which provides the basis of attributing a market model of neutrality to him. Dworkin has not sufficiently recognized the deep tensions between the perfectionist and neutralist aspects of his work.

of deliberation will no doubt vary a good deal. Judgements about which elements of culture are valuable and merit support will often be difficult to make and sometimes will be controversial. So while the state has a responsibility to ensure that the context of deliberation is sufficiently rich, this does not mean that the state must necessarily pursue perfectionist policies.

Despite the fact that a type of perfectionist judgement is compatible with this conception, I think it may still legitimately be viewed as embodying a characteristically liberal ideal of toleration. After all, it does not aim at the eradication of any comprehensive view of the good. Rather, it permits state action designed to secure the background cultural, intellectual, and informational conditions most conducive to autonomous choice of conceptions of the good. Moreover, because it rejects the legitimacy of mandatory and prohibitive perfectionism it is inconsistent with all the coercive measures the state might adopt in defence of (or assault upon) particular conceptions of the good held by some of its citizens. A tolerant state must permit individuals to lead their lives according to their own convictions about the good even if the state believes that some conceptions of the good have greater value than others. Liberal tolerance is therefore inconsistent with measures aimed at the enforcement of 'personal morality'. Finally, as I shall argue below, this ideal of tolerance is not open to the charge that it allows government to pursue policies that unfairly privilege particular conceptions of the good.

PERFECTIONIST STRAINS OF EGALITARIANISM

So far I have identified the two competing ideals of neutrality and tolerance which are present in Dworkin's theory. I now want to focus on the connection between these ideals and the underlying egalitarian framework of Dworkin's liberalism. Dworkin does not generally argue directly for either neutrality or toleration. Rather, he develops arguments against perfectionism which indirectly provide the rationale for the different constraints on state activity reflected in the two ideals. On this approach, egalitarian liberalism must embrace an ideal of neutrality or tolerance because the varieties of perfectionism which might otherwise seem attractive to a Dworkinian liberal are open to serious objection. The explanation of this indirect approach to the defence of familiar liberal doctrine is found in the egalitarianism which animates Dworkin's liberalism. The egalitarian thesis with which Dworkin begins does not lead inexorably to perfectionism but, at first glance, it seems to provide the resources with which to justify a wide range of state perfectionist measures.

Recall Dworkin's depiction of liberalism as an interpretation of the fundamental premiss that 'the interests of the members of the community matter and matter equally' (Dworkin 1983: 24). He claims that our most basic interest is in leading a good life— a life that is in fact good. Together these ideas suggest that the 'government must act to make the lives of those it governs better lives, and it must show equal concern for the life of each' (Dworkin 1987: 7). Dworkin believes that a crucial element of showing appropriate concern for everyone's interest in leading a good life involves providing everyone with an equal share of resources with which to lead their lives. However, the mere provision of resources is not sufficient to ensure that the lives individuals lead are good lives. The problem is that the convictions about the good that guide actions and determine how resources are employed can be mistaken. Individuals may, as a result of mistaken convictions, pursue lifestyles that fail to be good. But if the state has a responsibility in making the lives of its citizens good then surely it should implement policies that both prevent individuals from leading bad lives and direct them to lives that are, in fact, good. This argument establishes the prima-facie justifiability of a wide range of perfectionist policies. As Dworkin says, 'Why should people not use whatever political power they have in a democratic society to improve the lives they and others lead, according to their best judgement about what a good life is?' (Dworkin 1991: 41). These considerations do not show that the state is always justified in implementing policies which have as their aim the promotion of valuable lives and the elimination of defective conceptions of the good. The state must have compelling evidence that a given perfectionist policy will contribute to the leading of valuable lives. Nonetheless, all the types of perfectionism I have identified—prohibitive, mandatory, and the two varieties of educative perfectionism— could, in principle, be justified by appeal to the idea that government has a responsibility to improve the lives of its citizens. Thus, at a fairly abstract level, egalitarian liberalism is surprisingly compatible with perfectionism.

There are, however, severe obstacles to the justification of pervasive state perfectionism. Dworkin's advocacy of some variety of liberal anti-perfectionism depends on a series of arguments that purport to show why, despite the apparent affinity between the egalitarian ideal and perfectionism, there must be certain restrictions on what the state may do to ensure that citizens lead good lives. Liberal tolerance and liberal neutrality represent different interpretations of the degree to which the scope of state activity must be constrained.

Prima facie, the underlying egalitarian considerations would seem to provide support for liberal tolerance over justificatory neutrality. Whereas liberal tolerance is compatible with the forms of state perfectionism that aim at improving the circumstances in which citizens deliberate about the good life, the market model of neutrality forbids the demonstration of concern for citizens which involves any type of perfectionism. Liberal tolerance places fewer restrictions on what the state can do to improve the lives of its citizens. Because Dworkin does not distinguish clearly between neutrality and tolerance there is a problem determining just how far the anti-perfectionist arguments that he develops circumscribe the scope of state action. By solving this problem we can determine whether the anti-perfectionist arguments justify adopting the more restrictive ideal of liberal neutrality or are compatible with the modest perfectionism associated with liberal tolerance.

There are three principal arguments for the view that the activity of the state in promoting particular conceptions of the good must be highly circumscribed. I shall label these arguments: *the epistemic access argument, the endorsement constraint argument,* and *the fairness argument.*[13]

---

[13] These are not uniquely Dworkinian arguments. For example, a version of the epistemic access argument is examined by Simon Caney (Caney 1991: 460–5). Kymlicka emphasizes the endorsement constraint argument in his account of liberalism (Kymlicka 1989a: 11–13). Rawls considers whether his account of justice is fair to conceptions of the good (Rawls 1993: 195–200).

THE EPISTEMIC ACCESS ARGUMENT

The epistemic access argument is essentially a pragmatic argument against the possibility of success in the designing and implementation of perfectionist polices. It has two related dimensions. First, it draws attention to the fact that it will be difficult for governments to identify accurately the ideals of the good that the government should be concerned to advance. Government judgements about these matters are fallible and prone to error. In practice, it will be difficult to identify the ideals which are genuinely valuable and which merit state sponsorship. This difficulty is compounded by the fact that different ideals may be appropriate for different individuals. It will be difficult for government to determine which perfectionist ideals are appropriate for different individuals. Second, even if the appropriate ideals can be identified it will be extremely difficult to design policies which actually succeed in improving the lives individuals live by advancing some conception of the good. The instruments of government policy are often quite blunt and may not be sufficiently sensitive to the diverse needs of different individuals. Individuals are often better placed than government officials to decide not only what sort of life is worth pursuing but also how best to pursue it. Officials lack the requisite epistemic access to reliable information about what sort of lives are good for different people and how to design policies which succeed in making people's lives better. Dworkin suggests that the probability of error is quite high: 'officials will make mistakes of different kinds. They may do a bad job of deciding which lives are good ones for different people; indeed they are likely to do so' (Dworkin 1991: 97).

This argument does not establish that perfectionist policies are doomed to failure but it does present an important obstacle to the justification of perfectionism. The forms of perfectionism most vulnerable to the epistemic access argument are prohibitive perfectionism and mandatory perfectionism. These forms of perfectionism depend not only on the successful identification of ideals that should be promoted but also on the appropriateness of using the rather blunt and potentially dangerous coercive power of the state to advance ideals. A responsible government would have to have extremely good evidence that successful sponsorship of a conception of the good depended on the use of coercive measures. In general, it seems unlikely that the requisite evidence could be amassed. By contrast, educative perfectionism—in either of its forms—is less vulnerable to the epistemic access argument precisely because it does not involve the special considerations that are relevant to the justification of the use of coercive force by the state and because it continues to assign responsibility to individuals for the choice and implementation of conceptions of the good.

The epistemic access argument is the simplest and least developed of the arguments Dworkin considers. It does not provide decisive grounds for discriminating between the market model of neutrality and liberal tolerance. It would provide a rationale for neutrality to the exclusion of tolerance only if it could be plausibly maintained the government can never identify valuable options worth sponsoring. But this seems implausible. Government judgement about such matters may be prone to error but it seems unlikely that it is so systematically defective that government can play no direct role in enriching the environment in which individuals make decisions about how to lead their lives. Thus the epistemic access argument cannot justify the stringent constraints on state activity imposed by liberal neutrality. Of course, this does not imply that it will be easy for governments to determine the circumstances in which educative perfectionism is justified. The epistemic access argument suggests that the tolerant state must be cautious about the perfectionist policies it pursues.

THE ENDORSEMENT CONSTRAINT ARGUMENT

We initially encountered the endorsement constraint argument in Chapter 2. It holds that leading a valuable life has two necessary elements. First, the components of a person's life—experiences, projects, commitments, and the like—must be such as to make the life genuinely good or valuable. Second, the value of these components must be recognized and accepted by the person herself. A self-respecting person must lead her life by her own lights and have the conviction that her commitments are the right ones for her. She must, in other words, endorse the conception of the good by which her life is led. Moreover, the endorsement must be genuine and it must be secured in circumstances conducive to rational appraisal of ends. Genuine endorsement is the product of unmanipulated critical reflection and understanding. Therefore, the circumstances in which deliberation about the good takes place must be conducive to this sort of reflection. Endorsement which is traceable to fear, confusion, ignorance, or indoctrination is not genuine (Dworkin 1989: 484–7).

The difficulty that the requirement of genuine endorsement presents for prohibitive and mandatory perfectionism is twofold. First, these forms of perfectionism are simply unlikely to satisfy the requirement of endorsement. Forcing people under the threat of legal sanction (especially criminal penalty) to conform to certain conceptions of the good is unlikely to meet with the endorsement of those who reject or are indifferent to the conception of the good the state seeks to promote. As Dworkin observes, 'no self-respecting atheist can agree that a community in which religion is mandatory is for that reason finer, and no one who is homosexual that the eradication of homosexuality makes the community purer' (Dworkin 1985: 206). Second, even if coercive measures ultimately succeed in generating some type of endorsement, as when a person is converted to a new view after a period of coercion, this endorsement is unlikely to be the sort which reflects meaningful critical evaluation of the view. So Dworkin plausibly suggests that 'we would not improve someone's life, even though he endorsed the change we brought about, if the mechanisms we used to secure the change lessened his ability to consider the critical merits of the change in a reflective way' (Dworkin 1989: 486).

Although the endorsement constraint argument plays an integral role in arguments for state neutrality, it does not provide a basis for adjudicating between neutrality and liberal tolerance. Liberal tolerance is not vulnerable to the endorsement constraint argument because the educative perfectionism it permits does not deny individuals the opportunity to lead their lives according to their own views. Nor does it undermine the circumstances needed to achieve reflective and critical endorsement. Indeed, because liberal tolerance allows the state to broaden and enrich the circumstances of deliberation, the considerations associated with endorsement may actually strengthen the case for liberal tolerance.

THE FAIRNESS ARGUMENT

The most complex and interesting argument developed by Dworkin against all varieties of state perfectionism is the fairness argument. This argument holds that perfectionist policies are problematic because they violate egalitarian standards of distributive fairness. Perfectionist policies favour certain conceptions of the good over others in a manner that is tantamount to giving extra resources (i.e. a more-than-equal share) to some individuals at the expense of others. Dworkin's theory of distributive justice requires that individuals have an equal share of resources with which to lead their lives. By skewing the distribution of resources, perfectionism seems to represent a departure from the very foundations of egalitarian liberalism. Since this argument seems to provide an objection to all types of perfectionism, it may provide a rationale for adopting justificatory neutrality and rejecting liberal tolerance. It is, therefore, worth investigating in some detail.

The fairness argument appears to present a special problem for liberal tolerance because it implies that any departure from the sort of neutrality embodied in the market model leads to distributive unfairness. This argument draws upon the equal opportunity costs account of fair shares described by equality of resources.

The putative difficulty with perfectionism is that it distorts the pricing system of the market in a way that upsets the equal distribution of resources. Suppose, for instance, the government decides to subsidize the publishing industry and the literary community because it believes that reading good books contributes to the leading of valuable lives and the market, left to its own devices, will not provide a sufficient supply of good books. Dworkin argues that this policy would violate distributive equality because 'if a decision is made to produce and sell goods at a price below the price a market would fix, then those who prefer those goods are, pro tanto, receiving more than an equal share of the resources of the community at the expense of those who would prefer some other use of the resources' (Dworkin 1985: 195). The subsidization of fine literature would provide a social environment in which it was easier for literary types to pursue the projects they find valuable. But people with different views of the good would find the environment less hospitable to the pursuit of their projects. For example, sports fans would have less money to spend on sporting events because some portion of their income, in the form of taxes, is devoted to helping the publishing industry. By contrast, the market seems to respect each person's basic entitlement to an equal share of resources by ensuring that aggregate opportunity costs are equal. The market 'allows each person's social requirements— the social setting he claims he needs in order successfully to pursue his chosen way of life—to be tested by asking how far these requirements can be satisfied within an egalitarian structure that measures their costs to others' (Dworkin 1987: 31). Notice that the argument does not depend on doubting the soundness of the judgement that some lives are more valuable than others. Rather, it purports to show that it is inappropriate to allow such judgements to influence resource distribution. Even without appeal to the technical notion of opportunity costs, the argument has a good deal of intuitive appeal: your chosen life plan may, in fact, be more valuable than mine (and perhaps I would be better off changing my convictions to match yours) but I should not have to subsidize the implementation of your projects merely on that account. I am entitled to an equal share of resources to devote to the pursuit of my own projects.

This is a powerful argument. It seems to provide an obstacle to the justification of both coercive and non-coercive forms of perfectionism because all perfectionist policies alter the relative costs of different lifestyles. If the argument is sound then the market model of neutrality best fits with Dworkin's conception of distributive equality. The state must refrain from implementing policies predicated on the judgement that some human activities and projects are more valuable than others because such policies will have the effect of skewing the distribution of resources in favour of those who concur with the state's favoured conception of the good. Opportunity costs will not be equal because the true costs of the conception of the good advanced by the state will be artificially depressed. Persons with competing conceptions of the good will unfairly subsidize the cost of the conception which the state supports.

However, the fairness argument does not provide a conclusive case against every type of perfectionism. In particular, pluralistic educative perfectionism of the sort compatible with liberal tolerance need not fall prey to it. To see this we need to look more closely at the rationale for leaving determination of the fair cost of different conceptions of the good exclusively to the market.

THE GOOD LIFE: IMPLEMENTATION AND DELIBERATION

The fairness argument depends on a certain characterization of the relationship between our interest in leading a good life and the distribution of resources. Specifically, it proceeds from the supposition that our interest in leading a good life is advanced by making the distribution of resources as responsive as possible to our individual convictions about what life is worth leading. On this picture, resources are viewed primarily as means to the realization of the convictions we actually hold. Our interest in leading a good life is therefore advanced by acquiring the resources we need to give effect to these convictions. The requirement of justice, that each person's interest in leading a good life be shown equal concern, is then plausibly construed as requiring that each person have 'an equal share of resources measured by the cost of the choices he makes, reflecting his own plans and preferences, to the plans and projects of others' (Dworkin 1987: 27). The distributive scheme is fairer when 'it offers more discriminating choices and is thus more sensitive to the discrete plans and preferences people in fact have' (Dworkin 1987: 27–8). The fairness argument emphasizes that dimension of our interest in leading a good life which consists in being able to implement our projects. I shall call this the *interest in implementation*. When the implementation dimension of our interest in leading a good life is stressed, perfectionist policies that aim at making certain convictions easier to implement are problematic because each person is only entitled to an equal share of resources with which to give effect to her convictions.

The interest in implementation is, however, only one aspect of the broader interest we have in leading a good life. We also have a crucial stake in being able to deliberate critically about our convictions. Our views about the good are fallible so it is important that the social environment in which we live provide us ample opportunity to assess and revise our ends as well as to pursue new projects if we come to believe that our current ends are somehow defective. Showing concern for the deliberative dimension of our interest in leading a good life—our *deliberative interest*—involves securing a social environment which is conducive both to critical reflection about ends and to possible revision of ends. The noteworthy feature of this deliberative interest is the special way in which it construes the value that resources have for individuals. Unlike the interest in implementation it is difficult to differentiate the content of each person's deliberative interest. In the case of this interest (unlike the interest in implementation), it is difficult to identify the differentiating features of each person's interest. We cannot readily identify, in advance, the specific resources or opportunities that will actually be employed in meeting a particular person's deliberative interest. Instead, there are likely to be a variety of resources which seem generally conducive to meeting a person's deliberative interest, but any one of these may, in the event, play no role in satisfying a particular person's deliberative interest. Consider, for instance, the contrast between the resources I need to implement my plan to be a tennis player and the kinds of resources that speak to my deliberative interest. What I need to pursue a life as a tennis player is quite specific—rackets, courts, coaching, etc. As long as I believe that tennis is the good life for me, I shall be concerned to acquire the resources that permit me to pursue it and I will have no direct interest in acquiring or using other available resources. In other words, my conception of the good gives content to my interest in implementation. It provides the standard by which the value of available resources can be assessed and provides me with a reason to acquire and use certain resources. Since different people will have different conceptions of the good, resources for the implementation of ideals will have different values for different people.

My deliberative interest has a different character. If I want to be able to assess and perhaps revise my convictions about the good life many resources may prove useful. For example, a general arts education, access to a good library, or exposure to a diverse culture with vibrant examples of different lifestyles and ideas of the good might all assist my deliberations. Yet, in the course of deliberation about my ends, I may only avail myself of some of these resources or I may profit from them to different degrees. However, I cannot exactly determine in advance how specific features of my social and cultural environment will in fact contribute to the process of deliberation or which ones will prove especially valuable to me. My current conception of the good cannot be reliably employed to assess how exposure to various elements of the social and cultural environment will contribute to my deliberations. Indeed, the content of a person's deliberative interest is largely independent of any particular conception of the good. Moreover, if we accept that most people's basic capacities for deliberation—e.g. their native cognitive abilities—are roughly equal, then there will be no significant difference in the content of anyone's deliberative interest. In other words, circumstances conducive to the exercise of this form of individual autonomy will be the same for all who share the same degree of autonomy and most people are autonomous to roughly the same degree.[14] On this construal of the deliberative interest, it is plausible to hold that all persons have effectively the same interest in the provision of an environment that nourishes and facilitates the exercise of their deliberative capacities. It is in everyone's deliberative interest to be provided with a context of deliberation that features a rich repertoire of valuable options and diverse opportunities for exploration and learning (cf. Dworkin 1985: 229). The deliberative interest is served by the provision of such a plurality of valuable options because we are best able to consider the merits, for ourselves, of different alternatives against a background that displays such a plurality. Moreover, should we revise our ends, we are better placed to explore and pursue new ends. Of course, the deliberation of different individuals is likely to be affected to varying

---

[14] This is not to deny that the basic deliberative capacities of some people may be impaired in ways that give rise to special entitlements to resources. Nothing I say here implies, for instance, that people with learning disabilities do not have a claim to special educational resources. Obviously, the educational system should be sensitive to what different individuals need in order to develop their cognitive and intellectual abilities.

degrees by different elements of the social and cultural environment. You may come to appreciate something valuable by lis-
tening to opera while I may benefit from exposure to abstract
art. Nonetheless, our deliberative interest consists in the provision of the general conditions for effective deliberation. We
cannot accurately predict how the component features of a
context of deliberation will influence a given individual's
deliberations.

Two claims are being advanced here. First, our current conception of the good often does not serve as a reliable guide to
determining how our deliberative interest is best met. Second,
our deliberative interest is advanced when we are situated in a
social context of deliberation that presents us with a wide range
of valuable options. By way of support of these points, consider
the analogy that can be drawn between our interest in having
access to a good library and our interest in a culture that
displays a wide variety of valuable options. The suggestion is
that we can view our interest in having such a culture as parallel
to our interest in having access to a good library. Valuable
cultural options are like books in a library. Both afford us an
opportunity to learn about and to explore ways in which we
might lead our lives differently. Having access to a good library
clearly contributes both to our interest in implementation and
our deliberative interest. Thus a library provides me with resources that help to facilitate the implementation of my current
plans. I can improve my tennis serve by consulting appropriate
instructional texts. Similarly, a library addresses my deliberative
interest. If I become dissatisfied with tennis I can take advantage
of the library to discover and explore other options. I may find
that literature has more to offer than I previously realized. There
will, of course, be many parts of the library that I never actually
use. But surely it would be a mistake to conclude that I have no
deliberative interest in the maintenance of the portions of the
collection that I never have occasion to make use of. Notice how
the interest in implementation associated with my current view
about how to lead my life does not illuminate my deliberative
interest very well. *Qua* tennis player I am concerned that the
library have good books on tennis. Having access to great works
of literature is not of immediate concern to me and thus I may
fail to recognize how it is important. Inevitably, most of the

books in the library will not figure directly in either my deliberations about the good or my efforts to implement my particular
plans. Yet since my convictions are fallible and subject to revision, I have a strong interest in maintaining a good library.
Notice the importance that attaches to the library having a
diverse collection of *good* books. A library that was either
narrowly focused on a single area of interest or that only offered
a huge collection of third rate works would not address my
deliberative interest as well as a library that boasts a fine collection of good books. The options presented to us by our culture
play a role in deliberation that is similar to the role played by
books in the library. The presence of a range of different options
supplies us with a framework, as well as with material, for
deliberation. Cultural pluralism of this sort gives us an awareness of other opportunities we might pursue and permits us to
explore them. Just as our deliberative interest is best served by a
library with a diverse collection of good books, our deliberative
interest is best served by a culture that presents a rich repertoire
of genuinely valuable options.

Recognizing the complexion of the deliberative dimension of
our interest in leading a good life has two important consequences. First, it explains why the market is not likely to protect
our deliberative interest adequately. Goods purchased in a market setting will tend to reflect each person's interest in implementation. This is because it is easier for individuals to identify
the resources they need to implement their plans than to identify, on an ongoing basis, the resources which contribute to their
deliberative interest. A person's conception of the good can
provide a clear indication of what is likely to be of value in
pursuit of her plans. By the same token it is more difficult for
individuals to identify the features of their social environment
that may contribute to effective deliberation. Our conception of
the good cannot reliably guide our preferences in this context
because we want to know what sort of environment is most
conducive to developing our views of the good. So the importance we attach to the pursuit of our current convictions is likely
to obscure the importance of the character of the broader environment in which we form and develop our convictions. For
example, it is likely to be difficult for me to see the point of
contributing to the local opera company when all I want to do

is play tennis. The bias we tend to display, particularly in market contexts, for the interest in implementation is quite understandable. After all, our primary concern is to lead a good life. Reflection on the good life is only one means to achieving that end, albeit a very important means. The unexamined life may not be worth living but the merely examined life is not much good either. Nonetheless, we need to give appropriate theoretical and institutional recognition to both aspects of our interest in leading a good life. Market enthusiasts often emphasize the dynamic capacity of markets to respond efficiently to consumer preferences and thereby improve people's lives. However, one unfortunate aspect of some celebrations of the market is a tendency to exaggerate the significance of interests in implementation and to give short shrift to the significance of deliberative interests which are not immediately expressed in consumer preferences. Because the deliberative interest is not always effective in shaping consumer demand, market-supplied deliberative resources can be inadequate. There is also the potentially more disturbing possibility that market forces can actively distort conditions of deliberation. Clever marketing and seductive advertising can lead us to adopt preferences which would not withstand deliberative scrutiny. So for various reasons, unfettered market forces cannot be relied to serve our deliberative interests.

The second consequence of recognizing the importance of the deliberative aspect of our interest in living a good life is that the fairness argument can no longer be construed as providing an objection to all varieties of perfectionism. Pluralistic educative perfectionism escapes the fairness argument precisely because it addresses the deliberative interest and not the interest in implementation. It is in keeping with Dworkin's egalitarianism to believe that the state has an obligation to ensure that the interest in deliberation is adequately protected. As I have argued above, the market cannot be relied upon to address this interest. This explains why the state may legitimately try to design policies that ensure a sufficiently rich context of deliberation for everyone. Suppose that a state, with this end in mind, identifies valuable features of the social and cultural environment and undertakes to support them because the ordinary operation of the market places them in jeopardy. It thereby protects each individual's deliberative interest by securing a rich deliberative context. No one can complain that more resources have been devoted to the deliberative interests of some people, to the exclusion (or at the expense) of others, because each person's deliberative interest is effectively identical. The deliberative context is the same for everyone and thus everyone benefits (to the same degree) when the deliberative context is improved.

It is true that this sort of pluralistic educative perfectionism can have the consequence that some conceptions of the good will be easier to implement than they would have been in the absence of state activity. Take Dworkin's example of opera. State subsidy of opera, which is justified by appeal to the contribution opera can make to the overall deliberative context, will still make *Carmen* cheaper for opera lovers. But this is not unfair because a rich deliberative context provides the appropriate background against which opportunity costs can be measured. If 'the resources people have available, with which to pursue their plans or projects or ways of life, [should] be fixed by the costs of their having these to others' (Dworkin 1987: 30) then we need to determine the background against which people formulate their plans and projects. Presumably, the background should be one conducive to effective deliberation about these ends. Thus, the true opportunity cost of opera—the price at which it is available given the preferences everyone has for it— should not be determined by asking how much people situated in an impoverished context of deliberation would pay for it.[15] Rather, the cost should be fixed by how much people who are situated in a rich context of deliberation would pay for it. If opera contributes appropriately to the deliberative context (and this of course may be a controversial claim), then it is reasonable that the background against which the costs of different lives are determined—including the cost of attending opera—should include state-subsidized opera.

The provision of cultural goods because of their contribution to deliberation is interestingly analogous to the protection of free speech. In liberal societies the state may protect freedom of

---

[15] This claim is consistent with the principle of authenticity which I discussed in the previous chapter.

speech for all citizens and require that all citizens contribute to the costs of its provision. Some resources of the publicly financed judicial system are directed, for instance, to ensuring that rights of free speech are adequately protected. Similarly, there are government regulatory agencies that are charged with ensuring adequate public access to means of mass communication. These state activities give recognition to the fact that protecting free speech often requires more than mere government forbearance. Yet the provision of free speech contributes more to the implementation of some people's convictions than others. One might argue that the people who depend on free speech in order to implement their ideals are unfairly subsidized by those for whom free speech does not help implement their life plans. The resources spent to underwrite free speech and which benefit people with plans that depend on free speech are provided partly at the expense of people for whom free speech does not contribute to the realization of their plans. The latter group might prefer that the former group pay the full price of the provision of free speech which only they use. However, sharing the costs of the protection of free speech is not unfair because of the special contribution made by free speech to the context of deliberation. We all have the same deliberative interest in the protection of free speech. It is only after this interest is adequately satisfied that the problem of the resources devoted to each person's interest in implementation can be broached.

Notice that the fairness argument still provides a decisive objection to sectarian educative perfectionism. That form of perfectionism attempts to justify an allocation of resources on the ground that a particular conception of the good should be adopted and pursued by the citizens of a state. It speaks to the interest in implementation and not to the deliberative interest. Sectarian educative perfectionism is objectionable precisely because it gives some people more resources to devote to the implementation of their plans than others. The fairness argument provides an important argument against most varieties of perfectionism. However, because it does not undermine the legitimacy of pluralistic educative perfectionism it does not establish that a liberal egalitarian state must adhere to the ideal of liberal neutrality. Liberal tolerance remains an open and attractive option.

CONCLUSION

I hope the upshot of the foregoing arguments is now clear. A comprehensive form of liberalism that proceeds from a fundamental commitment to equality is more compatible with liberal tolerance than with a market model of liberal neutrality. As we have seen the ideal of liberal tolerance fits well with the egalitarian impulse that Dworkin locates at the heart of liberalism. Moreover, liberal tolerance provides a solution to the familiar tensions faced by liberalism which I noted earlier. Tolerance can explain liberalism's traditional hostility to using the coercive apparatus of the state to enforce controversial conceptions of personal morality. But it also explains how a liberal state may simultaneously be justified in supporting valuable features of the social and cultural environment. Liberal tolerance thus provides a way of reconciling liberalism's seemingly divergent elements.

8

Conclusion

THIS book is mainly about the specific account of liberal equality defended by Dworkin. Nonetheless, the critique of liberal
equality is relevant to more general issues concerning the connection between liberalism, justice, and markets. I began the
examination of liberal equality by noting traditional egalitarian
worries about the inequalities generated by markets. Despite
Dworkin's highly innovative and clever attempt to reconcile
distributive equality with the market these concerns remain
alive, both in the real world and in the idealized world of
equality of resources. However, I have also tried to show that
there are broader issues concerning the adequacy of the market
model. Adoption of this model, as either a heuristic device or as
a guide to structuring actual political communities, can lead us
to ignore important dimensions of human interests which need
to be accommodated within the design of real social institutions.
Non-market theories of equality and non-market institutions
are needed if we are to deal adequately with such issues as
the circumstances of deliberation, the significance of culture, or
even the distributional significance of risk-taking. The danger
endemic to a project such as Dworkin's is that appropriate
consideration of such interests will be neglected in the eagerness
to apply market-based solutions to problems. As we have seen,
the market can be employed to supply seemingly elegant solutions to perennially difficult issues. The seeming theoretical
flexibility of the market contributes, I believe, to the current
enthusiasm about the power of the market as a device for
understanding and eliminating injustice. Yet if the arguments of
this book are sound, much of the putative power of the market
as a tool for the articulation and realization of egalitarian justice
is illusory. So in addition to providing a comprehensive critique
of Dworkin's theory, I hope my analysis has succeeded in justi-

fying a more cautionary attitude to the power of markets to advance the cause of justice.

In my remaining remarks, I will make no attempt to recapitulate the various criticisms I have advanced of Dworkin's ingenious attempt to harness the market as a device for the articulation of egalitarian justice. Liberal equality is a powerful and attractive theory but it fails to provide the best interpretation of the abstract egalitarian thesis. The great strength of Dworkin's contribution to liberal theory lies not in the details of equality of resources but rather in his illumination of some of the basic moral ideals which animate egalitarianism. The view that impartial moral concern is the starting point for political philosophy is not original to Dworkin. However, his work on equality has, I believe, deepened our understanding of this important idea. Egalitarian theory has been enriched and made more complex by Dworkin's insight that a fair distribution of resources should be both ambition-sensitive and endowment-insensitive. The insistence that egalitarian concern for each person's life must be compatible with recognition of a principle of individual responsibility precludes the possibility of interpreting equality in purely welfarist terms. Similarly, the recognition that the needs of disabled persons must figure prominently in a theory of liberal equality is important, especially given the usual neglect of this topic. The idea that considerations of distributive equality cannot be isolated from discussions of the nature of ideals of liberty, neutrality, or tolerance is also important. In all these areas, and many others, we learn much from Dworkin's subtle analysis even when it is flawed. Yet this book is primarily a critique of central aspects of Dworkin's theory. It is appropriate, therefore, that I conclude with a few observations about some general difficulties which are endemic to the market interpretation of equality.

In the previous chapters, I have focused on various specific deficiencies of a theory of liberal equality which is predicated upon idealized economic markets. A theme of many of the criticisms which I have developed is that the market fails as a device for interpreting equality because it distorts the moral ideals which it is supposed to illuminate. This distortion takes two main forms. First, the nature and significance of certain human interests is not reliably captured by the market-guided interpretation of abstract equality. We have seen, for instance, how a narrow focus on the distribution of private resources by the market leads to a distorted understanding of the needs of disabled persons. And we have seen how the importance which attaches to insulating individuals from unreasonable risks is given improper recognition in Dworkin's theory. The commitment to the market weakens the interpretation of the abstract egalitarian thesis because the market processes which give life to the theory cannot adequately distinguish the relative significance of different kinds of human interests. Second, in some instances, commitment to market devices supplants concern for the underlying moral ideal which is supposed to ground use of the devices in the first place. For instance, the hypothetical insurance markets which play such an important role in Dworkin's theory are so complex that it is easy to lose sight of the objectives they are meant to serve. It is perhaps inevitable that the theory yielded by simplifying interpretive devices will not perfectly match our considered judgements about the nature of justice. And, of course, there is an attraction to using procedural devices to construct a theory if such devices can help us avoid controversy in the identification and weighing of different interest. However, I think that the kinds of distortion introduced by reliance on devices raise a serious problem about this approach. In the final analysis, egalitarian theory may have to be messier in the sense that it may have to grapple directly with complex controversies about the nature and weight of diverse human interests. In sum, it is doubtful that all the relevant dimensions of egalitarian concern can be captured by an elaborate market algorithm or any other sophisticated procedural mechanism.

In addition to the general problem of distortion, there are two more general difficulties which the reliance on idealized models of market interaction create for Dworkin's theory. I will call these the problem of *exclusion* and the problem of *distance*.

EXCLUSION

Despite its striking originality, Dworkin's project is, in one important respect, quite characteristic of contemporary liberal political philosophy. Liberal theory is concerned, to a large part, with the justification of principles that can fairly regulate relations between responsible adults who are capable of forming and pursuing their own conceptions of the good life. For the purpose of developing my critique of Dworkin's theory I have implicitly accepted this presupposition. We have seen how Dworkin contends that the demands of distributive justice and various liberal ideals are illuminated by reflection upon the interaction of mature, responsible agents in idealized economic markets. I have argued that reliance on the market does not succeed in illuminating the egalitarian ideal even when use of this device is restricted to consideration of the entitlements of adults. Recall, however, that the abstract egalitarian thesis instructs us to give consideration to everyone's interests, not just the interests of responsible adults. This means that a comprehensive theory of justice must directly address the interests of children. Once children are included within the ambit of egalitarian concern, we can detect a further limitation of the market as a device for the articulation of egalitarian justice. The root difficulty is that children, especially very young children, do not fully display the characteristics that are needed to make reliance on the market as an interpretive device seem at all plausible. Crucially, the arguments invoking the market assume that individuals can be held responsible for their choices and are able to assess rationally the risks and likely consequences of their decisions. Children cannot be presumed to have these capacities.

It is perhaps unsurprising that the immigrants to Dworkin's imaginary island arrive without children. For it is difficult to imagine how Dworkin's theory could even apply to children in the first instance. We cannot suppose that the entitlement of children to resources can be modelled by their choices in a hypothetical auction of resources. Nor can we simply assume that parents can be relied upon to ensure that the interests of their children receive full consideration. Children should not be assigned to the periphery of a theory of justice. Yet it is difficult to see how children can be appropriately accommodated within the structure of equality of resources. This suggests that there is a problem of exclusion created by reliance on the market. The theoretical apparatus which Dworkin deploys is insensitive to the distinctive status and interests of children and thereby tends to exclude consideration of these matters.

This problem of exclusion is reflected in the fact that some crucial problems concerning children and families are difficult even to formulate within the market structure of equality of resources. Consider, for instance, the arguments in the last chapter concerning neutrality and tolerance. As I addressed it, the debate concerning the appropriate attitude of the state vis-à-vis different conceptions of the good is conceived as a problem about the relationship between the state, and autonomous adults. On this construal, we can see how the market can be used to model an ideal of neutrality. But consider what is left out by setting up the problem in this way. Since children initially lack both a conception of the good and the capacities to evaluate the options they may be faced with, the ideals of neutrality or tolerance cannot be applied to children in any straightforward manner. There are, however, important issues associated with these matters which liberal theory should address directly. For instance, what prerogatives ought families, the state, and community groups have when it comes to shaping the environment in which children develop their views about the good and their capacities for assessing different conceptions of the good? How far should parents be permitted to inculcate controversial religious or ethical convictions in their children? Should a liberal state ever underwrite or assist such efforts? It is difficult to see how we can even begin to address such problems meaningfully by appeal to an ideal market.

Similar puzzles arise when we reflect upon how the inclusion of children within a liberal theory of equality greatly complicates the problem of tracking the twin requirements of ambition-sensitivity and endowment-insensitivity. Dworkin's theory holds that economic inequalities which are traceable to the choices of individuals can be fair and, in some settings, he is confident that the operation of the market can track ambition-sensitivity appropriately. Once children are added to the mix, however, the problems do not seem amenable, even in principle, to a market solution of the sort which Dworkin employs in the case of adults. For instance, to what degree (if any) should economic inequalities which can justifiably exist between mature adults affect the opportunities of children? How far should wealthy parents be able to confer advantages on their children which are beyond the means of other families? These problems are not merely minor subsidiary matters which can be dealt with independently of a general theory of equality. Rather they are problems which should occupy a central place because they touch on the source on the central conduits of inequality in contemporary liberal society. So the fact that children cannot be incorporated comfortably within the market framework of equality of resources is not a trivial matter. It reflects the exclusionary tendencies of a device-dependent theory of justice.

DISTANCE

Constructing a theory of political morality should not be merely an intellectual enterprise. Fidelity to the truth, as we understand it, is a noble commitment which political theorists should take seriously. However, the impulse to explore the nature of justice does not arise out of intellectual curiosity alone. We care, often passionately, about the moral character of the actual communities in which we live. We want our lives to be good and our societies to be just. We consult political philosophy to help guide our deliberations about how we might improve the world in which we live. Good political philosophy helps us to diagnose injustice in the real world and to envision feasible ways in which we can move closer to a genuinely just society. So although there is a sense in which political philosophy trades in unrealizable, utopian ideals of justice, there is also a sense in which it should be a source of practical wisdom. There can, however, be a tension between these aspirations of political philosophy. On the one hand, if our deliberations are too circumscribed by a concern only for ideals which are realizable, we may become complacent about genuine injustice. On the other hand, if our reflections about justice are too abstract or idealized then the theory we develop may have little practical utility. Political philosophy needs to avoid both complacency and, what might be termed, excessive distance from the real world.

The idealizations upon which Dworkin's theory depends create unnecessary distance between theory and the real world. Equality of resources requires us, in the first instance, to imagine a model of egalitarian concern which is far removed from anything that is even remotely possible. Of course Dworkin recognizes that the description of a just distribution of resources provided by equality of resources is highly idealized. Indeed he tells us that perfect liberal equality can be imagined only in an 'ideal ideal world' (Dworkin 1987: 46). This is an unattainable fantasy-world where both the initial auction and the hypothetical insurance market schemes function perfectly. Somewhat closer to our world is the 'ideal real world' where significant technical obstacles to the attainment of perfect liberal equality exist but where there is widespread acceptance of and support for the realization of genuine equality. By Dworkin's own admission, reflection on the 'ideal ideal world' provides little direct illumination of the meaning of equality in our world. In order to derive practical conclusions about the upshot of a commitment to equality of resources we need to develop a special theory of improvement which allows us to track the meaning of equality from the 'ideal ideal world' to the 'ideal real world' and finally to the 'real real world'. Needless to say, the theory of improvement which is needed to bridge the distance between the conception of perfect liberal equality and the real world meaning of equality adds a further layer of complexity to Dworkin's interpretation of the abstract egalitarian thesis.

The distancing of ideal theory from practical moral concern is, to some extent, unavoidable. The articulation of a theory of political morality requires that we be able to envision an ideal of how things might be. And there is a benign sense in which Dworkin's theory simply urges us to exercise our powers of moral imagination. However, I think the claim that perfect markets are intrinsic to the best interpretation of equality creates more distance than is necessary. The recommendation that we build a theory of equality around ideal market models is, perhaps, unnecessarily taxing on our moral imagination. After all, in equality of resources we begin by imagining a world which cannot exist. In this respect, the theory is very distant from an understanding of any practical manifestation of egalitarian concern. Instead of first modelling egalitarian concern in the fantastic world of perfect economic markets perhaps we should seek to interpret the implications of impartial moral concern for our world more directly.

REFERENCES

ACKERMAN, B. (1980). *Social Justice in the Liberal State*. Yale University Press, New Haven, Conn.

ALEXANDER, L., and SCHWAZCHILD, M. (1987). 'Liberalism, Neutrality and Equality of Welfare vs. Equality of Resources', *Philosophy and Public Affairs*, 16/1: 85–110.

ARNESON, R. (1989). 'Equality and Equal Opportunity for Welfare', *Philosophical Studies*, 56: 77–93.

BARRY, B. (1989). *Theories of Justice*. Oxford University Press, Oxford.

BENNETT, J. (1985). 'Ethics and Markets', *Philosophy and Public Affairs*, 14/2: 195–204.

BICKENBACH, J. E. (1993). *Physical Disability and Social Policy*. University of Toronto Press Incorporated, Toronto.

BUCHANAN, A. (1985). *Ethics Efficiency and the Market*. Rowman & Allanheld, Totowa, NJ.

——(1989). 'Assessing the Communitarian Critique of Liberalism', *Ethics*, 99/4: 852–82.

BUCHANAN, J. (1975). *The Limits of Liberty: Between Anarchy and Leviathan*. University of Chicago Press, Chicago, Ill.

CANEY, S. (1991). 'Consequentialist Defences of Liberal Neutrality', *Philosophical Quarterly*, 41/165: 457–77.

CARENS, J. (1981). *Equality, Moral Incentives and the Market: An Essay in Utopian Politico-Economic Theory*, University of Chicago Press, Chicago, Ill.

——(1985). 'Compensatory Justice and Social Institutions', *Economics and Philosophy*, 1/1: 39–67.

COHEN, G. A. (1986a). 'Self-Ownership, World-Ownership and Equality', in F. Lucash (ed.), *Justice and Equality Here and Now*. Cornell University Press, Ithaca, NY.

——(1986b). 'Self-Ownership, World-Ownership and Equality: Part 2', *Social Philosophy and Policy*, 3/2: 77–96.

——(1989). 'On the Currency of Egalitarian Justice', *Ethics*, 99/4: 906–44.

COHEN, L. J. (1981). 'Can Human Irrationality be Experimentally Demonstrated?', *The Behavioral and Brain Sciences*, 4: 317–31.

DICK, J. (1975). 'How to Justify a Distribution of Earnings', *Philosophy and Public Affairs*, 4/Spring: 248–72.

DWORKIN, R. (1977). *Taking Rights Seriously*. Harvard University Press, Cambridge, Mass.

——(1981). 'What Is Equality? Part I: Equality of Welfare; Part II: Equality of Resources', *Philosophy and Public Affairs*, 10/3–4: 185–246, 283–345.

——(1983). 'In Defense of Equality', *Social Philosophy and Policy*, 1/1: 24–40.

——(1985). *A Matter of Principle*, Harvard University Press, Cambridge, Mass.

——(1986). *Law's Empire*, Harvard University Press, Cambridge, Mass.

——(1987). 'What is Equality? Part III: The Place of Liberty', *Iowa Law Review*, 73/1: 1–54.

——(1988). 'What is Equality? Part IV: Political Equality', *University of San Francisco Law Review*, 22/1: 1–30.

——(1989). 'Liberal Community', *California Law Review*, 77/3: 479–504.

——(1991). 'Foundations of Liberal Equality', *Tanner Lectures on Human Values*, vi. University of Utah Press, Salt Lake City, Utah: 3–119.

——(1993). 'Justice in the Distribution of Health Care', *McGill Law Journal*, 38/4: 883–98.

——(1994). 'Will Clinton's Plan Be Fair?', *New York Review of Books*, 41/1–2: 20–5.

FRIED, C. (1983). 'Distributive Justice', *Social Philosophy and Policy*, 1/1: 45–59.

GAUTHIER, D. (1986). *Morals by Agreement*. Oxford University Press, Oxford.

GREENE, M. R. (1968). *Risk and Insurance*. South-western Publishing Co., Cincinnati.

GUEST, S, (1991). *Ronald Dworkin*. Stanford University Press, Stanford, Calif.

GUTMANN, A. (1980). *Liberal Equality*. Cambridge University Press, Cambridge.

——(1985). 'Communitarian Critics of Liberalism', *Philosophy and Public Affairs*, 14/3: 308–22.

HURKA, T. (1993). *Perfectionism*. Oxford University Press, Oxford.

——(1995). 'Indirect Perfectionism: Kymlicka on Liberal Neutrality', *Journal of Political Philosophy*, 3/1: 36–57.

JACOBS, L. (1993). *Rights and Deprivation*. Clarendon Press, Oxford.

KAHNEMAN, D., SLOVIC, P., and TVERSKY, A. (eds.) (1982). *Judgement under Uncertainty: Heuristics and Biases*. Cambridge University Press, Cambridge.

References   227

KROUSE, R., and McPHERSON, M. (1988). 'Capitalism, "Property-Owning Democracy", and the Welfare State', in A. Gutmann (ed.), *Democracy and the Welfare State*. Princeton University Press, Princeton, NJ.

KYMLICKA, W. (1988a). 'Liberalism and Communitarianism', *Canadian Journal of Philosophy*, 18/2: 181–203.

——(1988b). 'Rawls on Teleology and Deontology', *Philosophy and Public Affairs*, 17/3: 173–90.

——(1989a). *Liberalism, Community, and Culture*. Oxford University Press, Oxford.

——(1989b). 'Liberal Individualism and Liberal Neutrality', *Ethics*, 99/4: 883–905.

——(1990). *Contemporary Political Philosophy: An Introduction*. Clarendon Press, Oxford.

LAMORE, C. (1987). *Patterns of Moral Complexity*. Cambridge University Press, Cambridge.

LANGTON, R. (1990). 'Whose Right? Ronald Dworkin, Women and Pornographers', *Philosophy and Public Affairs*, 19/4: 311–59.

LEFTWICH, R., and SHARP, A. (1980). *Economics of Social Issues*. Business Publications, Dallas.

MACINTYRE, A. (1981). *After Virtue: A Study in Moral Theory*. Duckworth, London.

MACLEOD, A. (1985). 'Economic Inequality: Justice and Incentives', in D. Meyers and K. Kipnis (eds.), *Economic Justice*. Rowan & Allanheld, Totowa, NJ: 176–89.

MILLER, D. (1989). *Market, State and Community: Theoretical Foundations of Market Socialism*. Oxford University Press, Oxford.

NAGEL, T. (1991). *Equality and Partiality*. Oxford University Press, Oxford.

NARVESON, J. (1983). 'On Dworkinian Equality', *Social Philosophy and Policy*, 1/1: 1–23.

——(1988). *The Libertarian Idea*. Temple University Press, Philadelphia.

NOZICK, R. (1974). *Anarchy, State, and Utopia*. Basic Books, New York.

RAKOWSKI, E. (1991). *Equal Justice*. Oxford University Press, Oxford.

RAWLS, J. (1971). *A Theory of Justice*. Oxford University Press, London.

——(1985). 'Justice as Fairness: Political not Metaphysical', *Philosophy and Public Affairs*, 14/3: 223–51.

228   *References*

RAWLS, J. (1993). *Political Liberalism*. Columbia University Press, New York.

RAZ, J. (1986). *The Morality of Freedom*. Oxford University Press, Oxford.

ROSENBERG, A. (1987). 'The Political Philosophy of Biological Endowments: Some Considerations', *Social Philosophy and Policy*, 5/1: 1–31.

SANDEL, M. (1982). *Liberalism and the Limits of Justice*. Cambridge University Press, Cambridge.

——(1984). 'The Procedural Republic and the Unencumbered Self', *Political Theory*, 12/1: 81–96.

SCANLON, T. (1975). 'Preference and Urgency', *Journal of Philosophy*, 72: 655–69.

——(1982). 'Contractualism and Utilitarianism', in A. Sen and B. Williams (eds.), *Utilitarianism and Beyond*. Cambridge University Press, Cambridge.

——(1993). 'Partisan for Life', *New York Review of Books*, 46/13: 44–51.

SCHEFFLER, S. (1992). 'Responsibility, Reactive Attitudes, and Liberalism in Philosophy and Politics', *Philosophy and Public Affairs*, 21/4: 299–323.

SEN, A. (1980). 'Equality of What?', in S. McMurrin (ed.,) *The Tanner Lectures of Human Values*, i. University of Utah Press, Salt Lake City, Utah.

——(1985*a*). 'Rights and Capabilities', in T. Honderich (ed.), *Morality and Objectivity*. Routledge & Kegan Paul, London.

——(1985*b*). 'Well-Being, Agency and Freedom: The Dewey Lectures 1984', *Journal of Philosophy*, 82/4: 169–221.

——(1992). *Inequality Reexamined*. Oxford University Press, Oxford.

TAYLOR, C. (1985). *Philosophy and the Human Sciences: Philosophical Papers*, ii. Cambridge University Press, Cambridge.

TREMAIN, S. (1996). 'Dworkin on Disablement and Resources', *Canadian Journal of Law and Jurisprudence*, 9/2: 343–59.

VARIAN, H. (1985). 'Dworkin on Equality of Resources', *Economics and Philosophy*, 1/1: 110–25.

WALDRON, J. (1993). *Liberal Rights*. Cambridge University Press, Cambridge.

WASON, P. C., and JOHNSON-LAIRD, P. N. (1972). *Psychology of Reasoning: Structure and Content*. Batsford, London.

YOUNG, R. (1992). 'Egalitarianism and Personal Desert', *Ethics*, 102/4: 319–41.

INDEX

abstract egalitarian thesis 5–6, 202–3
Ackerman, B. 80, 190
ambition-sensitivity 9–13, 49–52, 75, 114–17, 153–4
  market theory of 53–4
  see also hypothetical insurance market
Amish 199 n. 11
Arneson, R. 7
artificial devices 4–5, 20, 219–20
auction device 21–3

Barry, B. 1 n. 1
baseline liberty/constraint system 169, 176–82
Bennett, J. 23 n. 3, 29 n. 6
Bickenbach J. E. 79 n. 1, 81 n. 4
brute luck 20, 50, 79
  and disabilities 79, 98
  and talents 110–11
Buchanan, A. 30
Buchanan, J. 1 n. 1

Caney, S. 203 n. 13
Carens, J. 115 n. 5, 117–18, 153
Chamberlain, Wilt 150–2
children 16, 183, 221–3
choice 46–8, 76–8, 115–17, 222
  see also ambition-sensitivity
circumstances of authenticity 15–16, 37–9
Cohen, G. A. 7, 112 n. 3
Cohen, L. J. 97 n. 12
communitarianism 166–7
conceptions of the good 186–7
constitutive bridge strategy 15, 171–5
  as equivalent to interest strategy 182–6
  structural problem of 174–5
  vs. dogmatic constitutive strategy 170–1
context of deliberation 200–1, 212–16
cultural pluralism 213

deliberative interest 209–16
democracy 12 n. 8
desert 116
Dick, J. 115–16
disabilities 13–14, 79–82
  and basic human capacities 122–5
  and equality of welfare 92 n. 11
  marginalization of 107, 120–8
  private property as compensation for 105–8
  see also talent
distance, problem of 223–4
distortion, problem of 218–20

economies of scale 74–5
education 38–9
effort 50, 52, 76–7
endorsement constraint 33–6, 162–3, 205–7
endowment-insensitivity 9, 114, 222–3
envy test 21–3, 28, 53–4, 58, 65, 86–9, 176–7
epistemic access argument 204–5
equality of resources 7–12, 21–3, 26–7, 51, 157, 168–70
equality of welfare 7, 10, 24–5, 28
equality through time, problem of 46–7
examples:
  Alice and top income insurance 144–7
  Anna and Brian 123
  apples and oranges distribution 22
  Deborah and Ernest 142 n. 19
  Feodor and Prudence 70–2
  golf and tennis retirement lottery 55–60
  Helen 105
  income redistribution 137–9

MacIntye, A. 166 n. 5
Macleod, A. 115 n. 5
market:
  and deliberative interest 213–14
  and disabilities 87
  and equality through time 46–7,
    51–2, 56–7, 63–5, 73–5, 77–8
  and initial equality 22–3, 30–1,
    37, 40, 43–4
  as model of neutrality 192,
    207–9
  perfect competition 23, 30
  in political philosophy 1–3,
    218–20
  and public goods 193–4
  role in Dworkin's liberalism 2–4,
    11–16
  and unequal talents 111–15
Mill, J. S. 33, 161
Miller, D. 116
minimum income 134, 150
model of challenge 35
model of impact 35
moral hazard 145
moral intuition 17–18
mutual advantage 1

Nagel, T. 17, 49
Narveson, J. 1 n. 1, 80, 87
naturalism 48, 52
Nozick, R. 45 n. 1, 112 n. 3, 150,
  156

objective value of resources 30–1
occupational choice 76–7
opportunity costs 13, 25–7, 53,
  61–2, 208–9, 215
  true opportunity costs 175–81
option luck 50, 98–100
organ transplants 87–8

paternalism 54
perfect liberal equality 83
perfectionism 187–8
  and equality 201–3
  forms of 198
person/circumstances distinction
  83–6
personal resources and impersonal
  resources 82–6

pornography 188 n. 4
preferences:
  external vs. personal 62 n. 8
  formal properties of 29 n. 6
  intrinsic mistakes and
    instrumental mistakes 29–30,
    40–1
  and objective interests 27–8
primary goods 6–7
principle of abstraction 172,
  177–83
principle of authenticity 42–4,
  172–3, 184–5
principle of correction 172
principle of independence 173,
  184–5
principle of security 172, 184–5

Rakowski, E. 55, 80 n. 3, 116, 133
  n. 12
Rawls, J. 6, 20, 48–9, 80, 112–13,
  116, 140, 199 n. 11, 203 n. 13
Raz, J. 34, 36, 199 n. 11
respect for persons 31–2
responsibility 8–11, 98–9
  and entitlement 47–9
  see also choice
risk taking 57–61, 65, 67–72,
  96–8
Rosenberg, A. 79 n. 1, 113 n. 4

Sandel, M. 166 n. 5
Scanlon 31 n. 7, 41
Scheffler, S. 48, 78
Sen, A. 7, 80, 111 n. 3
state support for art and culture 39,
  192–7
  failure of public goods
    approach 194–5

talent:
  and ambition thesis 125–8
  assumption of equal talent 20,
    51
  and difference of degree
    thesis 121–3
  and independence view 119–20
  unequal talents, problem of
    110–15
  vs. disability 110–13, 119–20